Matt Woodcock is a former news[...] and ministers in York. Matt is a re[...] *Thought* on the *Radio 2 Breakfast Show.*

Follow Matt on Twitter @revmattwoodcock

Praise for Matt Woodcock's first book,
Becoming Reverend: A Diary:

'an irreverent, often squeamishly honest account that… reveals too the trouble Woodcock and his wife had trying to conceive … Woodcock wanted his account of the process to be "earthy". It certainly is.' *The Sunday Times*

'hilarious and surprisingly human … an unlikely trainee vicar's laugh out loud memoirs' *Daily Mail*

'a typically hilarious and yet at times quite poignant read. Because the thing about Woody – sorry, The Rev Matt Woodcock – is that he never holds back.' *The York Press*

'In his new book, *Becoming Reverend: A Diary*, Matt spills all sorts of truths about his trials as a trainee vicar, while also attempting against the odds to become a dad. His diary is… devout and raucous, funny and serious, earthy and spiritual.' *The Yorkshire Post*

'*Becoming Reverend* [sets] out to lift the lid on what life is really like to be a 21st Century vicar – dealing with everything from his struggles with life … at vicar training college and low sperm counts.' *Hull Daily Mail*

'Refreshingly honest, frequently hilarious and genuinely moving, *Becoming Reverend* is a surprising and inspiring read. Even if you think church isn't for you – in fact, especially if you think that – this book probably is.' *The Reverend Kate Bottley*

'It is laugh out loud funny in places, but also moving and humbling as Matt's outrageous honesty and witty self-deprecation take you along with him in his journey … inspiring, challenging, humbling and very funny.' *The Reverend Jules Middleton, pickingapplesofgold.com*

Also by Matt Woodock

Becoming Reverend: A Diary

Being Reverend

A DIARY

MATT WOODCOCK

CHURCH HOUSE
PUBLISHING

Being Reverend: A Diary

Church House Publishing
Church House
Great Smith Street
London
SW1P 3AZ

ISBN: 978 1 78140 201 6

Published in 2020 by Church House Publishing

The opinions expressed in this book are those of the author and
do not necessarily reflect the official policy of the General Synod or the
Archbishops' Council of the Church of England.

British Library Cataloguing in Publication data

A catalogue record for this book is available from the British Library

Cover design by www.penguinboy.net

Cover photo by Jerome Whittingham

Typeset by ForDesign

Printed and bound in Great Britain by
CPI Group (UK) Ltd, Croydon
CR0 4YY

For Neal and Irene x

Prologue

B*gger. What have I done?

That was my first thought as I stood in the deserted Hull Trinity Square this morning.

It was my lowest moment.

Just a couple of hours before the curtain went up on our Live Nativity. The greatest story ever told, about to start in Hull city centre – with real camels, sheep, a donkey and a large cast of reluctant local characters. Road closures in place for the procession from Queen Victoria Square to Trinity Square. Police and stewards in hi-vis jackets and walkie-talkies ready to manage and direct the hordes.

Months of planning, fundraising and mouth ulcers. Front page headlines. My confident boasts of a 'Christmas spectacular never to be forgotten' being spouted in radio and TV interviews.

Now here we were – finally.

It was absolutely slinging it down.

Beyond torrential.

Of course it was.

This was the day my promise to God 18 months ago to do church in a new way was supposed to come to pass. The Bible kept shouting at me back then to 'make a way in the wilderness and streams in the desert'. 'Here I am Lord – send me,' I'd arrogantly prayed, echoing the words of the prophet Isaiah.

I can't remember a time when I felt more sorry for myself. More furious with God. More regretful that I had ever had this stupid idea in the first place. Now I was struck with the painful realization that I was about to be humiliated in front of a city I'd grown to love and admire with all my heart.

I'd be a laughing stock. No one would come. The sodden streets would be empty.

I allowed myself a few self-pitying tears. Tilted my head back to let the massive rain drops wash them away. They were unrelenting, noisily slapping onto the Old Town cobbles.

My shepherd's costume was already soaked. I was a picture of drenched hessian. I took a despairing look round the square – our 'Bethlehem'. The hastily-erected stable at the front of Holy Trinity Church looked as if it was about to take off in the strong wind. Hay was swirling everywhere. Large puddles had formed where our Mary (Lyndsey, a barmaid) and Joseph (Gareth, a welder) would be huddled with baby Jesus (Sidney, their son). I'd have to get them to bring some wellies. Wrap the Saviour of the world in a swaddling cagoule.

A text message pinged onto my phone from one of my friends. Loads of them had promised to come and support me. Now they weren't going to.

'Too wet', it read.

'Sorry, Woody. Break a leg.'

I wanted to crawl away and hide. I felt sick with a sense of crushing disappointment and failure.

I'd given this job everything. Worked relentlessly to try and grow Holy Trinity and make things happen. This was supposed to be the big crescendo. The moment of it all being worth it. The time of harvest after months toiling in the fields.

I could feel all my hope, confidence and optimism draining away. I foraged for my wallet photograph of my wife Anna and the twins. Our girls.

The sparkly-eyed, full-of-life faces of Esther and Heidi stared back at me. I felt better. They wouldn't care if no one turned up. Anna would wheel them down in the double buggy however relentless the rain. I imagined them in their cute pink splash suits pointing and waving at the camels as if they were the most fascinating, amazing thing they'd ever seen.

But I hadn't gone to all this trouble to entertain my own kids. I checked the time, swallowed hard and looked to the heavens again for some inspiration ...

In the Beginning...

As a Church of England minister, there are probably some things I should never admit to.

Like the fact I sometimes don't particularly like going to church. Or the clothes we wear, the traditional hymns we sing and the prayers written for us to pray. Too often the C of E's ways, rituals and culture feel as alien and uncomfortable to me as accountancy.

Or wearing a monocle.

I'm Sky Sports News and Oasis in a world of Radio 4 and Shostakovich.

At least I actually believe in God. That often seems to be the only thing I have in common with my clergy colleagues.

And even then it's not straightforward. There's a myriad of views on what we think God is like and what he thinks about all aspects of human existence. Enduring difference and tension are part of the deal in our expression of Christianity. It makes my head spin.

Thank heavens, then, for Jesus. Finding him – or him finding me – is still the very best thing that's ever happened to me. (And I was at Bootham Crescent in 1985 when York City beat Arsenal 1–0 with a last-minute penalty in the fourth round of the FA Cup.)

I've never found a better, fuller, happier, more challenging, adventure-filled way to live than the Jesus way. Since we got acquainted I've never been able to shut up about him.

The truth is though, despite that, on many Sundays I've been perched on the wooden razor we call a pew, daydreaming about lying somewhere hot while sipping something cold, wondering why I'm an Anglican at all.

I've always felt a bad fit for the Church of England. My boredom threshold is too low. My excitement threshold is too high. I don't like organs.

I remember having a moment of epiphany at a service I attended a few years ago. The whole experience was like a *Mr Bean* sketch. Arriving at the church, the 'welcome' was as stiff and hostile as if I'd walked into my grandma's front room with my shoes on. The grunting old guy handing out the hymn books made me feel as if I'd shot his dog. The shuffling priest at the front looked forlorn and preoccupied. His reciting of the prayers and flowery liturgy reminded me of the begrudging and irritated way I used to ask for directions to the train station in school French tests.

As I walked out from the cold gloom into the glorious morning sunshine, I made a promise to myself. When I became a reverend I'd do things differently. I wouldn't just be another breast-beater wailing about how bad things were in the Church of England. We had enough of those. I'd actually try to do something about it. I'd seek to be an agent of change in whatever little corner of God's world I found myself. I'd be focused and relentless in offering people the chance to find or grow in faith in a way that stirred their senses. Leave people with an enthusiasm to do a bit of good and seek a fairer world. I'd do Jesus with bells on. I'd reach out to those rarely seen in so many of our churches – like the under-60s and lads. The skint and the struggling. Wherever I did 'church' and whatever it looked like, I'd try to make it feel as if you were walking into the morning sunshine.

That was the theory anyway. That was the hope and the prayer. Naive? Arrogant? Misguided? Maybe.

Leaving theological college in Durham, I was given the chance to put my big dreams and confident words into action in the centre of Kingston upon Hull at Holy Trinity Church – the largest parish church in the UK but with a tiny congregation. It was the last throw of the dice for this 700-year-old church.

It's fair to say it wasn't easy to persuade my wife Anna to move to Hull. She's the second-best thing that's ever happened to me. We'd been on quite a journey together to get to this point. She'd put up with a lot supporting my calling to the priesthood and two years' training at vicar school. Then there was our infertility and multiple rounds of IVF treatment. And, suddenly, thanks to those test tubes, more fertility than we'd ever dreamt of – our twin girls Esther and

Heidi. After all that, Anna was pretty sure she'd be nestling into the bosom of supportive family and friends for a while. Her own bosoms were at breaking point. Sore and tender from the devouring mouths of our thirsty girls. Somehow I managed to change her mind. Or God did. We all moved to Hull.

My diary accounts of that fraught and colourful time became my first book, *Becoming Reverend*. My mum and grandma loved it. That made me happy.

I kept writing my diary every night in our new church house in Hull. Kept recording what happened – however brilliant, bad or embarrassing. Because it's one thing becoming a reverend, but what about *being* one? It's one thing having twins, but what about raising them? This is that story. My first eighteen months at Holy Trinity as a so-called 'pioneer minister' with a brief to make change happen. My efforts to grow a church and grow a family.

So, *Being Reverend*, then. Lord have mercy …

Year One

Tuesday 5 July

My first day as a fully licensed, fully frocked, fully clueless ordained Church of England minister. Anna and the babies waved me off to Holy Trinity on the steps of our new home. I feel a bit guilty that we've been housed in a warm, modern, detached house in a tidy cul-de-sac full of friendly people with manicured front lawns. Not what I imagined for us. I just need a Volvo and a golf membership now to complete the picture. I cycled away in my black shirt and dog collar, waving and blowing kisses. Gap jeans tucked into my 'Daddy Smells' socks, my Chile 62 Adidas Originals hard down on the pedals. After all that theological study and the intensity of vicar school I felt ready to change the world.

My new boss, the Reverend Dr Neal Barnes, greeted me at the church door with a beaming smile. He has kind eyes and thinning chestnut hair that isn't long for this world. He clutched a copy of his prayer book as excitedly as a seven-year-old holding candy floss at Disneyland. 'I've got the chapel ready for us to pray, Matt!' he gushed. I don't want to let him down. He's waited more than a year for the cavalry to arrive, but I'm very aware that the dynamic might not work, with my other colleague, the Reverend Irene Wilson, in the mix too. She's an unpaid priest in her sixties with a particular gift for reaching out to the homeless and marginalized. Her goodness intimidates me. The Bishop of Hull has put faith and money into this team, but we are so different. Three reverends with nothing in common except our Christianity. It could be disastrous.

Neal led me to the top of the tower of Holy Trinity after prayers. The narrow, snaking staircase went on forever. He wanted to give me an aerial view of Hull's Old Town, the extent of our parish boundary and a brief history of the area. The nearby docks were smashed to bits during the Second World War. Trinity was left unscathed as the Luftwaffe used it as a marker for their attacks.

A couple of brave guys had the job of standing on the church roof through the night to check for bombs and fires. I imagine those hours were prayerful.

I was later introduced to some of Holy Trinity's key people, the stalwarts who have faithfully kept things going. They know how close the church came to being mothballed. I hit it off with Gordon Barley. He's known as 'the cheerful verger' and I can see why. Such a warm demeanour, sparkly eyes and a huge, rubbery smile. We'll get on. David Stipetic, keeper of the bells and clocks, was a bit more guarded but fascinating nonetheless. One of the veteran volunteers – a widow – told me that welcoming visitors on the door had saved her from a life of loneliness. People are candid round here. I like it.

However, it was a relief to finally get out into the community. It's where I need to spend most of my time. The Old Town is like something from a Dickens novel. Cobbled, atmospheric streets with stories to tell. Narrow, half-hidden alleyways, striking Victorian architecture and old-fashioned shops. Pubs are everywhere. I wondered about the interesting people inside propping the bars up. I looked at my watch. Bit too early.

I introduced myself everywhere with a cheesy, 'Hello, I'm the new rev in town – lovely to meet you!' Some people were taken aback. Most were friendly. They told me how hard it is round here to make ends meet. Many are struggling. They crave revival. A reversal in fortunes. If Trinity is to survive and do its job properly, we must become good news to the Old Town in every sense. Engaged and practically helpful – as well as a hotbed of spiritual exploration. Our church is in a blind spot right now. A huge historic irrelevancy.

I had a significant hour with a bar manager called Allen Slinger. He runs the Kings Bar & Lounge, one of the hostelries opposite the church in Trinity Square. Nice guy. Keen. He asked if the church would be interested in being part of the Hull Trinity Festival in September. Definitely! It could be a big early win. Allen said it was the first time all the publicans in the Old Town had come together to try something new. A weekend of live music is planned in any venue that wants in. 'People have deserted this area over the years and we hope this will help bring them back,' Allen told me. We talked about the possibility of a big live music stage being erected in the square, just in front of the church doors. I just kept saying yes to everything Allen asked me.

Yes. Yes. Yes. I get the sense that if we are to awake this giant, it's a word we'll need to get very good at saying.

Wednesday 6 July

I don't know if it's possible to help turn things around at church in the way and at the pace I think it needs to while I'm up to my neck in baby girls. I was noticeably exhausted, bleary-eyed and grumpy all day. Properly focusing on anyone or anything was a struggle. I blame Esther. She was up and down all night demanding Anna's breast and a clean undercarriage. If Holy Trinity is going to be transformed, the girls will need to be better sleepers – and less frequent defecators.

Thursday 7 July

I was introduced to one of Holy Trinity's infamous welcomers today – volunteers who stand at the church door and greet people. He was a spindly, elderly chap called Selwyn, straight out of the pages of *David Copperfield*. The conversation went like this:

Me: 'Hi Selwyn. I'm Reverend Matt Woodcock, the new pioneer minister here. Pleasure to meet you!'
Selwyn: 'I know who you are Mr Woodcock! I'm an atheist – you won't convert me!'

Then he shuffled off. Selwyn is one of our key Welcomers. He makes a point of telling visitors that the very notion of God is entirely ridiculous. We have a long way to go.

Friday 8 July

Anna made a friend at twins' club this morning. They've arranged to go for coffee. I'm so proud of her. She's making this work. She's embracing Hull. I'm beginning to see how important this move is for Anna. I'm convinced that she's thriving on the adventure. She'd never admit it, though. Ever since we met at the church youth club as kids, she's been cautious, sensible and spectacularly content. Comfortable with what she knows. Happiest with her family, close friends and working in York council's environmental health department. It's astonishing we ever made it romantically. I'm not comfortable with anything. I've raged against contentment for years. All those weekly letters we sent to each other at university have a lot to answer for. Our bond grew with every lick of those second-class stamps.

I can remember the exact moment when I fell in love with Anna. She reached into the open window of my maroon Ford Fiesta to plant a peck on my cheek to wish me happy birthday. That was it. I loved her from that moment on and knew I had to spend the rest of my life with her. She took a bit more convincing, mind you. I pursued her relentlessly. And now here we are. Still in love and now in Hull. It's funny how life works out.

Fridays are my day off. It wasn't a great one. I immersed myself in the New Testament book of Romans in preparation for my sermon when I should have been on a quest for excitement and adventure. Later, Anna was too tired for any bedroom shenanigans. A combination of dairy farm-level breastfeeding and late-night winding is playing havoc with her libido. Mine seems remarkably unaffected. Funny that.

Saturday 9 July

Another dreadful night's sleep. I can't remember the last time I wasn't aggressively roused by at least one piercing scream. The girls seem to take it in turns. I've noticed that Heidi's wails are marginally less shrill. I took Anna tea and toast in bed and encouraged her that she's doing an amazing job. I burnt it a bit and smeared it in lemon curd instead of her favourite Marmite, but she was grateful for the gesture.

Got down to church early to spend time with the Saturday morning cleaning crew, or 'Gordon's holy dusters', as they're called. It wasn't long before I found myself becoming acquainted with a Henry Hoover.

I'm getting a feel for how desperate things are at Holy Trinity. Considering its size, historical significance and breathtaking architecture, so few people actually come inside. The visitor numbers are tragically low. We're talking handfuls at weekends. It doesn't surprise me that it's losing £1,000 a week. That's not sustainable. People have to belong before they begin to believe. They have to know that they are allowed in. I decided to walk my patch.

My dog collar is a gift. Why would you not wear one if you're a rev? They are a magnet for interaction and conversation. It didn't take long for it to work its magic. Striding around the Old Town's indoor market, the chats came thick and fast. People were keen to give me their thoughts on dire rugby league referees, the afterlife and 'the f***ing council'. A bloke in the sandwich queue shared a colourful story about getting 'the runs' during an all-inclusive holiday in Turkey. I passed on the egg mayonnaise bap.

The traders are something else. Old school. I met a guy who had sold socks for 30 years, and another flogging dusty vinyl records. He told me he was an atheist. People love telling me that. I like unpacking what they mean by it. I left the market encouraged.

I noticed a battered sign on a building down the north side of church: St Paul's Boxing Academy. The door was open. I could hear pumping dance music playing and bags being pummelled. Something stirred within me. I swallowed down the fear and walked in. Kids were sparring in a ring watched by their parents. Huge tattooed men in red and blue vests were dotted around the place in various states of pugilistic exertion. No one noticed me at first. I froze a bit. My mouth lost all its moisture. I'm cringing now, but I eventually shouted out something like: 'Hello everyone! I'm one of the vicars from the church next door. How are you all?' What was I thinking? The gym was suddenly transformed into a Wild West saloon. The music cut out. Everyone seemed to stop and stare fiercely. I'm sure I saw tumbleweed roll past the medicine balls. Mercifully a voice finally sliced through the silent tension. It was one of the coaches, Paul. 'I'm so glad you've come in, Reverend! I've been wanting to speak to someone from the church. We need somewhere to park and wondered if you could help us?' That was it. Tension lifted. The music came back on. People went back to hitting things.

Paul was lovely. We immediately connected. He filled me in about the club. They're all volunteers and coach hundreds of adults and kids at various sessions throughout the week. They've been there for years but no one from Holy Trinity has ever popped in. It's literally opposite – ten yards from our door. The club is doing the work we should be doing. I want to learn from them.

Paul let me into the ring so I could show him my Prince Naseem impression. Chin out, dancing around, wild swings. I'm not sure he was that impressed, to be honest. I've arranged to meet him for coffee next week. This felt very significant.

This afternoon when I got home I recreated my moves to Anna and the girls in the front room. They weren't impressed either. Tomorrow is a big day. My first service at Holy Trinity. It's fair to say I'm bricking it.

Sunday 10 July

Lots to report and reflect on. Holy Trinity's two morning services are like the rest of the place – pretty desperate but full of potential. They call the 9.30 a.m. an 'informal family service'. I saw little evidence of that. The congregation consisted of about 20 people in the twilight of middle age (if I'm being polite). Apart from Esther and Heidi there was only one other child. His parents looked well uncomfortable. They had the faces of a couple who are clearly thinking: 'As soon as little William is baptized – we are out of here!' As for the informality, it was pretty stiff, wordy and dull. People seemed afraid to relax or laugh or show any discernible evidence of joy. And yet, it could be brilliant. Sam, one of our licensed Readers, radiates warmth and welcome. I'd come back on the strength of his lovely demeanour. I'm staying positive.

I'd got down to church early and had a brew with a homeless guy called Dave. He's currently sleeping in the doorway of the docks office. He was refreshingly candid about his plight. He became addicted to alcohol years ago and has been sleeping rough ever since. Dave doesn't want to be housed. He chooses to sleep rough. Interesting. 'Less hassle,' he told me. 'I get left alone.' A little team led by a saintly volunteer called Dot open Holy Trinity early on Sundays to provide hot drinks and toast for rough sleepers. This is why I love the church. Little acts of Christian kindness going on all over the place. Little indicators of Christ working in the lives of ordinary people. Helping guys like Dave. Keeping them warm and fed and loved.

The sound of our Sunday worship intermingled with the sound of the poor and destitute being served. It's what the church should be like. Admittedly, the misty-eyed romance of the moment was lost a bit when one of the homeless guys belched really loudly during the prayers. His timing was genius. I couldn't help snorting with laughter as Jean prayed for the situation in Sierra Leone.

My most significant encounter was with a former bodybuilding champion called Jamie. I spotted him shuffling in late to the 9.30 a.m. in a muscle vest. His calves were bigger than my torso. I raced to catch him at the end. Jamie said he had wandered into Holy Trinity about four weeks ago during a terrible time in his life. He felt immediately at peace and has been back ever since. I've arranged to see him next week.

The 11.15 a.m. service was robed and very formal. Neal interviewed me so the congregation could find out who I was and where I'd come from. I did my best to liven things up. But either the flock were afraid to laugh or my jokes and stories were very, very unfunny. I could hear Anna giggling, but she doesn't count. There was a 'bring and share' lunch at the end so we could get to know everyone. I ate my bodyweight in Gala pie.

Monday 11 July

I'm in Caffè Nero reflecting on my first week. I think our flock recognize the need for change but perhaps don't want it at my pace. I've discovered the holy dusters have nicknamed me 'Tigger' because they say I can't sit still. It could have been worse. I can tell I'm already doing our church secretary's head in. Chris is one of the stalwarts who have kept the place open these past few years. I told him that I went for a run last night. He bit back: 'Can you go for one now? You're exhausting us all!'

I've discovered that Holy Trinity owns a nearby house that someone could live in for next to nothing. That got me excited. It could accommodate a children's and youth worker. Trinity hasn't had one in its 700-year history. I wonder if my cousin Ben would be up for it? He's too comfortable in York working for my old church. Our need is greater.

Attended a meeting with all the Old Town bar and pub owners tonight to talk about Hull Trinity Festival. They were quite excited at my invitation for them to use the church for acoustic acts and bouncy castles.

Tuesday 12 July

A historic day for Esther and Heidi. Each noticed that the other one existed for the first time – and that it was funny to throw dinner in each other's faces. It won't be long before they learn that it would be even funnier to throw it at us.

I took the St Paul's Boxing Academy coaches up the Trinity tower tonight. They're very keen to engage with us. Apparently they have one of the country's best amateur bantamweights on their books. He's called Luke Campbell. One to watch for next year's Olympics, they reckon. They think he's good enough to win a medal.

Wednesday 13 July

Visited Jamie the bodybuilder at his house. He told me that his life had fallen apart in recent years. He's on a lot of painkillers just to stay functional. He proudly showed me pictures of his glory days competing with the best musclemen all over the world. Lots of huge, spray-tanned blokes in tiny trunks struggling to combine a smile with a flex. Coming down from those kind of highs have taken their toll on Jamie. He said he experienced God in a very tangible and powerful way when he randomly walked into Holy Trinity. He has many questions and spiritual dots to join. He asked me to pray for him. I committed to helping him find some answers. Jamie said he wished Holy Trinity was a bit livelier. Me too, Jamie, me too.

Thursday 14 July

The babies are making us physically more unattractive day by day. An old bloke stared back at me in the bathroom mirror this morning. And rarely have I seen Anna look less vibrant and bright-eyed. Her sensational olive skin seems to be losing some of its lustre. We shuffle, creak and sigh round the house like nursing home residents.

I gently and quietly tiptoed in to say goodnight to the girls when I got back tonight. I ever so delicately realigned Esther's blanket before creeping out. Cue piercing scream.

The rest of the night went something like this:

1. Anna silently and furiously mouthing *'I've just got her to sleep!'* and bounding past me to settle her.
2. Hushed row in the kitchen about my alleged loud, clumsy ways.
3. Calmer discussion about how hard things are and how much our lives have changed.
4. Cuddled agreement that we wouldn't want it any other way.
5. Swoop Anna over my shoulder and fireman's lift her to bed.

Friday 15 July

Great day off in the glorious nearby market town of Beverley. I enjoy basking in the comfort of affluent little places like this sometimes. There's good breeding everywhere. All the blokes seem to dress like Hugh Grant. All the women carry those handbags with the expensive-looking clasps. The cafe conversations are so refined. I listened in on two bejewelled ladies next to me dissecting a classical recital they'd been to. Apparently the wind section were crap.

I couldn't help working on my sermon for this Sunday. It's my first one at Holy Trinity so needs to set the right tone and get people excited about mission.

Sunday 17 July

Made a schoolboy error in the sermon. In the hope of a few easy laughs to settle me down, I told the people which Hull rugby league team I preferred. It turns out the rivalry between Hull Kingston Rovers based on the east side of the River Humber and Hull F.C. on the west is fierce. They really don't like each other. I think they'd actually put it a bit stronger than that. I began my preach by singing the KR anthem 'The Red, Red Robin' and saying I preferred them because of the colour of their kit. The Hull F.C. half of the congregation gave me the death stare. Some could barely bring themselves to look at me afterwards over coffee. The Rovers fans fawned over me like I was some sort of conquering hero. I seem to have alienated and offended 50 per cent of our church. So that went well then.

Monday 18 July

Esther was up constantly last night. Does she ever sleep? She can't be human. Her cry is the most horrendous noise I've ever heard. I'd endure days of listening to pneumatic drills or fingernails being scraped down blackboards if my ears didn't have to be exposed to it. It's a good job Jesus didn't have kids. He wouldn't have got much done. Sometimes I wonder if that's why the disciples with young families were so keen to drop everything and follow him.

Anna and I had another row in the kitchen. The constant stress of Esther's wailing is causing big tensions between us. Anna said that I was useless. I said she could be doing a better job. We didn't mean it. Our judgement is being impaired. We're drained of compassion, sensitivity and grace. Peace eventually descended on the house at about 10 p.m. I attempted to muster a holy moment in my study. They are becoming scarcer as the cries get more frequent. I lit some candles, put on Rachmaninov and settled down for some soothing Bible and prayer time. This was literally the first thing I read: Judges 21.10 '...put to the sword those living there, including the women and children.' Ouch.

Tuesday 19 July

I'm discovering that Holy Trinity doesn't seem to do 'normal' days. A Muslim student came into church today to tell Neal and me that she wanted to change her religion. Neal made his excuses and left me to it. Thanks for that. The girl was terrified that her parents were trying to arrange a marriage for her that she didn't want. Her plan was to quickly convert to Christianity before they flew out to the Middle East to make the arrangements. She was under the impression that it was something she signed rather than an informed decision of the heart. I did what I could to explain the Christian basics. I can't imagine the personal cost and potential family estrangement involved in her changing religions. I felt completely ill-equipped to help her. She wandered dejectedly back out into the Old Town, half-heartedly saying she'd call back in 'some time' if she needed any more clarity. Sadly, I don't think she will.

Paul gave me a personal coaching session at the boxing club tonight. It was a welcome distraction. Between my ragged jabs and uppercuts, he asked me to tell him how I found God. It was a bit weird to be punching a heavy bag really hard while talking about being transformed by the Prince of Peace. The footwork is the hardest skill to master in boxing. Fighters must make great dancers. Their movement is so balletic.

Wednesday 20 July

I sat with one of the homeless guys on a bench outside church on my way in. He was in a bad way. His face was all smashed in and he sobbed into my jacket. I put my arm round him and tried to be of comfort. Last night he'd been sitting in a doorway outside one of our neighbouring pubs when he saw two lads throwing loose change at an elderly guy. When he told them to stop they set on him, kicking and punching him in the face. A lady from the pub spotted them and shouted at them until they went away. Incredibly, as he was telling me this, she walked past us. I commended her for being such a good samaritan – and a potential lifesaver. He couldn't thank her enough. It was a beautiful moment. Apparently she popped into church later on to drop off some clothes for the homeless. She's also offered to help us serve tea and toast to them on Sunday mornings. Showing kindness does special things to people! It makes us feel good. It compels us to do more to help. This place is a living parable.

Thursday 21 July

Brought back down to earth today. Thoroughly depressed after my first Hull Deanery Synod meeting. It's supposed to be a time for the churches in our little area to encourage each other, share challenges and inspirations and plot a way ahead. It made me feel like tying bricks to my feet and jumping into the Humber. Some grim statistics were read out about church attendance in the diocese. Sunday attendance has dwindled to 16,500 – and is projected to go down to 12,000 within five years.

'We must do more,' the secretary said, tamely. 'Right, next item. Church lead thefts …'

I should have said something. I should have bolted the doors and forced everyone to stay in that room until we had at least discussed what 'doing more' might look like. Doing fewer things would be a start. Making our services less stuffy, less dull, less incomprehensible to the vast majority of ordinary people. Less like feeling you want to be anywhere else on a Sunday morning. That would be a start, surely?

Friday 22 July

My day off. Back to York to catch up with some of my old mates. You'd have thought I'd moved to the Outer Hebrides or something. None of the lads seem remotely interested in coming to visit. I went to The Nags Head with Ollie. Nothing's changed between us since our school days. We still annoy and entertain each other in equal measure. Strolling home fairly late, it gave me a little reminder of my old life. I miss it sometimes. Time escaped us as Ollie and I had the mother of all heart-to-hearts and sought to untangle decades of complex friendship. Ollie thinks I let him down badly years ago. We spent hours talking God too. He now wants to rekindle his dormant faith. I hope so, but we'll see. They all say that after too many bottles of Desperado. I remember the night he became a Christian at Pathfinder Camp in North Wales. We were 13, I think. I was sat next to him at the evening meeting where we were encouraged to make a step of faith. I could tell Ollie was having 'a moment'. I teased him for it. I seem to remember his first words as a new disciple of Jesus Christ were: 'P*** off, Woody!'

Earlier a woman at the hairdressers asked if I believed in angels. She said she saw two in a dream about her mum who is in the middle of cancer treatment. I said I did believe in angels and that I'd pray for her mum.

Saturday 23 July

Last night with Ollie was a terrible idea. From about 5.30 a.m., Esther and Heidi seemed to take enormous delight in finding the noisiest toys they could and playing with them really, really vigorously. As close to my head as possible. Hiding the toys didn't work. Their screams were even more unbearable. I spent the late morning trying to sneak in some secret snoozes without being detected by Anna and her mum.

We went to my lovely niece Honor's sixth birthday party at my sister Amy's house. She's loving her Catholic primary school. She crosses herself more than the Pope. I invented a game on a skateboard for all the kids. No necks were broken.

Sunday 24 July

Bad start to the day. 'The Holy Trinity website is TERRIBLE!' I shouted to anyone who'd listen as I breezed into the vestry. Our church secretary Chris's face reddened. It turns out he maintains the Holy Trinity website. 'You are going too fast for us!' he exploded. 'You're trying to change everything. We can't keep up. You'll be gone in a few years and we'll have to pick up the pieces!'

Chris stormed out, slamming the heavy door behind him. Neal ran after him to calm him down and suggested we needed a period of calm reflection about the future of the website.

Minutes later I was leading the 9.30 a.m. service – still shell-shocked by the verbal battering. Sharing the Peace with Chris as preparation for Holy Communion was a bit awkward but very necessary. It took on deeper meaning for both of us. I'll add the church website to the list of things that I should probably never mention again and meet Chris to apologize. I need to bust out some Atticus Finch moves on these Trinity stalwarts. Seek to step into their shoes. See things from their perspective. Why did God call me here? I seem to be doing more harm than good at the moment. I long to be a minister in Mauritius or the Cayman Islands. The people on those beaches need Jesus too.

Monday 25 July

Cousin Ben has decided to stay at his own church in York rather than come here. I understand but I'm gutted. He's just what we need. Please send us someone, Lord.

I've persuaded one of the choir dads to put up his bouncy castle in Trinity Square on Saturday afternoon. We need to get stuff happening out there at weekends. I'm going to get my guitar out and busk some Oasis tunes.

Tuesday 26 July

I was given a tour of the *Hull Daily Mail* newsroom by the editor, John Meehan. He's a great guy. I felt that familiar ache to be back at one of the desks, ringing round my contacts, sniffing for a story. Those seven years as a reporter for the *York Evening Press* were some of my finest. No day was ever the same. I still miss the deadline adrenaline rush. Competing with my ace reporting pals like Alex for the front page and then nestling into the Spread Eagle pub after the paper had gone to bed to toast our triumphs and wallow in our failures. John persuaded me to let them do a 'news to pews' feature story on me. It gives me the chance to lay out my vision for the pioneering work at Trinity. My smiling mouth looked massive in the pictures their photographer took.

I drove one of my fellow curates to a rookie clergy training gathering this afternoon. He's super spiritual. No sooner had I put on my Spotify car mix than he suggested a prayer and worship time. He didn't draw breath. I'm glad I wasn't driving to Scotland.

Wednesday 27 July

Neal is the most encouraging, releasing leader. I know I couldn't do his job. Being the boss of Holy Trinity looks horrible. So much admin. So many meetings and people to please. It's like a monster that needs constantly feeding. Neal has been a year in the job. His weary face gives the impression it has been far longer. He keeps pushing me to be bolder and braver. He doesn't seem to be able to say 'no'. It's like a red rag to a bull. My respect levels for Neal and Irene are going through the roof. Precious, affirming clergy comrades. We are united in turning this place around.

Thursday 28 July

I went down to the newsagent early doors to see what the *Hull Daily Mail* had written about me. 'After writing about bad news, it was time to spread good news.' This was the headline on page 3. I'm dreading the church reaction to some of my quotes. This one in particular: 'I think church should be about prayer and parties – not misery and quiche.' They also wrote a leader piece about me. It said:

Hats off to Reverend Matt Woodcock. The former reporter has given up the news for pews. And top of his agenda is to inspire today's youth. Matt, who has just joined the city's Holy Trinity Church, believes tradition plays a key role in his religion. But it is clear Matt believes the future of the church lies in engaging with young people and making religion relevant to their lives. He wants young people to enjoy faith and believes the way to do that is by making the Church into a place of 'prayer and parties'.

Cringe!

Pretty nervous tonight. I launched my first exploring Christianity course (called the Start Course) in our front room for Jamie and John, the two massive bodybuilders who've started to come to our 9.30 a.m. service a bit. They told me they want to know if God is real and what difference he might make. I said I'd help them find out. I've never been in a confined space with such large, bulging humans. It was a special time. They are very open about faith and admit to being on a journey of discovery. John said he doesn't love himself so struggles to love anyone else. It's great to have Anna in the sessions. The lads loved her. I noticed her eyeing their remarkable biceps with a worryingly keen interest.

Friday 29 July

Just started reading a biography of the poet R. S. Thomas. Talk about complex. He did not like people by all accounts. Not the most helpful trait when you are a priest and paid to shepherd them. Thomas read in the mornings, went birdwatching in the afternoons and visited his human flock in the evenings. Not a bad rhythm to a day. He was in a constant wrestle with God about what bits were true or not. He looked at nature and found it hopelessly cruel as well as mind-blowingly beautiful. It drew him to the divine as well as alienating him.

Shopping nightmare in Morrisons with the girls. Why did I even think that I could manage this task on my own? Wheeling that trolley with them sat in their little seats was ridiculously stressful. Young mums tutted and sighed unhelpfully loudly as I tried to manoeuvre the damn thing towards the English Mustard shelf without maiming anyone. I just don't know how Anna remains so unruffled. We later strolled to The Minerva in the sunshine for a quick pint.

Saturday 30 July

The bouncy castle was put up in Trinity Square this afternoon. In hindsight, I probably should have filled out a health and safety form or a risk assessment or something, but I was determined to generate some life, laughter and energy out there. It's such a beautiful square that is criminally underused at weekends.

The bouncy castle queue proved to be a place of real spiritual encounter. I became engaged in bone-deep conversations with four dads who had brought their kids for a jump around. One said he'd spent over a decade in prison and had a son he was trying to bring up right. 'I'm worried about the cruel world he's growing up in,' he said.

Dad number two was very large and worked in construction. We got onto the subject of building a faith. He said he'd be willing to try church as long as it was lively, not dull and joyless. 'How about somewhere in between?' I asked, hopefully.

Another bloke was a police officer who'd had a belly full of misery working on some grim cases. The job had made him cynical about the world and the people in it.

The last conversation in the line was with a young dad with a tough, hard face and eyes that had probably seen a bit too much of life's harsh realities. Tears filled his eyes as he shared the complex web of broken family relationships. 'Is there anything I can do for you?' I asked. 'You can pray,' he replied. So I did – right there in the queue. Giddy, excited squeals from the young bouncers provided a soundtrack for my heartfelt intercession.

I saw out the afternoon in the square busking some Oasis songs on my guitar. 'Cast No Shadow' and 'Rockin' Chair' sounded OK but the rest were pretty bad. 'Talk Tonight' was an embarrassing car crash of scuffed chords and lousy vocals. I was underwhelmed by the public's reaction, to be honest. They dispersed quite rapidly once the novelty of a vicar playing below-average versions of Oasis songs had worn off.

Sunday 31 July

I tentatively introduced a contemporary worship song to the 9.30 a.m. service this morning. The reaction from some of the old guard was beyond frosty. It didn't surprise me that the most positive feedback came from those newest to church. I feel like we're wading through decades of cobwebs and dust in an effort to make the church shine.

Irene's sermon was timely and brave. She challenged folk to embrace change. It helped that Churchwarden Tim's article in the church magazine was centred on the same theme. He wrote that change was absolutely necessary if Trinity was to stay open. What a legend. It won't have been easy for him to write that publicly.

Afterwards in the clergy vestry Irene confessed that she'd been worried about working with me. 'I now see what God was up to putting you, me and Neal together,' she told me. 'Our gifts complement each other. We've got the same heart and passion. We can do this, Matt.'

Monday 1 August

I kept up with my promise to do circuit training at the boxing club tonight. I chatted to a particularly fierce-looking guy between agonizing planks and sit-ups. He had several gold teeth and an array of alarming scars. One of the coaches shouted over: 'Don't listen to his confession, Rev – you'll be here all night!'

Tuesday 2 August

I began another six-week Start Course with four more people in the church vestry this lunchtime. It's designed to help them explore Christianity in an informal way. To be fair, we never got much further than some of their colourful personal and family troubles. They're all out of work and beset with personal issues. One of the lads had a huge love bite on his neck. I had some fun with that. My kind of group.

Friday 5 August

Hull people have an edgy honesty and natural friendliness that is so endearing. I want to be more like them. It feels like I've come home. I fell in love with the attitude of the waitress in the pizza restaurant tonight: 'What's your hottest pizza?' I asked her.

'The Vesuvio,' she replied. 'But it's a complete rip-off for what you get. I wouldn't pay for it.'

I'd return to this place just on the strength of that one comment.

Saturday 6 August

I spent a moving morning in the company of some of Hull's Normandy veterans. They're reluctantly retiring their regimental flag in a special service at church tomorrow. It will hang here until the last shred of it drops to the stone floor. Most of the guys are in their nineties now and wanted to do it while they still could. I spoke to one veteran who was spewed out onto the beach on that bloody first day of D-day in 1944. He articulated some of the fear he felt. German bullets cut so many of his friends down before they even reached the sand. Another guy told me that as soon as the war was over they were expected to just return to work as if nothing had happened. Many were physically unharmed but carried inner trauma after witnessing things no human being ever should have to. What a privilege to be among them. Generations of us owe them our freedom. This is where a big civic church like ours can really give them something back. A place to mark their sacrifice so we never forget.

One of the guys from the boxing club came into church today. During his morning run, he told God that if it started raining he'd believe in him. Minutes later it began to drizzle.

Sunday 7 August

The first shoots of new growth are beginning to emerge at Trinity. The merest hints that a new community is developing. A little gaggle of new people and their kids chatted in the cafe area after the 9.30 a.m. service. I looked on them with love, eavesdropping into the lovely buzz of conversation. New life is slowly being breathed into this church's dry bones. Ezekiel 37.5–6 came to mind:

> *This is what the Sovereign Lord says to these bones: 'I will make breath enter you, and you will come to life. I will attach tendons to you and make flesh come upon you and cover you with skin; I will put breath in you, and you will come to life. Then you will know that I am the Lord.'*

Bodybuilder Jamie told me that he'd prayed that his racing pigeons would all return unharmed after a big storm last night. They not only returned, but he won the competition, pocketing £200. 'Praying works, Matt!' he laughed.

Anna's mum is staying for a few days. I'm convinced that her sausage casserole might be what heaven tastes like.

Monday 8 August

Sent off a letter to the *Yorkshire Post* in response to their grumpy columnist's opinion piece about people not behaving in church. It really annoyed me. He doesn't get it. I wrote:

> *As a newly-ordained minister, I found the Rev Neil McNicholas's column (*Yorkshire Post, *August 4) a very good example of why the established church is in sharp decline.*
>
> *Of course I sympathise up to a point with some of his more extreme examples of wedding and baptism guests causing chaos in the pews. But I would remind him of the former Archbishop William Temple's comment that 'the church is the only cooperative society in the world that exists for the benefit of those who are not its members'.*
>
> *I would argue that our churches should first and foremost be places of welcome, relevancy, joy and prayer ... The Rev McNicholas is right that, to a great many people, Church is a 'foreign place' ... and [they] don't know 'what is required of them'.*

But whose fault is that? I would argue that the finger of blame should not be pointed at the brides with plunging necklines, beer-swigging baptism guests or out of control kids, but rather at the Church leaders themselves.

I'm glad that's off my chest.

Tuesday 9 August

Riots and looting have been sweeping across big cities like London and Manchester. The level of destruction has been shocking. We were braced for it kicking off in Hull tonight. Rumours were swirling all over Twitter that the Princes Quay shopping complex – just round the corner from Trinity – would be targeted. It was closed early as a precaution.

Wednesday 10 August

Hull is quiet so far but down south more riots have broken out. Sixteen thousand police are now on the London streets. There were rumours again on social media of a riot in the city centre tonight. I dashed out to offer support and pastoral help. Blessed are the peacemakers and all that. All was quiet. Not sure what I could have done if anything had erupted. I don't know if dog collars are good deterrents to bricks going through shop windows. I did see two lads hanging off the Andrew Marvell statue in Trinity Square. They threw an empty Coke can at my feet. I picked it up and put it in the bin. Thought better of saying anything. They looked extremely happy at the idea of jumping up and down on my neck.

One of our cleaners at Trinity collared me this afternoon. He said that some of the elderly folk were confused about my role. I think he meant that *he* was actually confused about my role. 'What are you actually here to do, Matt?' he asked, pointedly. I said I was here to help change happen. To be a catalyst for new life and growth. He robustly disagreed with the need to modernize the way we do church. He is desperate to keep things the way they are. He is afraid of the unknown.

'We're never going to change, Matt,' he said firmly.

'I disagree, Peter,' I replied politely. 'God is always doing a new thing, whether we like it or not. Aren't you excited about that?' He didn't seem to be. He went back to rubbing the church brass, only a bit more furiously. I'm glad we talked. I like Peter. I clearly need to win over some more of our entrenched faithful. They'll take some shifting.

Thursday 11 August

Plucked up the courage to go for a drink in Ye Olde Blue Bell with my dog collar on after work. I don't think they see many vicars ordering pints of Sovereign in there. I got some funny looks. Only one or two seemed hostile. I sat with the paper listening to the flow of conversations. The topics included fishing, a fight breaking out after a pub lock-in last weekend, the price of cars and the Hull job market. It was fascinating. Only by doing this can I really seek to minister in a relevant way to the people round here. I need to know what they care and worry about. What they find funny and sad. What they believe. I need to frequent these places more often. It needs to be normal for drinkers in the Old Town to find a reverend propping up the bar beside them. I can do this.

I've had an idea. Why not have some sort of service out in the community? A pub would be ideal. I need to go where the people are, rather than naively think they will just come to us. The verse from John 10.10 keeps popping into my head: 'I have come so that they might have life, and have it to the full.' 'FULL' would be a good name for a pub service.

Friday 12 August

I've written a press release for the local paper to announce that Holy Trinity is now on social media. I said it better than that.

I received a worrying text from bodybuilder Jamie. He said his mum had been diagnosed with cancer. He went out all day drinking to numb the pain. Now he feels guilt-ridden and wretched. I called him and did my best to offer comfort and support. He let me pray for him at the end of our long conversation.

Got a load of sausages and burgers for a church barbecue I'm organizing tomorrow. There's no real culture of people meeting together socially at Holy Trinity. I'm trying to change that.

Saturday 13 August

Hardly anyone turned up to the barbecue this afternoon. It was well embarrassing. Absolute waste of time. Why the hell do I bother?

Sunday 14 August

Massive communion chalice fail this morning. It was all going so well. I'd been passing the cup along the rail like an old pro. Then I came to a twitchy teenage lad. He went to take it from me but then changed his mind at the last second. He pulled his hands away. The chalice ricocheted off his chest, splattering the blood of Christ all over him. Unfortunately he was wearing a white T-shirt. He looked like an extra in *Die Hard*. A stream of wine flowed down the length of the chancel in the cracks of the stone floor. I got the lad out of there to get cleaned up. Only everyone noticed. What a nightmare!

A disappointing weekend, then. I had such high hopes for it. Warming this church up socially is proving harder than I thought. I thought the barbecue would be a smash hit. Anna says I need to dial down my massively high expectations. 'Things won't change overnight,' she said. 'Give them time.' The trouble is that time is in such short supply. There isn't that long to properly turn things round. I hope Jamie is feeling better tonight. I'll check in with him tomorrow. I'm going to get Neal to show me his chalice technique next week. Onwards.

Monday 15 August

My little press release went in the *Hull Daily Mail* today virtually word for word. It said:

> *It may be 700 years old, but now Holy Trinity Church, Hull, has been given a twenty-first-century makeover and joined the digital revolution. The UK's largest parish church is now on Facebook and Twitter in an effort to communicate with a virtual as well as a physical flock. The church's leaders will be uploading regular news, views, videos and pictures about church and city centre life.*

Of course I didn't mention the fact that 98 per cent of our congregation think a tweet is something blue tits do.

Tuesday 16 August

A guy came into church to ask me about my work as a pioneer minister today after hearing me on the radio giving an interview to Radio Humberside. He had hair like Robert Plant from Led Zeppelin and vacant eyes.

'God has told me that the end times are coming soon,' he said.

'OK,' I replied. He didn't look like the kind of bloke you disagreed with.

Wednesday 17 August

Waves of human need are crashing over me. I'm struggling to cope. A very distressed Iranian lady came in today to ask me to write a supporting letter for her immigration court hearing. She's terrified about being sent back. I've had to pass it onto Neal to handle. He'll have to get advice from the bishop's office to find out if we can help her.

One of the lads from the Old Town starts IVF treatment tomorrow. I could totally empathize with his worries and fears. The IVF journey can be so cruel and unforgiving, and yet when it works, such an incredible gift. He'll need to allow people to support him. Strong blokes are hardwired never to show weakness or vulnerability. I encouraged him to offload. To not pull his punches, so to speak. By the end he was keen for me to pray for him – as long as no one would see. We hid behind his van in the church car park.

These summer days are going too quickly. Waking up to glorious sunshine makes everything feel better. I'm still not sure about the clergy shirt, shorts and flip flops look, but I'm too hot to care.

Monday 22 August

Esther and Heidi have brought Anna fully alive. It wasn't long ago that she was shrouded in a deep sadness at us not being able to have kids. Ministering to my friend from the Old Town as he begins his IVF journey has brought it all back. Now Anna radiates a special joy and thankfulness. There's a sparkle in her eyes. A new-found bounce. Which is remarkable given what the girls demand of her. It was heart-melting to watch her play with them in the garden this afternoon. Ducking in and out of the washing on the line, she was making them squeal with laughter. It was the most heavenly sight and sound. I ran down to give them horsey rides on my back. Soon we were all squealing. However hard my day and slow the progress of turning things around at church, I have this. I take them all for granted too much. I need to write on a blackboard 100 times at the start of each day: 'My family is more important than my church. My family is more important than my church. My family is more important than my church ...'

Tuesday 23 August

Busy day in church. There were encouraging numbers at lunchtime prayers. Afterwards a local artist came in to ask if he could paint my portrait. He's been looking for a 'suitable' minister to capture on canvas to enter into a competition. He paints his portraits from photographs. I posed for him slouched on a chair in the chapel while he snapped away. 'Can we try one with you not grinning?' he asked. I did my best. The mean and moody look isn't my strong point.

Thursday 25 August

I can't seem to persuade anyone to join our little revolution at Holy Trinity and start some youth and children's work. I'm not giving up, though. We're going to turn this thing around. Pray and they will come.

Dot, one of our church volunteers, shared Pat's story with me today. He helps Dot out with the tea and toast for the homeless on Sunday mornings and comes to our 11.15 a.m. service. He is the hardest looking human being I've ever seen in the flesh. Somehow Dot ended up regularly visiting him in prison. Her kindness and compassion is helping to turn his life around. After he left prison she agreed to take him in. Pat might look like he's about to bite your nose off, but he is now committed to being a man of peace. I want to get alongside Pat. He has a lot to teach me.

Friday 26 August

Since church secretary Chris verbally roasted me over my harsh website reflections, he can't help me enough. He's taking care of the Trinity Music Festival logistics. Seeing him measuring up the stages in our car park with the organizers filled my heart with joy. It's a sign that the Trinity old guard are embracing the new.

For once the girls went down without tears or poo tonight. It put Anna in a very good mood. We ate chicken biryani and watched the film *Sideways* for the umpteenth time. I adore the spiky interaction between the two lead actors. 'I'm not drinking ****ing Merlot!'

More nights like this, please.

Sunday 28 August

I gently encouraged Irene to preach with her own authentic voice. Theological college seems to have knocked it out of her a bit. From the pulpit, she has a tendency to sound like the Queen Mother ordering another gin and tonic. Irene has got so much to say to ordinary people about the love and impact of Christ and has one of the most naturally pastoral hearts I've ever come across. I'm trying to drink in her kindness and compassion. I'm slowly getting the courage to gently feed back to my colleagues. I expect them to do the same with me.

We desperately need a children's and youth worker. I can tell the kids are getting restless and bored during morning worship. Our precarious number of new families won't stick around if being in church is more stressful than being out of it. We can't let that happen. A quality crèche and Sunday school is the answer.

Monday 29 August

We joined the bank holiday crowds going to Hornsea. I love this town. It's the proper seaside. So much character. The whiff of other people's fish and chips was everywhere. From our seafront bench I watched the contented expressions as families tucked into their haddock and mushy peas with wild abandon. It was only 10.30 a.m. Spotted this lovely sign outside one of the Hornsea churches: 'The creed of an unsophisticated old lady: "I goes to bed thankful and I wakes up hopeful."'

A proper day off restores the soul. I made the girls laugh by arsing around on a stone lion statue. After playing in a pretty little park decorated with neat rows of garish flowers, we went for a quick pint. The barmaid had a face like thunder and a potty mouth. She clearly felt that actual customers were a huge cross to bear. A massive inconvenience to her texting and smoking. We sat outside in its pathetic excuse for a beer garden but were driven away by the wasps. They were friendlier than the barmaid. Grim pub aside, the four of us left Hornsea feeling much better about the world and each other than when we first drove in. It dawned on me on the drive back that we actually have two daughters to take to the seaside! Amazing.

Tuesday 30 August

I wrote to the BBC's *The One Show* today to ask if they'll feature our quest to recruit Holy Trinity's first youth worker in 700 years. We need Gyles Brandreth on the case.

Wednesday 31 August

A potentially very significant day. All my flesh pressing around the Old Town might have paid off. Lee Kirman, landlord of The Kingston, called to ask about the possibility of staging Hull's massive annual real ale and cider festival inside Holy Trinity. He told me that the organizers – Hull CAMRA (Campaign for Real Ale) – currently pay the council thousands to stage it in City Hall. Punters have complained that it's too small and too hot for the beer. I reassured Lee that we have the room – and it's *always* cold. Apparently one of the CAMRA committee was lamenting to Lee about their issues and thought he was joking when he mentioned my name and said I'd be up for it. I'm totally convinced already that it should happen. What better way to connect us to the ordinary people of this city? They may not come in for Sunday worship yet, but they'll probably come in for a delicious ale. This could put us on the map. It sends out the perfect message that we are here to serve. The missional potential is huge. I've just got to persuade everyone else at Trinity that it's a good idea. Not everyone will be happy about beer in church. I think I can do it. This could be the big one.

Sunday 4 September

We seemed awash with new people at the 9.30 a.m. service. Word is clearly spreading that this church has a pulse. They just kept coming in. Church virgins many of them.

A lovely young family brought in their six-month-old daughter, who they want me to baptize. I bonded with them. With so many newbies I gave the worship a much more relaxed start. I explained clearly what was going on and why we were doing what we were doing at every stage of the liturgy. I used John Keane's painting 'Fairy Tales of London (1)', which hangs in the Ferens Art Gallery, in the confession. I said the mother in the picture is so often how we come into church: burdened, harassed and distracted. I held what I hoped would be a powerful silence while we called to mind those things. The moment was ruined a bit when one of the drunk homeless guys walked to the front and shook my hand furiously. 'Thanks for the tea, Rev!' he shouted repeatedly, until I eventually coaxed him back down the aisle. Not exactly the holiest of moments. Then the hymn words on the projector screen were different from the ones the band were singing. It was comedy hour.

Total chaos. I caught Neal and Irene's eye. We burst out laughing. We wouldn't want to be anywhere else.

Tuesday 6 September

I presented Jamie with his first Bible this afternoon. He said he'd poured all his booze away. He seems determined to quit for good.

Wednesday 7 September

I'm burning out. I know things are going well but it's all coming at a cost. I feel wired. I need the comfort and peace of a quiet, darkened room. I was too snappy with people. A Salvation Army captain didn't show up for a meeting which annoyed me. I only just managed to resist sending him a snotty email.

I pushed the babies round town for a bit this afternoon in the buggy. I carelessly forgot to put the wheel lock on while browsing in a shop window. Out of the corner of my eye I saw the buggy begin to roll towards the road. It was like that slow-motion Union Station scene in *The Untouchables*. Mercifully a guy walking past stopped it just in time. I didn't feel it was necessary to mention the incident to Anna.

Thursday 8 September

The bishop led a session for us curates this morning. He talked about the book *The Contemplative Pastor* by Eugene Peterson. It made me paranoid that my urgent, frenetic approach to church and ministry was wrong. Not contemplative enough. 'Busy people are either vain or lazy,' the bishop said. I'll get my coat.

I excitedly pitched an idea to Mark the organist about the forthcoming harvest service. The church will be packed with kids from the local all-boys secondary school, Trinity House. I'm determined to spice things up and get their attention. They've been bored to within an inch of their young lives in previous years. I said to Mark that I wanted to get a couple of pupils up at the front to play an icebreaker game at the start of the service. I suggested 'Name That Tune' on the organ. 'Please can you learn the *Match of the Day* theme and that new Lady Gaga song?' I asked hopefully. Mark's eyes rolled into his forehead. He sauntered off muttering something. Was that a 'yes'?

For the first time, the girls recognized us as their parents when we picked them up from nursery tonight. Joy flooded our hearts. Then we got home and changed them. The contents of Esther's nappy were so foul and inhuman that I did a little burp of sick into my mouth.

Friday 9 September

I'm listening to a lot of hip hop lately. It reminds me of being 13 again in Nicky Jefferson's bedroom in Newborough Street, York. Two white kids in shell suits with large clocks and stolen VW car signs round their necks. We spent far too much time pretending we lived in Compton, Los Angeles. Rediscovered this nice line from Public Enemy's Chuck D: 'Believe in something or you'll fall for anything.'

I don't know why I read R. S. Thomas on my day off. He is the ultimate joy hoover. How about this for a cheery few lines to help you feel better about the world: 'So now in winter hateful is the sea,/Hateful its low and melancholy roar;/And yet most hateful is thy memory,/My sole companion on the lonely moor.'

Saturday 10 September

I took a couple of the St Paul's Boxing Academy coaches for lunch today. We discussed forgiveness and the problem of evil between mouthfuls of coronation chicken and curly fries.

Sunday 11 September

A grim morning meteorologically but, in the end, spiritually far brighter. I'd walked into the 9.30 a.m. service a bit despondent. There weren't many who'd braved the rain. Most of the newbies seem to have left. I wondered what the point of it all was. Neal didn't help my mood, to be honest. We both like to be in early to arrange the church furniture in a certain way. I fear we're both on the spectrum. He moved the lectern to a spot that wasn't right. I shifted it, he moved it back, I shifted it. Finally he told me – loudly and irritably – that the placement of the lectern was his job, not mine. I muttered. He muttered. We avoided each other for a while.

It was one of those mornings when everyone looked hacked off when they shuffled into the chancel for worship. I could tell they were wondering why they'd got up early to come to a very large, very cold church to sit on a very uncomfortable pew. I delivered the welcome and a dour opening prayer in keeping with the mood of the place. Then I spotted him. Danny. He looked like Shaggy from *Scooby-Doo*. Unkempt and sleepy with a scraggly ginger beard. He looked wonderfully out of place in his cool tweed jacket and Converse trainers. It turns out he is a new student at Hull College. He got wasted the other night and felt like he needed to come to church for the first time. He wasn't sure how you actually find one so he ended up visiting the Hull tourist information centre to ask for some advice. The baffled woman at the desk asked him: 'Have you tried that big one up the road in the Old Town? It's called Holy Trinity. I'm sure they do services.' I've arranged to meet Danny for coffee next week. He seems to be looking for deeper meaning in his life. He didn't seem to be fazed by the fact he pretty much made up our youth intake this morning – and he's 21. Having him here this morning was a huge encouragement. Danny made the sun come out.

Monday 12 September

I'm feeling relaxed and refreshed. Things have gone well with the in-laws staying here. There's a newfound warmth and generosity of spirit between us all. I'm enjoying their company. Our massive bust-up on holiday in Bamburgh just before we moved to Hull feels a lifetime ago. We all carry the scars from that week, but I see now how important it was to get us to where we are now. Our frustration with each other was finally verbalized in a big showdown in the holiday home. We told each other how we really felt. Loudly and with great enthusiasm. All those years of suppressed dissatisfaction came pouring out. Driving away the next morning, I didn't think we'd ever be able to be in the same room again. Now here we all are, actually getting along OK. Not so much as a barbed comment or dramatic tut to speak of. It's major progress. We'll laugh about Bamburgh one day. But not yet. Too soon.

I collected my giant copy of Rembrandt's *The Return of the Prodigal Son* for my office wall. It will do me the power of good to stare up at it as I work. It speaks to me in such deep, affecting ways. The way the father holds his son with one large, masculine, powerful hand and one soft, feminine, gentle hand. It's my Christ holding me. I need constantly reminding that he sees me the way the father does his lost son.

Anna busted me in the throes of a glorious power snooze this afternoon. I tried to convince her I was trying out a new meditative prayer technique. 'What, snoring your head off?' she said. No compassion, that woman.

I was live on Radio Humberside's version of *Desert Island Discs* tonight. The presenter James Hoggarth shares my love of Oasis. He played 'Wonderwall' for me. We talked about my pioneering work and hopes and dreams for Holy Trinity. I always feel on the edge of spouting something wildly inappropriate. I said: 'For too long we've been a church that says "no". My job is to make sure we start saying "yes".'

Tuesday 13 September

I've heard nothing from *The One Show* about running a feature on our youth worker situation. Clearly Gyles Brandreth has a lot on his plate.

I sat with two street drinkers I'd noticed in Trinity Square this afternoon. They spoke candidly about their lives in slurred speech and then asked to be blessed. As I got up to leave, one said: 'I've got terrible liver problems, Father!' before cackling out a throaty laugh and draining an entire bottle of Diamond White.

Neal and I have finally negotiated the format of the Trinity House harvest service. I gently tried to encourage him to think more creatively and not settle for what they've always done before. I'm on a mission to leave these hundreds of schoolkids not feeling as if they'd rather be in double maths than engage with church and faith.

Wednesday 14 September

Visited bodybuilder John at the dialysis clinic this afternoon. He's just started coming to our 9.30 a.m. service a bit and told me he has to be hooked up to a machine three times a week. I was surprised to find him engrossed in the Bible I gave him a few weeks ago. 'There's lots of this I don't understand,' he said. I agreed. We talked through his questions. I left him with more to think about.

Coach Paul made us do extra time in the plank position at boxing training tonight. I was in danger of barfing over the blue crash mats and passing out. 'Blame the vicar for these extra 10 seconds,' Paul boomed. 'He's not working hard enough.'

Thursday 15 September

Current addictions: NFL; hip hop; custard creams; saying 'Wasaaap!' when I answer the church phone.

Two contrasting encounters today. I arrived at Trinity this morning to discover a homeless guy called Graham fast asleep outside the side door. Chip wrappers and dance music CDs were scattered around him. I got him a brew and a KitKat. We talked about his life, favourite fag brand, the existence of God and his experiences of taking ecstasy. Graham said he ended up on the streets after frying his brain taking too many drugs during his clubbing days.

I then met student Danny for a coffee to discuss how he ended up at Trinity on Sunday. He's lovely and wants to explore Christianity big time. Danny is a keen electric guitarist. I can't wait to unleash him in the Sunday worship. He has signed up to do our next Christian basics course. This is significant. Things are moving.

Friday 16 September

A waste of a day off. I was grouchy and impatient with the girls all day. Fatherhood is just too hard. I find it fairly unpleasant so much of the time. Is that normal? Trying to do family life and ministry at this pace is not working. I don't see how I can be a competent husband and dad and a pioneering vicar. Getting ordained feels like a terrible idea today. My life used to be lovely. I also remembered today that Archbishop Sentamu has to decide this year if I'm fit to be a priest. He'll be monitoring and reflecting on my every move this probation year. I'm currently what the Church of England calls a deacon (from the Greek meaning 'helper', so Google tells me). You never stop being one, apparently, because our first and most important calling is to be servants. Foot washers. 'Once a deacon, always a deacon,' bishops love to pontificate at ordination services. I know that and agree with it, but it will be humiliating if I don't get my wings as a priest. Today, though, I don't care. I just want my old life back.

Saturday 17 September

Hull Trinity Festival is in danger of falling apart with only 13 days to go. The bar owners keep having bust-ups. There's so much mistrust and backbiting. I'm trying to hold them all together through the delicate art of diplomacy. Seeing all sides but being careful not to take any. I've persuaded my friend Pete to host an open mic night with me on the Friday night in The Kingston to kick off the festival. I'm going to be the compère and encourage mass singalongs. We're ramping up our vision to be a church of prayer and parties.

Sunday 18 September

Took the service at our daughter church, Holy Apostles on the Thornton Estate, this morning. As usual, only the Glenton family, Terry and Sharon and old Sid had turned up. As the sun was so glorious outside, I took my guitar out onto the church steps and played 'Give Me Oil in My Lamp' as loudly as I dared. A few inquisitive heads popped out of some windows in the high-rises. A couple of shady-looking blokes in caps and tracksuits were milling around. I shouted 'good morning' to anyone who walked past. The Glenton kids came out and joined in. The more we sang, the less embarrassed we felt. Eventually a lady with two adorable toddlers stopped to watch us. 'Are we allowed to come in?' she asked me warily. *'Absolutely!'*, I hollered back, a bit too keenly. Within minutes they all had a tambourine in their hands and the service was away.

This evening in Oscars Bar I met a guy who opened up to me about infertility. He's been through eight courses of IVF with his partner. His voice cracked as he told the story. His huge shovel hands gripped his glass of Stella more and more tightly. He said they'd now settled for a life without children. His story was so nearly our story. It brought it all back to me. Those moments when we discovered Anna wasn't pregnant. Her tears as we drove home from the IVF appointments. Nothing I said could make it better. And then it did happen. Anna's incredulous face when the nurse said she was pregnant. I looked at the guy and couldn't say anything. Why us and not them?

Monday 19 September

Inspired by this Brian Clough quote today: 'Don't send me flowers when I'm dead. Send them to me now, so I can enjoy them.'

Wednesday 21 September

I'm back with the four Morning Glory boys on retreat. Aidan, Jason, Sanjay and Rob. We've come away to the secluded Westwood Christian Centre near Huddersfield. The views over the Colne Valley are soul-restoring. Who would have thought we'd still be meeting after that random late-night whiskey session on the theological college retreat nearly three years ago? Our decision – by that roaring fire in the wilds of Northumberland – to meet weekly for prayer and bonding was so significant. It kept us on an even keel during that disorienting time. None of us have changed. I suppose we fall out a bit less. In typically theatrical style, Aidan read out a wordy reflection on what it meant for us to be together again:

Five men gathered, reacquainting, realigning, reimagining a call to pray continually; retelling, reminding, rewinding, recalibrating or just pausing to pray for people. A band of brothers, bountifully blessed by a beautiful being.

It went on. For quite some time. I think he means that we're going to talk a lot of crap over some bottles of wine and pray a bit.

Rob made a great soup and we talked about our situations and hopes and dreams for the future. It all got a bit emotional as we talked late into the night. I feel relieved to be in the presence of these boys again.

Thursday 22 September

Time away from Anna has given me some insights. We're like bickering strangers at the moment. There's a disconnect. We are at cross purposes. She seems to spend all our time together telling me off. I'm sure, in her case for the defence, she'd testify about my selfish attitude and excessive time away from the family. I see that. I want to be better. We need more quality time together. And fun. Lots more fun.

Eight days until the music festival.

Friday 23 September

The in-laws looked after the girls so Anna and I could get out for a few hours. We cleared the air over a couple of ales in Ye Olde White Harte. We agreed that things have not been good between us. We resolved to make it better. I'll try to be less selfish. She'll try to shout at me less often. Landlord Lee showed me the flyer for the Trinity Music Festival. It read: 'Open mic night at The Kingston, Friday 7.30 p.m. till late. Hosted by the "Mad Reverend" Matt Woodcock and Pete Hale!' Thanks, Lee.

Sunday 25 September

Felt so despondent as I looked out from our high pulpit at the 11.15 a.m. service to see a light smattering of elderly folk. They seemed to have deliberately placed themselves as far away from each other as possible. I had to draw on all my reserves of restraint and decorum not to stop the service during a particularly turgid hymn and shout: 'Does anyone actually want to be here, because you all look thoroughly miserable?!' They're expecting it to be dull and irrelevant. I see the blokes sneaking out for a fag. They'd rather kill themselves puffing away on a cold bench outside, than be on a cold pew inside having their life drained away in a tedium of words and liturgies that have no bearing on their real-life circumstances. And that's just our organist. I've clocked him creeping out with his baccy tin during our sermons. Rude – but understandable. If we can stop Mark straying outside then we can keep anyone in.

Meeting my best friend Lee back in York tonight was like balm to my weary soul. We did the quiz at The Sun. We cried with laughter when a guy in a neighbouring snug farted loudly in a lull between questions. It was sensational comic timing.

The music festival is in *five* days.

Wednesday 28 September

I peaked too early taking the school assembly at Trinity House this morning. I'd just about managed to hold their attention when I stupidly handed out some invitation cards for our harvest service. During the final prayers they'd been transformed into paper planes. It only took one to be launched at my head before the chapel was like a scene from the Battle of Britain. I said the final blessing kneeling for cover behind the lectern.

Thursday 29 September

Christ's words from the Gospel of Matthew resonated with me today: 'Are you able to drink the cup that I am about to drink?' Basically, are we willing to do what God is asking? Jesus had doubts and fears on the road to his crucifixion. It feels like a question relevant to my work in Hull at the moment. I know I'm not facing torture and death (I hope) but am I prepared to keep pouring myself out for so little reward? I'm not sure I've got what it takes to help turn this church around.

Danny the student said he wanted to meet me this afternoon. The negative way I was feeling, I feared the worst. He's leaving, I thought. He's found a shinier church with leaders who know what they're doing. He's lost his faith. 'Would it be OK if I got baptized?' he asked. I let out a whoop, jumped up and gave him a crushing bear hug. 'Is that a yes?' he said.

The Hull Trinity Festival is tomorrow! No going back now.

Friday 30 September

First day of Hull Trinity Festival. The first time the Old Town's pubs and clubs have come together to try to breathe new life into the area. This is massive. I turned up at the church early doors, nervous. The festival is just the sort of thing needed to get this long-neglected area up off its knees and back into the ring. If it fails, then the naysaying, negative doom-mongers (of which there are too many round here) will have a field day.

I was asked to officially open the festival with a blessing in the Kings Bar & Lounge. To my amazement, it was heaving. I said a few words of encouragement and then prayed for a 'banging weekend'. 'AAAmen!' the crowded shouted in unison. The festival was up and running.

I was apprehensive about hosting the open mic night with Pete. The idea was that we'd get a few local acts lined up to sing and get things bouncing as an acoustic duo. I hoped some random revellers would get up to sing. It helped that Pete is the most chilled-out human being I know. The Kingston attracts all kinds of life on a Friday night. I feared we'd get eaten alive, beaten or molested – maybe all at the same time. Many punters thought the dog collar was part of our stage act. Pete and I kicked things off with

'Wonderwall', 'Ring of Fire' and 'I Am the Walrus'. Terry from Holy Apostles then did a few solo numbers. The crowd went nuts for him. Something special was brewing in the place. As my confidence grew, I invited people in the crowd to get up and sing a song with Pete – 'the human jukebox'. One scantily-clad woman sang something resembling 'Wuthering Heights'. To call what she was wearing a dress would be a huge exaggeration. Two wild ladies did the Amy Winehouse version of 'Valerie'. They tried to carry Pete off with them. He looked helpless and afraid.

Word began to spread round the Old Town. More and more people poured in. You couldn't move for sweaty bodies and hoarse voices. You could feel the place bubbling over with joy. I can't think of another couple of hours like it in my life. I encouraged everyone to form into a massive group hug as we finished with an insane version of 'Suspicious Minds'. I then invited the entire pub to church on Sunday. They all promised to come.

Trinity Square was buzzing all night. Glorious live music seeped out of virtually every bar and pub. This was the dream. Pete and I were invited back to an after-party at one of the venues to meet all the owner's friends and staff. The goodwill towards Holy Trinity was overwhelming. I got chatting to a really nice woman at the end.

'What do you do for a living?' I asked.

'I'm a topless model,' she replied, casually.

'You?'

'A vicar,' I spluttered, a bit less casually.

She found it hilarious. We talked about her family and boyfriend. He looked like the blonde baddie out of *Avatar* – only less friendly. I offered to marry them at Holy Trinity if the time ever came.

Pete and I eventually wobbled home. We were exhausted but full of lovely stories about things we'd seen and people we'd spoken to. I officially love my job.

Saturday 1 October

Day two of the festival. We were still on a high this morning. I did briefly wonder if it was appropriate for me to be out that late in those kind of places. Am I being too edgy? Does this take pioneering too far? What would Jesus do? I think he would have been with us. I hope so, anyway.

Pete and I were back in Trinity Square at 8.30 a.m. I'm so grateful for his friendship. Whenever I call on him, he comes to help. We couldn't resist playing an impromptu set on the festival stage while no one was around. A little crowd had gathered by the end – mostly of hung-over landlords from the surrounding bars pleading with us to stop.

The weather was glorious all day and the festival venues were heaving. I had a significant chat with a barman who has eight kids with four different mothers. Another nightclub owner wanted to show me his place in action. He invited me into the DJ booth to address the crowd at about 2 a.m.

Me: 'Hi everyone! I'm Reverend Matt from over the road at Holy Trinity! It's lovely to see you all.'
Cue deafening cheer.
The DJ: 'Get yourselves down to Matt's church services in the morning – sort your f***ing heads out!'
Cue even louder cheer.
'Now get your hands in your pockets and help them out, you tight-arsed b******s!'

I looked out onto the packed dance floor and one of the nightclub staff was walking round with a large bucket collecting money for Holy Trinity. He was dressed as a giant pink condom.

Monday 3 October

Anna went back to work today as a council admin worker in York. She's missed it. She set off with the babies yesterday after church. The plan is that she'll stay at her parents and the girls will be looked after by them on one day and my mum on the other. I'll pick them up on Tuesdays. It's not ideal. I was hoping she'd have a rethink, but she loves her job and a promise is a promise. I miss them already. I'm too loud for the house to be this quiet.

Tuesday 4 October

Hundreds of pupils from our neighbouring all-boys secondary school Trinity House will descend on our harvest service on Sunday. Teenagers. Forced to go to church. Made to sit still and shut up. Bored to within an inch of their young lives. The toughest crowd of all. So I've had an idea for my sermon. I'm preaching about Zacchaeus, the vertically-challenged crook who climbed up a tree to get a better view of Jesus. His life was transformed when Jesus called him down and invited himself round to his house for tea. I thought I could act that bit out. Transform our tall pulpit into a tree and climb down it. I'll try to persuade Mark the organist to play the *Mission Impossible* theme tune during that bit. I'd do the rest of the sermon from a soap box right in the midst of the pupils. The point being to encourage them to get a better view of Jesus.

Bringing the church into disrepute aside, my only reservation is that our pulpit is high. Dangerously high for someone bedecked in ungainly, flowing robes. My vertigo kicked in a bit when I got up there and looked down for a bit of a rehearsal. This is a sermon illustration that could genuinely break my neck.

I visited Emma and Craig at their home tonight. Their daughter Ellie will be my first baptism at Holy Trinity.

Wednesday 5 October

Today when no one was around I practised the pulpit climb down for the harvest festival service on Sunday. It's doable. But perhaps a bit different in full clergy garb – and with the Lord Mayor directly below me. One snag or slip and it doesn't bear thinking about. I can see the headline: 'Reckless Rev in Lord Mayor death plunge!'

I found out that the Guildhall has about fifty weddings booked this year. We have hardly any. Couples simply don't know it's possible to get married at Holy Trinity. We need a communications offensive. Our weekends should be buzzing with blushing brides and babies getting dunked.

The girls are sleeping a bit better, thank goodness. Anna and I actually managed a conversation tonight – a real adult one! It felt like seeing each other again properly after a very long time. She's loving being back with her friends and colleagues on the council's environmental health and trading standards team. Going back to work has been so important to Anna. I didn't mention how much I missed them on Sundays and Mondays. It wasn't the right time. We snuggled into each other on the sofa. I've missed us doing that too.

I've downloaded Noel Gallagher's new song 'Let the Lord Shine a Light on Me'. For someone so publicly sniffy about God, his songs namecheck him an awful lot.

Thursday 6 October

Once again, I'm beset with a few niggling doubts about my suitability for this job. I felt so different to the other curates at the chaplaincy training last night. Listening to their experiences made me wonder if the way I do it is appropriate. I feel on the edge of appropriate the whole time.

We've decided to have a Trinity clergy meeting every Thursday morning in The William Wilberforce, a Wetherspoons round the corner. It used to be a bank. The old manager's office is the perfect place to pray, plot, share and generally disagree at great volume. Today we came up with an optimistic action plan for the next six months and agreed on our different areas of responsibility. Neal will seek to grow people's faith. Irene will help make sure they don't lose it. I will go out to see if people have any in the first place. Neal treated me to poached eggs. They were cold and the yolk wasn't runny enough. I didn't mention it.

A huge, fierce-looking bloke with brutal facial scarring and gold teeth asked me for a blessing in the chapel this afternoon. Admittedly, my first thought was, 'Why, what have you done?' If I was casting the new Martin Scorsese film, he'd be hired to play someone not very nice. We shared a holy moment. He scrunched his eyes closed, bowed his head, and opened his huge palms while I prayed. The guy who plays classical guitar in the church on Thursdays wasn't happy. He interrupted us with a rant – my loud praying voice was distracting him from his recital. I was fuming at his attitude. I politely encouraged him to stop complaining and show more compassion. I then introduced him to the muscly focus of my prayers. One look at my new friend and he couldn't be more accommodating. We were mates again pretty quickly after that. He went back to his recital.

Friday 7 October

A lovely visit from Sam and Jess today. One of my definite success stories has been setting these two up. They are beautiful people. I still remember Sam contacting me randomly when I worked at my old church in York to say that he was interested in faith. He found God and he quickly found his soulmate in those pews – Jess. Now she was 26 weeks pregnant. Her face was beaming sunshine as she patted and stroked her glorious bump. Anna and I filled their car up with all our excess baby stuff. Sam is full of nervous, giddy excitement. He confessed to having already bought a pair of industrial ear defenders to protect him from the cries. He'll learn.

Saturday 8 October

I've offended the Holy Trinity flower arrangers. They were aggrieved at me wanting to move their pulpit harvest display. Apparently it has been that way for the last 1,000 years or something. I called the chief arranger to apologize. She agreed to move it slightly. I've ordered *The Art of Diplomacy* by François de Callières.

Churchwarden Tim has got wind of my sermon plans for the harvest service. He's worried that I might kill myself. He made me climb down the pulpit a couple of times to prove that I would survive.

Sunday 9 October

I had the most extraordinary moment of clarity as I looked down at the 700-strong congregation who'd packed Holy Trinity for the harvest service. I was taken aback that the church was so full. Every pew was taken. My legs nervously spasmed behind the high pulpit. I could see the hundreds of Trinity House school boys. Bored and fidgety. The great and good of Hull were all in. The Lord Mayor, honorary aldermen, naval cadets and police chiefs. My bum was in squeak mode.

I'd got into church at 7.30 a.m. to practise the pulpit climbdown fully robed up for the first time. Seldom has a vicar looked more undignified. Then, just before the service I was engaged in a heavy pastoral encounter in the choir aisle. A distressed lady feared her husband had got cancer. She asked me to pray for him.

Neal began the service by walking around the pews dishing out raisins and Jaffa Cakes as a symbol of God's goodness and blessing. His theological point was a bit lost on the Trinity House kids as they swept into them like locusts. The school's steel band played a joyfully toe-tapping version of *Blessed Be the Name of the Lord*.

In the end I went for it. 'Please don't try this at home,' I warned. I nodded at Mark the organist. He launched into the *Mission Impossible* theme tune. I swung a leg over the side of the pulpit and tried to lever myself down. It's a bit of a blur after that. No one realized how close I came to falling. For a few horrible seconds I got stuck, dangling and stranded over the Lord Mayor's head. The congregation were going nuts. They thought it was part of the act. Their initial gasps of shock had turned into clapping, cheering and whistling. I thought I was going to die – and take others with me. Mercifully my foot eventually found something to stand on. My body sighed with relief. For a heart-stopping moment I thought I'd followed through. I hit terra firma and calmly walked to the soap box to finish the sermon. 'Jesus comes and meets us wherever we are,' I said. 'Whatever we've done or not done. He invites us to know him.' Never again.

Monday 10 October

On daddy day-care duties all day. I took the girls to a toddler group. It was excruciating. I was the only bloke there. I felt my parenting came under the closest of scrutiny.

I found out tonight that Tivvy, my Uncle Mike's best mate and the drummer in his band, has been diagnosed with asbestosis. Everyone's gutted for him. He wants to keep playing in the band until he can't physically do it. I've always liked Tivvy, he's such a character. He is one of many victims of asbestosis. It's an absolute scandal that so many men who built train carriages in York were exposed to it. They were led to believe it was harmless. Tivvy told me they used to have snowball fights with asbestos when they were apprentices. All the time they were unwittingly breathing in its killer dust. The compensation payments are scant consolation when you're facing death.

Friday 14 October

Bar manager Allen got in touch today with a proposal. Fired up by the success of the Hull Trinity Festival, he wants to hold an Old Town Halloween party in Holy Trinity, complete with revellers dressed as devils, vampires and witches. 'It's the ideal venue, Matt!' Allen said. 'We could hang zombies from the pulpit! How cool would that be?' I've got a lot of work to do round here.

Saturday 15 October

Uncle Mike and Deb came to stay tonight. They told me that Tivvy is still struggling to come to terms with his diagnosis. We went to City Hall to watch an AC/DC tribute band, and afterwards to The Kingston for a nightcap. I waxed lyrical about how earthy Hull is, but that I'd never seen any trouble. Just at that moment we looked out onto Trinity Square to see two rival stag parties knocking hell out of each other. The police were quickly on the scene to make arrests.

More curates' training at the magnificently named College of the Resurrection in Mirfield this morning. A pleasant lady talked about how we can generate more weddings in our churches. Then in a striking gear change, she went on to talk about looking after our mental health. Or 'preventing madness' as she put it. I'm way past that.

Sunday 16 October

I hate it when Anna and the girls go back to York on Sunday afternoons. The house is so lonely. I know that was part of the deal of us moving here – that she would keep her job in York. But it's not working for me. The loneliness of this job is brought into sharper focus. I know loads of people here, but close friendship isn't easy when you do my job. I should probably make more effort to have a few people round on Sunday nights. Too much thinking time and introspection isn't healthy for me. I have a tendency to wallow. My edges blunt. I find myself becoming immersed in depressing poetry and the music of Nick Drake. Never a good sign. I took solace in the film *Jerry Maguire*. It wasn't the same watching it without Anna.

Monday 17 October

I visited a lovely family tonight. Seeing people in their homes is one of the most important things I do. Matt and Julie have been coming to our morning service a bit. They're not sure why. Matt says he's looking for more meaning in his life. They asked me to share my story. I told them about my 'road to Damascus' moment. 'What's Damascus?' Julie asked.

Tuesday 18 October

Heidi is poorly tonight. We're blaming teething, but who knows? Her pained cries were unbearable. I hate not being able to make her feel better immediately.

No one turned up to Neal's exploring faith course. He'll need encouraging and picking back up. You can't help but take it personally.

Wednesday 19 October

I did my first school assembly at Adelaide Primary School. It's right in the middle of the Thornton Estate near Holy Apostles. The staff are amazing. I think I overdid it. I whipped the kids up into a state of frenzy, dishing out too many Haribos and Flumps. Some of the staff gave me the death stare as they sought to restore order and pull their classes down from the ceiling.

Thursday 20 October

A productive Wetherspoons session with Neal and Irene. Irene and I had a robust debate about how we best serve and integrate the homeless on Sunday mornings. Neal looked on at us like a kindly uncle. Irene's argument won out in the end. We will do it her way. I'm enjoying having a colleague to go toe-to-toe with. Nothing is left unsaid.

Just as we were leaving, Neal introduced me to a lady called Tamzin. She's desperate to have kids one day but the doctors have told her it's unlikely due to a chronic illness. She prayed about it recently and said a deep peace washed over her. 'I want to start coming to church,' she said. 'How do I join?'

Another lady came into Holy Trinity a bit later and spoke to Irene. She blurted out that she's desperate to come to church too. What's going on? People are actually asking to come! Our desperate prayers for growth seem to be working. We should really say them more often.

Friday 21 October

I'm engrossed in a book about the life and work of the sixteenth-century painter Caravaggio. I keep finding myself stroking my chin and nodding as I try to make sense of paragraphs like this: 'Caravaggio paints with a strong and unmistakable sense of the perils and powers of looking. His pictures both embody and evoke an acute and piercing gaze.'

Pete has got me a ticket to see The Stone Roses' big reunion gig at Heaton Park. Their music is art I understand. Everyone I know tried and failed to get a ticket. There is a God.

Saturday 22 October

Quote of the day: 'Anyone can start something new. It takes real leaders to stop something old.'

I had an interesting faith debate tonight with the bass player in a riotous local band called The Hillbilly Troupe. He's a committed socialist. I challenged him to think about some of his most treasured ideals and policies and compare them to the central teachings of Christ. 'I think some of the Labour Party have been reading the Gospels,' I argued.

I'm a bit worried about the tone and length of our special Sierra Leone service tomorrow. It could be a long one. A delegation from the country – including the bishop – has come over to visit in an effort to forge better links with Hull. I wanted to welcome the party in their native language. Chris has warned me against it. Apparently there are hundreds of local dialects. He reckons I'm bound to screw it up and say the wrong thing. Something like: 'Greetings, bishop – I see your wife has the face of a hairy walrus, yes?'

Sunday 23 October

I dropped a pastoral clanger just before the start of the 9.30 a.m. service. One of our elderly regulars told me that her son-in-law had just been diagnosed with cancer of the oesophagus. I blurted out unthinkingly: 'My aunty died of that last year.' The lady said she didn't appreciate being told that. After I made a grovelling apology, she agreed to let me pray for him in the chapel after the service. I'll cross off hospital chaplaincy as a possible career move post-Holy Trinity.

There were only twelve of us worshipping at Holy Apostles Church on the Thornton Estate this morning. We made a lot of noise, though.

Monday 24 October

Bed-ridden all day after a four-hour puke-a-thon. Must have been something I ate. Biblical bathroom scenes.

Tuesday 25 October

My insides were not ready for that bowl of mulligatawny. I texted Anna with regular bathroom updates. 'Too much information, Woody!' she messaged back. Fair comment.

Wednesday 26 October

We were roused eight times by Esther and Heidi through the night. We're breaking personal records. We keep saying that it can't go on like this. That there must be a point when they just sleep. Anna's parents are being so helpful and supportive. We'd be sunk without them. Divorced too, probably.

I presented congratulations cards to the three new pros at the boxing club. I also bought coach Paul a mug with a picture of Jesus giving the thumbs up on it. He seemed confused, and mumbled an awkward 'thanks' before walking off. Probably to hide in the toilets until I'd gone.

Thursday 27 October

Lovely belly laughs with Anna in Costa Coffee. We scoured the online reviews for the hotel we'll be staying at in Gran Canaria for the big family holiday next month. 'It's a dump,' one said. 'What a s*** hole!' another guest wrote. It shouldn't be this funny after all the money we've spent.

Friday 28 October

I'm still engrossed in my book about the Italian Renaissance painter Caravaggio. I understand it more now. I like this quote: 'Caravaggio lived his life as if there were only carnival and Lent with nothing in between. His pictures are the legacy of his Lenten days.' I can relate to that way of being. The all or nothing approach to life. I can do silent prayer or raucous party. Days of fasting or frantic feasting. I just can't seem to do the bit in between. God didn't make me with a moderation button.

Saturday 29 October

Halloween? I just don't get it. At the entrance of Tesco's yesterday there was a staff member – a large tattooed bloke – dressed in a werewolf mask with a massive crucifix round his neck. Tesco's were actually paying this guy to jump out and chase unsuspecting shoppers through the car park with a toy machete. I gave a little girly squeal when he pounced on me as I strolled out with my meal deal.

I spotted our new church caretaker, Andy, being shown round by Churchwarden Tim. 'Do you really want to work here?' he was saying to him. 'You must be mad!' Unbelievable.

A local artist called Martin Waters has transformed our north choir aisle with a poignant poppy installation. 'Poppy Drift', he calls it. Four thousand of them have been laid out on the stone floor. It's so simple and moving. Such a helpful focal point and gathering place for Remembrance Day. We're expecting a lot of visitors.

It's my first Christening tomorrow. I'm nervous. Wriggling babies, slippery baptism gowns and water are a potentially hazardous combination in my hands. I got the font filled and practised my baptism technique with Heidi's doll in preparation for it.

Sunday 30 October

I broke my baptism duck with Ellie Mae Smith this morning. She won't be short of birthday presents with seven godparents to spoil her rotten. Seven! The guests looked so uncomfortable when they walked in. Their language wasn't brilliant, either. Yet seeing the church so full and alive with people of all ages made my heart soar.

I struggled to get their attention at first. They were happily talking and texting away, entirely oblivious to anything I was saying. In the end I picked Ellie up as I preached and walked her around them. A hush came over the place. Pin drops became audible. The whole baptism suddenly made more sense as they became transfixed by the innocent beauty of this little baby.

My only issue with the baptism itself was the laborious liturgy. The prayer over the water seemed to go on for days. It lost the room.

Ellie's mum sent me this lovely text tonight: 'Thank you for the lovely service and present you gave us. My family thought you was very good and my uncle and aunty are coming to church next Sunday as they would like you to christen their children. See you Sunday!' Excellent.

It's our wedding anniversary today. Seven years. Lovely Rowena, a wonderful lady from my old church in York, sent her annual cheeky text to remind me just in case, but I actually remembered and all was well. We're saving our proper celebration for Gran Canaria. Anna got me a lovely card. 'Thank you for our two beautiful daughters,' she wrote. 'I can't believe we made them!'

Monday 31 October

I met the 'Hull Pavarotti', aka Leroy Vickers, at church this morning. He's up for doing a charity opera show in our nave. Lovely guy with sparkly eyes. He gave me a blast of 'Nessun dorma' from the pulpit.

Wednesday 2 November

Bodybuilder John prayed out loud for the first time at our exploring faith group tonight. He'd been inspired by what he called a 'Jesus moment' in his local shop. The bloke at the counter mistakenly gave him a £20 note with his change. John only noticed when he'd walked out. He told us: 'I don't know what's happening to me but I went back in the shop and told the guy his mistake. He was so relieved. He could have lost his job. That would never have happened in the past. I'd have loved keeping that twenty quid!' This was massive for John. A little tangible sign of personal transformation. Of Christ at work within him. His prayer was so heartfelt. I heard sniffs among the bowed heads. I finished by reading Revelation 1.17–18: 'Then he placed his right hand on me and said, "Do not be afraid. I am the first and the last. I am the Living One: I was dead, and behold I am alive for ever and ever!"'

Thursday 3 November

Shaun, a lad from the Old Town, stood me up again for our God chat. Probably a good job. I have a massive ulcer on my tongue. Talking hurts. I feel like a Marvel character who's lost his special power. Anna seems worryingly happy about it.

With difficulty I recited Morning Prayer with Irene. I didn't think the Old Testament reading would ever end. Afterwards we looked round a new homeless facility on our patch. It has a fab cafe and conference facilities. I love the fact that the residents get ensuite bathrooms and TVs. They're treated with proper respect and dignity.

Saturday 5 November

Up at 4 a.m. to drive to Manchester Airport. We're going on holiday to Gran Canaria! There are 24 of us in all. It's a big group full of big personalities. Aside from me, Anna and the girls, there's Grandma and Mum, my sister Amy, her husband Keith, their three kids, Joely, Honor and Phoebe, and Keith's mum, Anne. Then cousin Becky, her husband Matt and their brood, Artie and Lily. And not forgetting Uncle Ally and our third cousin-in-law 17 times removed or something, Emma, her husband Andy and their three kids, Frankie, Alfie and Alma. It will be absolute chaos. My family don't seem to do steady, quiet people with calm level heads. Everything is a big drama, highly emotional and very, very loud. I love it. I love them. But will I still be saying that by the end of this week? Unlikely. It will be a titanic battle just to get a word in. My heart went out to those people without young children on the flight. There were toys flying, toddlers screaming and cooing grandmas offering unwanted parental advice. The flight attendants struggled to keep order. Thank heavens for my headphones and the drinks trolley.

Our resort complex – the Paradise Lago Taurito Hotel and Aquapark in Playa Taurito – is basically cut out of the side of a mountain. It's surrounded by rocky wasteland. We've done well. It's lovely. I sympathized with our fellow guests as my family loudly swarmed through reception in search of keys and complimentary fizz. Last one into the pool was a Jelly Baby.

Sunday 6 November

Brilliant first day. Scorching sun, high-spirited bonhomie, games, water slides, ice creams and diving on and off inflatable flamingos. The kids seemed to enjoy it too. The water slides are terrifying. My swimming shorts continually became wedged in my bum cleft as I shot round corners, flew over humps and splashed into the blue.

It's been lovely to get reacquainted with my family. To catch up with their good news, bad news, hopes and fears. I love how open and unguarded we all are as a group. There's something very special about lying on a sun lounger having quality conversation and laugh-until-you-cry moments with the people you love most in the world. I hadn't realized how much I'd missed them.

Monday 7 November

Esther and Heidi are thriving here. They're constantly passed between different family members to be cooed at, cuddled and pampered. Except when they need their nappy changing. Funny that.

Tuesday 8 November

One of the great days. Mum looked after the girls so Anna and I could enjoy a wedding anniversary meal in Puerto de Mogán. It's an idyllic little fishing village a short bus ride from the complex. A place rich yacht owners go to eat expensive squid by candlelight. I caught myself staring into Anna's eyes over our starters, a ridiculous 'cat who got the cream' look on my face. She's still delicious. Is there a better look on a woman than a tight red dress and black high heels that make that clack-clack sound when they hit the pavement? I don't think so. I made an effort too. Cousin Becky's fancy-pants husband Matt lent me one of his expensive shirts for the night.

We strolled round Mogán's sensational marina. Balmy breezes were blowing. We began in a bar playing jazz music where I treated Anna to a Piña colada. It had one of those brollies in it and everything. The magic was spoilt somewhat by a lady with nasty sunburn sitting behind us. She had a nerve-shredding, hacking cough and seemed to be aiming her disgusting fag smoke our way. I tutted dramatically as we left.

We found the perfect place to eat at a table overlooking the marina. We talked about where we'd sail to if we could and which vessel we'd travel on. We splashed out on my late Aunty Lynn's favourite holiday wine, Viña Sol, in memory of her. I had an unbelievable onion soup and king prawns with garlic. I felt so special when they gave me a little bowl of warm water to wash my fingers. We popped into a little intimate place for coffee on the way back to the taxi. A Spanish guy was singing Chris de Burgh covers. He had an unfortunate lisp.

We arrived back at base camp to discover our group in raucous, well-oiled mood. For Anna and me it was like that moment in Cinderella when the clock strikes twelve. The spell was broken. Back to reality. They'd had an outrageous few hours, apparently, fully embracing the hotel's live entertainment and wacky games. Uncle Ally won a grandads' competition. He had to run out into the audience and find items of clothes. The ladies lent him their bras. Even Grandma. It irritated me when they kept saying things like: 'It was the best night *ever* – you should have been there.' I wanted to whisk Anna back to Mogán. There were no balmy breezes here. Just my family in their underwear, being really, really annoying.

Wednesday 9 November

The babies have been a nightmare all day. I'd want to challenge stockbrokers, London cabbies or air traffic controllers as to who has the highest stress levels. I reckon trying to get through a packed mealtime on an all-inclusive holiday with grouchy twin girls in high chairs would take some beating. I sucked in long, calming breaths by the salad bar. Comments about how we should be parenting from some of our party are about as welcome as haemorrhoids right now. If cousin Becky's husband Matt makes one more quip about my fathering skills I'm going to beat him with something heavy.

Thursday 10 November

This holiday has made me realize what a neurotic, terrified mess I am when it comes to Esther and Heidi. Having kids when you've been told you never will must be the cause of it. My protective instinct is out of control. I am a helicopter parent – always swooping in to avert this and that disaster every time the girls move. I'm doing the family's head in. I worry about everything the twins do, everything they eat, every sound they make. It's giving me mouth ulcers. Mum took me to one side and very gently and lovingly told me to get a grip.

Bodysurfed big waves with Matt and Keith this morning. We were like three bloated, sunburnt pigs in a washing machine on fast spin. I later went deep with Andy sitting by the pool. He told me why he struggles with church. 'I don't like it when they make out that only Christians can be good people. I'm not a bad person.' I tried to explain that the Christian faith isn't reliant on goodness but grace – the idea that there's nothing we can do to make God love us any more or any less. It's absolute and unconditional. But I sadly recognized the church he described.

We all gathered by the beach bar to watch the sun go down. A wonderful interlude. There was a palpable sense of community and easy joy. We told far-fetched stories and committed to future adventures we'd never embark upon. Widower Uncle Ally whispered to me and Matt: 'How do I meet someone?' It sounds like he's ready to make the first tentative steps towards finding a new companion. It's what Aunty Lynne would want, I'm sure.

An amazing day. I just wish I wasn't so paranoid about the girls choking on bread sticks.

Friday 11 November

Final gathering by the pool. We're ready for home. Someone did an impromptu quiz. 'Who invented the bra? (Otto Titzling)' and 'Who invented the toilet? (Thomas Crapper)' being the pick of the questions. I had another long debate with Andy about the essence of 'truth'. Keith and I went for a final late-night stroll. We agreed that the sight and sound of the moonlit ocean was good for the soul. A special holiday. Loved it.

Monday 14 November

I've put an advert in the *Hull Daily Mail* for a drummer to play in a new church band I want to get going. They'll play worship songs from this century.

Later I encountered a lady crying in the Holy Trinity chapel. Her father fought in the war on the German side. She was upset about our Remembrance Sunday services, claiming that we made out that German people didn't matter. I told her that there were no winners in war.

I started another Christian enquirers' course in our front room tonight. There were ten of us including Anna. There's a real mix of ages, personalities and views. I am literally starting from scratch with most of them. A couple of the younger ones had no idea what Easter was all about, aside from the bunnies and the chocolate eggs.

Tuesday 15 November

Esther is adorable. Even at 3 a.m.

The local artist who asked if he could paint my portrait a few months ago came in to show me his finished work today. I'm slouching really badly. He thinks he's captured something of my 'essence' and wants to enter it into the Ferens Art Gallery portrait competition. All the winners will get displayed in there. The idea of this pleases me a bit too much. Ecclesiastes 1.2 came to mind: 'Vanity of vanities! All is vanity!' It didn't last. I stupidly posted it on Facebook. Ollie, my York friend (and I use the term loosely), said it looked as if I'd had a stroke.

Friday 18 November

I've come away to Wydale Hall in North Yorkshire for a curates' teaching retreat. It could be a real face-melter. We're learning about human nature, sin and forgiveness. I particularly enjoyed the session given by a theologian of the more progressive/liberal persuasion. He was just more interesting and left field. A feather ruffler. I respect that. He claimed that God 'delights' in our imperfections and that original sin is a nonsense. Then one of our group piped up that we are forgiven by God without even asking for it. That comment heated things up a bit among some of the more biblically conservative curates. The room was suddenly peppered with many an impassioned 'Yes, but …'. I sat back and enjoyed the show, trying to work out what I thought. Profuse sweating was an issue for some of the group. The radiators were too hot. My friend Paul Bromley was like a walking lava lamp.

Saturday 19 November

We were set some interesting moral dilemmas in this morning's session. In one of them, an out-of-control trolley is on course to kill five people. We had the chance to divert it so only one person would die. Would doing so make us murderers? Interesting to chew over but no clear answers emerged.

Later we looked at our role in taking confession and how we personally absolve someone. There was some lively discussion over what we should do if a confessor divulges some nasty criminal activity. Technically, we were told that what's said at confession stays at confession. I hope I'm never in that position.

We endured a final gruelling session before we decamped to the bar. We had to split into groups to share and seek feedback about our ministries and talk about any issues we had with forgiveness. But I wasn't in the mood to share any more confessions. I sought absolution in a pale ale instead.

Sunday 20 November

One of the older female curates made a beeline for me during the Peace at our final Eucharist. 'Don't let them get to you,' she said, cryptically. 'Don't let them change who you are.' I was grateful but a little perturbed. Who did she mean by 'them'? What did she know?

Excellent news. I received an email from a lass who'd seen my advert in the local paper about the pub service band. She wants to audition as the drummer. Things are coming together!

Monday 21 November

I reluctantly agreed to be part of a Band Aid spoof video to raise awareness about Christmas events in the Old Town. Different people from across the city centre have each sung a line. I was filmed singing Bono's lyric from the pulpit in full clerical robes. 'Well, tonight thank God it's them instead of you!' I really went for it. Now a *Hull Daily Mail* reporter has called to ask if it was appropriate to spoof a serious song about the famine in Africa. I told him that I didn't think this was a story. 'I have no comment,' I said (probably a bit irritably). They were words I used to hate hearing when I did his job. High drama is never far away in this place. It's wearying me.

I'm reading *The Gospel and the Catholic Church* by Michael Ramsey. He was a proper theological smarty-pants. Full of insights, wisdom and deep concepts I wish I could grasp properly. For instance, I've no idea what he's fully saying in this paragraph, but it sounds brilliant:

> *Jesus knew whence he came and whither he was going. His church on earth is scandalous with the question-marks set against it by bewildered men and with the question-mark of Calvary at the centre of its teaching; yet precisely there is the power of God found, if only the Christians know whence they come and whither they go. They are sent to be the place where the Passion of Jesus Christ is known and where witness is borne to the resurrection from the dead.*

Answers on a postcard, please.

Tuesday 22 November

A day of wonderful contrasts. For the first half I was at St Bede's Pastoral Centre with Sister Cecilia for a few hours of quiet spiritual reflection. She set me up in a comfortable room in the basement. I went with no preconceived ideas about what to read or meditate on. Eventually I came across Psalm 62. I repeated these words over and over again: 'My soul finds rest in God alone; my salvation comes from him. He alone is my rock and my salvation; he is my fortress and I will never be shaken.' It made me feel good.

When I got outside I saw Rick Witter, lead singer from my favourite York band Shed Seven. I've always liked him. No one his age should be able to fit into jeans that tight. The band have got their Christmas tour starting this weekend. I said I'd pray it went well.

Our church guitarist Terry took me to Hull's iconic New Adelphi Club tonight. It's literally on the end of a Coronation Street-style terrace. All the greats have played there including Oasis and Radiohead. I fell in love with the place. We'd come to see The Hillbilly Troupe. They're a wild band. Like a mash up of The Pogues and The Clash. For the encore they sang the Hank Williams gospel song 'I Saw the Light'. I'm sure he never played it like this lot. It was a surreal joy to hear these gravel-throated, hard-drinking blokes singing, 'I wandered so aimless, life filled with sin./I wouldn't let my dear Saviour in./Then Jesus came like a stranger in the night./Praise the Lord, I saw the light.' It was a profound moment for both of us. We became lost in worship. Arms aloft. Hearts bursting with the presence of God amidst the sweat and lager. I didn't want it to end.

Wednesday 23 November

The girls have obliterated our sex life. Lord knows I love them more than life itself, but I can't remember the last time Anna looked at me lustily.

In other news – Irene is frustrated that Holy Trinity is so cold and unwelcoming. It's the opposite of her personality. Anyone who comes within ten feet of her immediately feels warm and valued, as if they're being reunited with their favourite great aunt. It's her gift. We make a good team. She wants to build up what we're doing inside Holy Trinity, while my propensity is to be out the whole time.

I welcomed two huge school groups into church today. The history and architecture of Holy Trinity is not my strong point. I floundered at their questions, mumbling spectacular inaccuracies about its age and structure. I sprinted off to find our fount of all knowledge, Jean Fenwick.

Thursday 24 November

A fruitful clergy meeting in Wetherspoons this morning. I'm developing a lovely relationship with the bar staff. Maybe too good. Neal was smiling wickedly when he came back with the lattes. Apparently the lady who served him asked for my number. She's in her sixties. At least.

We talked about how to improve our welcome at Holy Trinity. I suggested recruiting a few more people on the door who were a bit less hostile to Christianity. I also gently challenged Neal about whether he had committed to too many unnecessary meetings. I think they take his focus away from being with and ministering to people. He is a gifted listener – particularly among the verbal diarrhoea sufferers.

I finished my sermon for Sunday. It's all in the editing for me – what to leave out. Splurging the words then purging them. I like the challenge of preaching here because so many of the people are biblically illiterate, bored easily or don't yet believe. Our weekly challenge is to communicate deep spiritual truths in a way that they can understand, relate to and, heaven forbid, enjoy.

I finished the day at cousin Becky and Matt's house. Tomorrow we're swimming a mile for charity. Matt revelled in telling me that he is a passionate atheist but would go to church for as long as it took to get his kids into a decent school. At least he's honest. I don't think he's alone.

Friday 25 November

Our charity swim was in York at one of those large upmarket gyms where the flat whites cost a week's wages. The highlight was watching Matt get cramp in his big toe. Becky had to lay him out by the poolside as he writhed around in agony like a hairy white walrus. I happily breast-stroked past him, giggling with pleasure. 'Would you like me to pray for you?' I shouted.

Saturday 26 November

My relentless relationship-building is paying off. It was a joy to see the Tucker family up ladders helping to put up our massive church Christmas trees this morning. A few months ago they came into church for a look round. They'd lived in Hull for years but never been in. I went to see them a few times and kept inviting them to stuff. Now they feel like they belong and are getting stuck in. Make the effort to get to know people and they will come. I'm convinced of it.

The girl who saw our drummer advert in the paper came in for her audition today. Molly was accompanied by her parents and younger brother. They weren't big talkers. Molly has no church background whatsoever. Her nose is pierced and she wants to drum like Keith Moon. She's hired.

Sunday 27 November

Ellie's family haven't been back to church since her baptism last month. It's the hopeful optimism that kills you. I'm learning that crushing disappointment is part of being a reverend. Staying positive, fighting cynicism, going for it again – that's the hard bit.

One of our church helpers, Maria, confided in me that Neal keeps confusing her for another lady at Holy Trinity called Mary. He even thanks her for leading intercessions that she hasn't actually done. 'I don't have the heart to tell him,' she told me. I reassured her that I'd sensitively let him know. I'll look forward to it!

Monday 28 November

A significant day. I popped into a pub called The Mission round the corner from Holy Trinity to meet the landlord, Ron. He's a real character with a wonderfully generous nose. Half of the pub used to be a chapel where there was a significant ministry to destitute seamen spilling out of the docks. Before I said anything, Ron suggested that we could use the chapel space as a worship area once a month – for free. What a legend. It's the perfect place to hold an alternative service for those who would never come to Holy Trinity. This feels like a God door opening.

Tuesday 29 November

Our church council just keep saying 'yes' to me. In one meeting tonight they approved the church beer festival, the possibility of rock bands playing in the nave and the launch of a new service in The Mission in January. It's unbelievable. I have huge respect for them. It will have been so hard for some of the old guard to put their hands up tonight. Admittedly there were some pointed coughs and harrumphs about the beer festival. That was until I told them it would generate about £3,000 in two days. The hands shot up. Neal was a big persuading factor. He gave a stirring account of his visit to St Martin-in-the-Fields in central London. They managed to raise £36 million to complete a major restoration project and are doing some innovative things now for the community. The church is the heartbeat of the area. Neal spoke with such passion that transformation felt genuinely possible. He sold the vision. Forget central London – why not in central Hull?

One of the St Martin's fundraising board, John Robinson, is willing to be part of the revolution and drive a possible transformation through. He was one of the key people at the massive Hull pharmaceutical firm Smith & Nephew and the former chairman of Railtrack. Neal urged the council to think and pray big. It all feels up for grabs. It will cost millions to make the building fit for purpose. Neal got approval to begin to pursue the project in earnest. I floated out of the meeting. I feel as a clergy team we've been given a huge stamp of approval. Permission to crack on and make things happen.

Wednesday 30 November

Disappointing date night with Anna. We got on each other's nerves and turned in early.

Thursday 1 December

I soaked up what I could at a compulsory clergy day at York Minster this morning. The Bishop of Durham, Justin Welby, was the keynote speaker. He reflected on the current financial crisis carefully and articulately. He made the bold claim that the financial and consumerist 'idols' of current British society had 'fallen' and the church was ideally placed to respond. It was great content, but just once at these clergy gatherings I'd love to turn up and be surprised. Shocked, even. Welby and the day's other speakers were all essentially talking about change, renewal and transformation. That the time is ripe for it. The air is full of it. And that the church of Jesus Christ has the potential to bring it in. So why are they still making us sit on cold, hard pews freezing our butts off? Why are we singing hymns so outdated that they were written at a time when men with large sideburns commuted to work on horseback and had supper by candlelight? Today was a chance to model what change could look like. I'm learning that so many of our bishops love to pontificate about the winds of change. Clergy love to hear it. I worry, though, that until some of our own idols have fallen it just won't happen.

Friday 2 December

Day off. Anna and I strolled into town with the girls. I love it when I turn my phone off and I can be totally present. We went into Debenhams and I tried out a chair I could use for reading and prayer. It's perfect for my office. It reclines back and everything. Anna claims I'm doing too much 'reclining' when it comes to household chores lately. 'It's time to step up, Woody,' she said. I've committed to doing the dishes, cleaning the bathroom once a week and remembering that the bog brush isn't just for decoration.

Saturday 3 December

Stood up for the third time by Shaun for our God chat tonight. Jesus will have come back by the time he turns up.

Sunday 4 December

Shambolic scenes at our daughter church Holy Apostles this morning. I arrived 20 minutes early to find that the door wouldn't open. It was freezing. One of our few faithful members, Sid, was stood outside with his teeth chattering. In the end we held the service in the front room of the church-owned house next door. It was warm and – worryingly – comfortably fitted us all in. Ministry on this estate is brutal.

A life-size nativity scene has been erected inside Holy Trinity. Neal borrowed some mannequins from Burtons. Our Angel Gabriel is terrifying.

Monday 5 December

Esther is poorly. She puked and pooed all night. One moment you think they're invincible, the next they seem as vulnerable as tiny chicks in a nest. I went in to check on her an unhealthy amount of times.

I went to visit my priest friend, Adam, today. He's really struggling with his boss, who sounds like a joyless, heartless curmudgeon. They see the Bible and ways of 'doing' church very differently. It won't end well. He showed me round his patch. I found a joke shop and tried to cheer him up by putting on silly hats and a chef's apron that made you look as if you were starkers. It was lovely to hear Adam laughing. He's a beautiful soul doing brave things in a tough parish. I'm worried about his mental health. He needs more support. And a boss who's not a complete berk.

Tuesday 6 December

I've come up with a name for our new gathering in The Mission: 'FULL'. It seems to sum up what we're aiming for and trying to communicate. We will rage against emptiness. Offer an alternative way to live. It's a scourge round here. Its inspiration is Christ's words in John 10.10: 'I have come that they may have life, and have it to the full.' I'm bursting with ideas. I've gathered a little team of people to help me pull it off. Well, just Terry so far, but I'm praying others might get on board. He isn't the greatest singer. His guitar playing is technically suspect sometimes. But Terry means every word that comes out of his mouth and speaks the language of ordinary people. He knows the difference between living fully and running on empty.

He knows Jesus as his saviour and his friend. That's all I'm looking for really.

Wednesday 7 December

We've somehow managed to keep the girls alive for one whole year! We celebrated at Anna's parents in York with balloons, cake and party poppers that scared the life out of them.

Friday 9 December

I was invited to celebrate the first birthday of Oscars Bar by landlord Lee tonight. I took my new Nigerian buddy, Emmanuel. He comes to our formal Eucharist sometimes. He's a bit of a mystery. It wouldn't surprise me if he turned out to be a member of the Nigerian royal family.

Just before we left the bar, a large, scary skinhead bloke strode over to our table. He looked like Phil Mitchell. I wondered what I might have done to offend him. I thought I was toast. Then he broke into a lovely smile and offered to buy me a pint. 'I've been meaning to come to Holy Trinity with my girlfriend,' he said. 'When would be a good time, please?' This says a lot about how far we've come in quite a short amount of time. I feel so encouraged.

Terry and I are planning to host an open mic night at Holy Apostles. We hope it might stir some interest on the estate. Our Sunday morning worship sure as hell isn't. I've decided to perform The Beatles' 'Norwegian Wood' and 'Nowhere Man'. They're easy to play and make below average guitar players sound fabulous.

Saturday 10 December

It was the Hull council's Christmas festival 'spectacular' in Trinity Square today. The footfall wasn't brilliant. Apparently the fair rides only made £8 profit all day. I'm sure the ride operator didn't help.

He stood there pressing flashing buttons in fingerless gloves, moaning about 'freezing his t*ts off'. The whole thing was just a bit cheap and tragic. We struggle to compete with the main city centre drag. Trinity Square is just not somewhere shoppers wander to at the moment.

On a positive note, hundreds of people ventured inside Holy Trinity, despite the worst Santa I've ever seen. Mrs Claus must have been feeding him salad and green beans. He looked about ten stone wet through. I admire the council for trying to get things happening in the Old Town. This wasn't a 'spectacular' start – but it was a start.

I've hired a committed non-churchgoer to design our FULL logo and posters. He isn't cheap but the people we want to attract will see through his eyes. Anna would go bananas if she knew how much I was forking out for it. Holy Trinity is too skint to pay.

Sunday 11 December

I've gone public about the FULL pub service on Facebook. No going back now. I wrote:

> *We are launching a new Holy Trinity service on January 29th at 4 pm. It's called FULL. It's in The Mission pub, Posterngate. It will be pretty chaotic but, I hope, never dull. Expect worship, food, guests, space to think, talks, laughs and as much creativity as we can muster. Building a team of up-for-it people but room for more.*

The response has been good so far. Lots of goodwill. I need to sit down now and think and pray about what we're going to actually do. I'm worried it will flop. What if no one comes? What if only church people come? I need this to work. If it fails, Holy Trinity will retreat back into the comfort of the old. If it succeeds then I'm convinced anything is possible.

Monday 12 December

Irene and I have had a desk space built in Holy Trinity's dungeon-like bowels. We hoped it could be a place to have confidential pastoral conversations, too. It's like working in a medieval French prison – but better than nothing. One of our welcomers, Margaret, breezed in to tell us that she could hear our every word.

I'm reading a book about Mother Teresa – *Come, Be My Light*. I've been thinking a lot about light lately. It's the season for it. Teresa writes that she was called 'to light the light of those in darkness on earth'. We have a choice to be light. Every human being does. A choice to be people who make things better. Sounds good to me.

Tuesday 13 December

The Hull Collegiate School choir service at Holy Trinity was heavenly tonight. I was put next to Neal's daughter, Rachel. She had some of the main singing parts. It was like being sat beside Maria Callas. I didn't attempt to sing along. I just closed my eyes and allowed my soul to be taken somewhere lovely. Neal's in his element leading these formal occasions. His cadence and gentle patter is pitch perfect. I'm still a bit uncomfortable around the well-bred. They all seem so healthy, chiselled, rosy-cheeked and well-mannered. The men have silken, floppy locks and unbitten nails. The women look as if they've just breezed in from a Jane Austen film adaptation. They unnerve me. Make me feel like some kind of rough hired hand. I actually feel the urge to run errands for them.

I waffled my way through a Christingle service at Adelaide Primary School this afternoon. The best moment was when I wasn't saying anything. We turned all the lights off and the kids were left bathed in an awesome candlelight. It was magical. The Head has now asked me to be a school governor. In a weak moment, I said I'd do it. My attempts to avoid spirit-crushing meetings are failing badly.

My new workspace in the depths of Holy Trinity is now the warmest part of the building. Our welcomers, churchwardens and verger keep coming in to eat their smelly sandwiches and noisy crisps. It's very irritating.

Wednesday 14 December

The Christmas carol services are coming thick and fast. I already feel that if I have to sing 'Little Donkey' one more time I'll swing for someone.

This morning I met with a friend who recently told me he'd found a lump on his testicle. So I prayed for that. I'm an expert at praying for balls, after mine failed to generate anything useful in our IVF days.

Thursday 15 December

Esther has started dishing out kisses. Seeing her plant a wet smacker on Anna's lips turned my heart to blancmange. Heidi is too hyperactive to kiss. Nothing escapes her attention. Everything interests her. She seems on a constant quest to find the biggest source of potential danger in any room she's in. She's a magnet for sharp corners, big drops or anything that she can fit into her mouth that might choke her. Every day feels like a titanic battle just to keep her alive.

We're throwing a party tomorrow night at our house for some of the new people who've been coming to church.

Friday 16 December

Anna has had her first period for almost two years. The breastfeeding coming to an end has made it kick in again, apparently. She said it explains the brutal moods she's been in lately. I nodded quietly. It's still too early to offer an opinion on these matters.

I worked hard to get people talking and mixing at our party tonight. I used all my tricks to create a sense of buzz and energy – encouraging strangers to become friends. We'd invited some of the church's fringe people and occasional toe-dippers. It was an introvert's worst nightmare. They gave me murderous looks as I forced them to do a charade.

The *Hull Daily Mail* took a load of pictures of me at The Mission today. They're doing a story about the FULL service. I tried really hard not to look cheesy. Not easy when you're being propped up by the bar with a massive Bible in your hand.

Saturday 17 December

The *Hull Daily Mail* went quite big on the FULL story. Great headline: 'Service please – and I'll have an ale, Mary.' The opening paragraph said:

> *From pulling pints to pulpits and prayers – a city pub is being transformed into a church. The Mission pub serves alcohol throughout the week. But on the last Sunday of every month, the landlord will call time, so a church service can be held. For the first time in Holy Trinity's 700-year history, the church will be holding monthly worship at The Mission pub.*

They even published a short opinion piece. I found myself saying 'Yes!' and 'Amen!':

> *While Rev Woodcock has nothing against the traditional services, they can often be too prescriptive and not everyone's cup of tea. He has realized that one size does not fit all. Not only that, but the church needs to recognize it is now in the twenty-first century. We use computers instead of quill pens – why*

should religion be any different? If the idea takes off, who knows which other churches will follow.

Church was buzzing today. Loads of visitors. I did an acoustic set of carols and Christmas songs with Terry and a local busker. We called ourselves The Rockin' Rev and the Reindeers. I remembered to leave out the Parental Advisory bits from our version of The Pogues' 'Fairytale of New York'. Our Christingle service at 4 p.m. was heaving. Irene made it sparkle with warmth and Christmas magic.

Sunday 18 December

I received a surprising email from my old Portsmouth University mate Ian Kavanagh today. It's our first contact in years. It brought back memories. I didn't embrace the student life as well as I could. It's a regret. My first time away from home. One of very few northerners. No easy access home. I had to grow up fast – but never quite managed it.

Our little friendship group were such misfits. Always on the edge of the action. On a constant quest to meet girls and experience some of the free love we'd heard so much about. It never happened. We were caged by our own embarrassed awkwardness. Few girls ever looked at us romantically. I had one date in three years. Vicky Trunkfield. From the moment I nervously picked her up I knew she'd realized her mistake. I never saw her again.

Ian was important to me. In the best student tradition, we'd spend hours of emotional and cheap booze-fuelled intensity cursing our wretched lives. Often in fits of laughter. We were good at that. I was too intense for our group, really. Too extroverted. They often went to big lengths to avoid me. One afternoon I turned up uninvited for a party at Kev Holder's digs. There was no answer at the door. I looked through the letterbox to see my 'pals' huddled on the stairs. I heard Kev whisper: 'I think he might have gone.' I don't blame them. I wasn't the easiest.

Ian now lives in Brisbane, Australia with his wife and two kids. He still sounds the same. Still wonderfully awkward. A spoon in a world of knives. So happy that he got in touch.

Monday 19 December

I sent Dad my mini-sermon for tomorrow's lawyers' carol service to look over. His approval as a former journalist on a national paper is important to me. Probably too important. I'm sure Freud would have a field day. Sometimes I still feel like the young hack meeting Dad every Saturday morning in the Acropolis Cafe to ask him to check over my latest weekly *York Evening Press* column, desperate for it to be good enough. Dad's writing was highly respected among his journalist colleagues and I was determined to be that good. I remember he hated my first column. He actually told me: 'This is ****, Matt.' I hated him for it – but he was right. He mercilessly scrawled over it in that dreaded fine point red pen of his. Every week I'd push myself harder and harder, trying to learn. Trying to get better. Trying to make sure there was just a bit less red pen over my script. Finally, months later, he read that week's column, poised with his red pen, and didn't make a single change. 'You've got it,' he said. We never met in that cafe again.

Anyway, I was worried about my sermon script for the lawyers. It had to be good. There were too many sharp, clever, well-bred people in one room for my liking. It needed a going over with Dad's red pen. He got back to me tonight. 'Don't change a word,' he said. What a relief.

Anna and the girls being in York on Sunday nights is just not working for me. Mum said Esther's cries were deafening last night. There's nothing I can do to help from my bed in Hull. Every hour of sleep I have feels like a guilty one. Anna is determined to keep working in York. I think she's clinging onto the remnants of her old life. A difficult conversation is looming. How can I possibly tell her that I don't think her continuing to work away is healthy for us after all the sacrifices she's made to follow my calling? The answer is, I can't. It's got to be her decision.

I can't stop playing 'Spiegel im Spiegel' by Arvo Pärt. It's 9 minutes 40 seconds of breathtaking beauty.

Our final exploring faith session tonight. One of the group feels worried that he'll be stuck in a constant cycle of guilt if he accepts God. I tried to articulate the grace of Christ, but I don't think he's convinced.

Tuesday 20 December

I faced a roomful of judges, barristers, solicitors and their staff tonight at Holy Trinity's lawyers' carol service. In my opening welcome I said, 'I pray to God that this is the only context with which I ever have to stand before you.' Later in my homily, I gave some heartfelt reasons why Jesus was relevant to every human being. 'The defence rests,' I concluded. It seemed to go down OK. I got a few encouraging nods of approval and no one collared me afterwards to put across a counterargument.

I'd arranged an after-service party in the Kings Bar & Lounge for all those who came tonight. The choir kids devoured the buffet like a locust swarm before anyone important or legally-minded got anywhere near it. I was raving. One of the senior judges looked crestfallen with nothing cheesy or pastry-based to stuff into his learned, jowly face.

It turned into an epic night with Mark, Holy Trinity's notoriously louche organist. Organists and 'epic nights' are not words I would have put in the same sentence before Holy Trinity. Mark has become a soulful, special friend. We sank into deep conversation about love, faith and dilapidated organ pipes by the fire in Ye Olde Black Boy over a bottle of delicious Cabernet Sauvignon. Wonderful.

Wednesday 21 December

I've been trolled. Someone emailed me to accuse me of 'dangerous heresy' for wanting to hold the FULL service in the pub. He claimed that I'm all about entertainment and not the 'real Gospel'. He took the trouble to mock up a smiley picture of me with the words, 'There's no business like showbusiness.' I wish the Bishop of Hull would just speak to me in person.

I'm aching to be with the girls tonight. It's not healthy for us to be apart. I don't know how servicemen, oil-rig workers and errant husbands do it. I want to hold them. I want to crawl towards Heidi pretending to be a lion. I want a kiss from Esther. I want to comfort them when they cry.

I visited bodybuilder John in hospital during his dialysis session this afternoon. He was feeling down after all the knockbacks he keeps getting on the dating websites. I gently suggested that he might need to broaden his search criteria. Be a bit more flexible. Basically he only pursues a certain type of woman. Ones with certain physical attributes, let's say. 'The one for me is out there, Matt,' he said. 'I'm going to keep looking.' Fair enough.

I went round to see a new church family at their house for a pizza tea. They got the Wii out and invited me to dance to MC Hammer's 'U Can't Touch This'. I gratefully accepted.

Thursday 22 December

One of the lads I trained to become a reverend with has emailed me one of those round-robin family Christmas newsletters. I hate these things. They never fail to make me feel bad about what we aren't achieving as a family. Christians send the worst ones. Toby's daughter already seems to be fluent in two languages and can play the viola. She spends her lunchtimes ministering to her friends in the playground and praying for healing. She's four. Anna had to physically restrain me from sending back our own version. Something like:

> *The twins are driving us insane, our poor excuse for a marriage is barely functioning beyond wine and nappies and I can't remember the last time we prayed together. Life is horrible.*
> *Merry Christmas!*
> *The Woodcocks x*

Watched *It's a Wonderful Life* with Anna for the 400th time. We cried and cried and cried and cried. I haven't bought a single present yet.

Saturday 24 December

I was up with the larks to do my Christmas shopping. It was lovely to see I wasn't alone. Harassed-looking blokes were everywhere. There was a rush on in Boots. I grabbed armfuls of luxury bath products for Anna.

Good turnout at our crib service this afternoon and later at Holy Apostles. Loads of estate families turned up.

I've just had the privilege of preaching at Holy Trinity's midnight mass service. Revellers poured in from the Old Town pubs. Preaching from the first chapter of John, I built up a picture of darkness and light. I got Chris to turn all the lights off. 'We all know what it feels like to live like this,' I said. People understood, I think. Then I got a high-powered torch and beamed it around the place. I made the point that this is what happened when Jesus was born. No dark area of human life was immune to his light. 'The darkness has not overcome it.' I said that the gift of Jesus was for everyone – whoever you are, whatever you've done or not done in life. 'He's for you and you and you and you,' I said, shining the torch into the faces. I encouraged everyone to come and receive the bread and wine at the Communion rail. I heard people crying in the darkness. It was a moment where I felt that the Spirit of God had completely overtaken my words, my movements, my gestures. Then I turned the lights back on. Many came and received.

Sunday 25 December

I was grateful for my Christmas gifts from my family this morning. I did well. The pick of them were a multipack of Caramacs and a thermal vest to wear in Holy Trinity.

Tuesday 27 December

I'm really struggling to unwind after the Christmas mayhem at Holy Trinity. It was all so intense. It's hard to turn it off. People's needs and prayer requests don't just suddenly stop. I got this text from one of the lads who's struggling a bit: 'I could do with some prayer, Matt. I feel in a dark place right now. I'm getting stressed out with going back to work. That and the guilt is making me miss words when I'm in conversation. I get confused when I'm trying to process info in my head. I'm really trying not to feel sorry for myself.' I've offered to meet up with him in the new year. I also encouraged him to visit his GP.

Peter Kay's new book is offering some light relief. He has funny bones.

Wednesday 28 December

Unpleasant, long-buried memories of the moment I found out Mum and Dad were getting divorced returned to haunt me today. They were triggered when I met Mum in a cafe by the River Ouse in York. She wanted to tell me about the latest development in her love life. I'd rather not know a single thing about it to be honest.

I'm hardwired to cover her in cotton wool and do everything I can to stop her from being hurt again. It's not proving possible.

I knew from the tone of her voice that she had big news. In a nutshell, her ex-partner Barry has been back in touch. He wants her back. They broke up over two years ago when he felt things weren't working out. She's only just got over it. We all thought he was great – they seemed so perfect together. I truly want Mum to be happy but I'm fiercely protective after her heart was broken last time. I can tell she'll take him back. She loved him. I hope she knows what she's doing.

The point is, our conversation brought back the unwanted divorce memory. It was something about Mum's voice. I recognized it. It was her 'I've got big news' voice. Some aspects of our family life I just find too unbearable to dwell on. The divorce is one of them. I don't know why and I know I shouldn't, but I blame myself. I've always wondered if I could have done more to prevent it. I remember the dreaded phone call from Mum when I was at university just before some important exams. Always great timing in my family. I knew straight away from her familiar tone that it was all over. I couldn't face it. I wouldn't go home for the holidays or talk to anyone for months.

I've never been very good at coping when Mum is in distress. When she hurts, I hurt. Thank the Lord I was in my early twenties when it happened. How do little kids cope? My favourite Hull poet Philip Larkin never wrote anything more painfully true than in 'This Be The Verse': 'They **** you up, your mum and dad. / They may not mean to, but they do.'

I held Mum close after our coffee. Whatever she decides to do I'll support her and love her unconditionally. Well, I'll try. I feel better after writing this stuff down. I need to tell Anna how I'm feeling.

Friday 30 December

We went to see our lovely friends Sam and Jess at their pretty village today. It's the last time we'll see them as a family of two. Jess could give birth at any time.

Saturday 31 December

New Year's Eve. I don't think I've ever had a year like this one. So many life changes: babies, becoming a reverend, the death of Aunty Lynne, moving to Hull. Anna and I tried to make sense of it all looking out of the window in Mum's loft as we watched Chinese lanterns float into the black sky.

Year Two

Sunday 1 January

Another big year coming up. I'm struck by a sick feeling of dread. I'm plagued with negative thoughts about the FULL service starting, something bad happening to Esther and Heidi and Anna leaving me for the postman. I know one thing from the last year – when I neglect God my inner life goes pear-shaped. Here's my three resolutions:

1. Give church less.
2. Give Anna and the girls more.
3. Stop eating Colman's English Mustard with a tea spoon as if it's ice cream.

We got back to Hull this afternoon. I took the girls out for a walk in the rain so Anna could get sorted without bursting a blood vessel. I looked out over the windswept River Humber. I could see Holy Trinity jutting above the buildings in the Old Town. It felt as if we'd come home. Back to the place where God has called us. This city and these people have seeped into my bones. I'm holding nothing back this year.

Monday 2 January

I'm determined to take a more systematic, ordered approach to my ministerial life. Include an element of planning. Being so spontaneous and heart-led all the time will give me a cardiac arrest one day.

I'm amazed at how much mucus two little girls can produce. There's a constant flow of it out of their nostrils. We are continuously mopping it up. Heidi is reaching new heights of hyperactivity. Esther has finally stopped crying every time I pick her up for a cuddle.

This morning's plan was to walk to Kingston Retail Park. I'd sit in Costa and write while the girls quietly ate grapes and crackers. Anna would shop. I wrote one sentence before all hell broke loose. They simultaneously screamed the place down. I was red-faced, helpless and apologetic. No amount of shushing or pink wafers would stop them. So we lasted all of nine minutes before going to find Anna in Home Bargains. I'm determined to reach a more competent level of parenting.

It's Anna's birthday tomorrow. I intend to shower her in nice things and happy times.

Tuesday 3 January

Anna's birthday. I tried to do the whole presents and breakfast in bed thing but it was just too stressful. The girls were too keen on trying to choke themselves on wrapping paper, egg shells and ribbons. I so wanted Anna to feel a lightness of being today. She grafts like an old packhorse. Esther is constantly pawing at her, craving her full attention. Anna said she felt like a failure as a mum. I tried to cuddle away her tears and make her laugh before I left.

It was pure Frank Spencer in my first hour back at Holy Trinity. A storm swept over Trinity Square as I tried to manoeuvre my Hyundai into the car park. Beaten and ruffled by the driving wind and rain, I trapped my finger in the heavy Dickensian-style gate. It's a good job the square was deserted. I filled the air with pained profanities. I got inside to discover torrents of water pouring in through the church roof's leaky bits. I rushed to get the buckets out. Scrabbling my way to the cafe area in the gloom, I found myself face to face with three large Arab men wearing headscarves and holding sticks. I screamed. They were the Three Wise Men mannequins. I went into the chapel to still myself – and apologize to God for my bad language.

Amy called to say that Mum is going skiing with Barry. I predict they'll be moving in together soon. I'm praying she doesn't get her heart broken again. She's acting like a loved-up 16-year-old girl.

Tonight's birthday bubbly was my last drop of alcohol for a month. It's 9.30 p.m. and we are already in bed. I'm sitting up writing this. Anna has just made physical overtures but I can't face it. Nothing left. What's happened to me? I used to be a wild stallion! Now I'm turning into one of those tired old mules in a donkey sanctuary. Middle age is creeping up on me and I feel powerless to stop it.

Wednesday 4 January

I was in a foul mood this morning. Neal and Irene were at least ten minutes late to our diary meeting in Wetherspoons which didn't help. I struggle to hide my annoyance when people are late. I can't seem to stop myself mentioning it. We said morning prayers together and it thawed me out a bit.

A 15-year-old lad came into church to ask if he can be baptized alongside his grandma, Edith. She's 85. It's a 'yes' from me.

Christmas was too quiet for some of my Old Town bar manager friends. Allen said he nearly wept when hardly anyone turned up to his big New Year's party. I said I felt the same most Sunday mornings.

There's an awful smell in our workspace in the bowels of Holy Trinity. Every time someone walks in to see me they must think I've trumped. It's unhelpful and embarrassing. No one seems to know what's causing it.

Esther and Heidi's latest fascination: the stairs. They constantly want to try to climb them. Another reason to be stressed.

Thursday 5 January

Today I have been exactly six months in the job. It's all a bit of a blur. I've learnt so much about what it means to be a so-called 'pioneering' reverend. I think it basically involves making it all up as I go along and trusting God and the instincts he puts inside me. I hope that a little bit of how Neal and Irene minister might be rubbing off on me as well. In summary, I've still got a job, a faith and a marriage – what a relief! It will be interesting to see if Archbishop Sentamu agrees to ordain me as a priest in July. Has he seen enough potential in me during this rookie year?

I walked in on a kerfuffle (great word) at church between a couple of welcomers – and I use that term loosely – and a homeless guy. He'd gone in to fill up his flask with hot tea. Someone told him the kitchen was closed. The guy wasn't happy, understandably. I despair that this was even a discussion. In the end I took him into the indoor market to fill his flask. I felt my temper teetering on the brink so thought it best to get out and cool down. Neal needs to sort this out. Quickly. If we can't be a church that warms up freezing homeless people with hot tea we don't deserve to be transformed.

We watched *Revolutionary Road* tonight. It's too depressing for a Thursday in early January. Mind you, this Kate Winslet line was a belter: 'If being crazy means living life as if it matters, then I don't care if we're completely insane.' Amen.

I feel much less scared about FULL when I talk to Terry. He is fast becoming my wingman. My confidante and brother on the change journey.

Saturday 7 January

I found out that my old secondary school is compiling a history book. They want former pupils to write in their memories. I don't think my epic fight with Duncan Whitley in the dinner queue over who was more worthy of the affections of Vicky Robinson will make the final cut.

I visited Edith and her great grandson at their home in Bransholme. I'll baptize them together. At 85, this means the world to Edith. She wants the comfort of being baptized before she dies. I prayed for them both in her little front room. She cried happy tears.

Monday 9 January

A dead rat under the floorboards of our church workspace has been identified as the source of the terrible smell. Relieved I'm no longer the chief suspect.

I've got to preach on 2 Kings 21. The evil King of Judah, Manasseh. He didn't have a good bone in his body.

Mum and my sister Amy have fallen out. This is a bad one. They both called me to give me their side of the story. This is the last thing we need.

In better news, we heard tonight that Jess has gone into labour. Praying that all will be well.

Tuesday 10 January

A dark day. Molly Overton died in the arms of Sam and Jess at 11.30 a.m. today. It's utterly devastating. I received a frantic call from Sam at 7.30 a.m. I was still half asleep, and it felt like a terrible dream. 'There's nothing they can do,' he mumbled. 'They've got to turn the machine off.' He was trying to get hold of the Reverend John to baptize Molly before they had to let her go. Sam sounded shellshocked and delirious. I tried to stay calm but didn't know what to say.

We talked again at lunchtime. Jess had a long, arduous labour and finally gave birth at 5.07 a.m. It's not known why Molly's heart stopped. Sam and Jess held her and loved her for as long as they could before she slipped away. I can't get my head round it. Only a couple of weeks ago I was in their front room praying for them. Why did this happen? It seems so unnecessarily cruel. Jess is going back to the hospital tomorrow to hold and tend to Molly. It's a slow, healing process for the parents to say goodbye. I told Sam that I loved him.

I led the school assembly at Adelaide Primary School this morning. I looked out at the children and struggled to hold it together. It dawned on me that Molly would never be in a classroom. She'd never have friends to mess around with, favourite teachers to shower with end-of-term chocolate or school dinners to complain about. The world is just too awful for words sometimes. I did a question-and-answer session at the end. One of the kids asked: 'Matt, what is the purpose of life?' I batted back a stock answer. At times like this, I wish I knew.

Wednesday 11 January

I wondered what it was like for Sam to wake up this morning. The reality of yesterday hitting him. I want to snap my fingers and make everything right for Sam and Jess. We are heartbroken for them. I feel guilty when I laugh or experience a moment of joy.

Irene and I are being forced to work in the surrounding coffee shops. The stink of the dead rat has become unbearable.

For a bit of light relief I phoned up my Morning Glory buddy, Jason, at his church in Surrey this afternoon pretending to be the Bishop of Guildford. He suddenly put on the most hilarious posh voice and gave spluttering, fawning answers. 'Certainly, Bishop. Of course you're right, Bishop. Anything you say, Bishop.' He really didn't appreciate the prank. He soon went back to his normal voice and called me all manner of unrepeatable things.

Friday 13 January

A long heart-to-heart with Sam over the phone tonight. He shared his experience of the last week in heartbreaking detail. We cried together as he recounted the moment Molly slipped peacefully into the care of Jesus. I believe he is holding her until they can all be reunited in glory one day. It's a fuzzy hope sometimes, though. A hope to cling to, rather than to sit nonchalantly with. Sam said that before Molly breathed her last she opened her eyes and looked at them. 'I wanted to die with her,' he said. 'Go with her. Be with her.' They had to sign the birth certificate and death certificate at the same time.

After Molly had died, Jess got the chance to bathe her and put on her nappy and the tiny clothes she would have gone home in. It's all part of the bonding and healing process for a grieving mother. The funeral is next week.

I hoovered my car this afternoon to try to think about nothing. Carrying the pain of others is exhausting. Cleaning the car forces me to withdraw into myself and clear my mind. My new duster helped. It was therapeutic to wipe away the dust from the dashboard.

Saturday 14 January

I'm reading *Goodnight Mister Tom* for the hundredth time. The tears came from the first page. It's such a testament to the power of love, kindness, gentleness and healing in the face of life's darkness. I became connected to my 13-year-old self as I sank into the story. The happy memory of being engrossed in it on my bed at home in Murray Street. Properly falling in love with books for the first time. I'd love to go back and have a word with that lad. Calm him down a bit. Mister Tom always reflected something of the character of Jesus to me. Zach's death still leaves me desolate and angry. It's the most despairingly unfair death in the whole of fiction.

Anna has been engrossed in a book about how parental conflict impacts children. Apparently it's crucial that babies can see their parents making up. Witnessing reconciliation is supposed to be a crucial part of their development. We've certainly become more conscious of how often we disagree. Our house too often simmers with a silent tension.

Sunday 15 January

Our church services were uplifting today. The atmosphere charged. We weren't doing anything particularly differently. God just seemed more present with us. It was lovely. I've stopped trying to explain or understand the sacred mystery of these moments. Now I just try to enjoy them.

Neal's sermon was a belter. The best I've heard from him. It was bold and challenged us about why and how we worship. I've noticed his eyes fill with tears and his neck go red sometimes when he makes a passionate point in the pulpit. He was glowing this morning.

I sat in on the FULL band practice this afternoon. Hardly any of them have been going to church for more than a few weeks. You would never plan to do a new church service like this, but this is where we are and this is who we've got. They sounded OK. In tune.

Monday 16 January

I've had an exciting exchange with cousin Ben. I contacted him again about the possibility of him coming here as our youth and children's worker. He now sounds keen. I'm trying not to get too excited but this would be incredible. Ben's musical ability goes without saying but his labrador-like faith would give us all a lift. I said I'd arrange a meeting between him and Neal.

I'm using this belting Desmond Tutu quote to conclude my sermon on Sunday: 'Good is stronger than evil, love is stronger than hate; light is stronger than darkness; life is stronger than death: victory is ours through him who loves us.'

Tuesday 17 January

We visited Sam and Jess at their home tonight. It was a hauntingly sad encounter, but special too. They showed us pictures of Molly.

She had a thick thatch of Overton hair. Sam and I walked up the hill to the village church where Molly will be buried. It was frosty, deserted and serene. We played 'When I Survey the Wondrous Cross' on the iPod in the darkness of the church. Sam collapsed into my arms, sobbing and wailing. I held him until he had nothing left.

We sat outside on the church steps looking up at the stars. We talked about the enormity of the universe and the mystery of life. Sam said he craves to be with his Molly. Wishes it could have been him who went instead of her. I said he needed to live now more than ever. Live it to the absolute fullest in memory and in honour of his daughter. We walked back in silence. The air still. The dead stars shining down on us.

Wednesday 18 January

Sam and Jess have asked me to read their tribute to Molly at the funeral on Friday. They write:

We are so proud of our darling daughter, Molly. She may have only had just over six hours of life with us but she lived them to the full. She has touched so many peoples' hearts and lives and changed our lives forever. We have marvelled at her beauty and her amazing character and strong spirit, as she tried to breathe for herself despite having a ventilator, as she kicked her legs despite being so poorly; those kicks were so familiar to us throughout the pregnancy. She gripped our fingers and looked us in the eye as we spoke to her and cuddled her. We are so thankful to God that she died peacefully in our arms. We know that Molly is safe with Jesus, free from any restrictions that her earthly body may have given her. We will miss her every moment and every breath of our lives but we look forward to the day that we can be reunited with her in heaven.

Cousin Ben came to visit Holy Trinity today to explore the possible youth worker job. Neal is worried about how we will pay for his salary. Mere details.

Thursday 19 January

Neal and I clashed a bit about the youth worker post. I'm convinced that we should step out in faith and go for it. If we don't commit to young families and kids at this stage then we are sunk. Jesus didn't come to seek and save only those in their sixties, seventies and eighties. If enough of us sponsor the post financially it's perfectly possible.

I think I overstepped the mark in getting my point across. I know I have to accept and respect Neal's decision – even if he is spectacularly wrong. A few deep breaths needed on this one, I think.

Irene led the new first praise service for some of the older folks this morning. I love her warm style and the way she makes everyone feel included. I went door-to-door round the parish leafleting about the FULL service. Some of the Old Town residents seemed happier about a vicar at their door than others. It's Molly's funeral tomorrow.

Friday 20 January

Jess's anguished face as Molly was lowered into the grave will stay with me for a long time. Her wicker coffin was heartbreakingly small. Sam and Jess chose 'How Great Is Our God' as the first song. It's a measure of their faith and trust in Jesus that they could still sing that. Despite the horrors of the past few weeks they believe that, in the end, all will be well.

Saturday 21 January

My sister Amy and I had a heart-to-heart today. We went to some places with each other that we'd never been to before. We should have had this conversation years ago. Her and Mum falling out has brought a lot of things to the surface. I got to her house early. I secretly hoped they'd all still be in bed. All the curtains were closed and the lights were off. It looked promising. I knocked as quietly as I could. Hearing nothing, I started walking off when the door opened. Amy burst into tears almost immediately. I made tea and toast.

We talked about the past. Mum and Dad. We acknowledged how horrible we used to be to each other. I love my sister. We might never be close, but I hope she knows that. We embraced until it was awkward and I drove back to Hull. Families.

Monday 23 January

Some of the most important spiritual lessons I learn are in the most unlikely of places. This morning it was on the cycle path underneath the A63 flyover. The smashed glass strewn everywhere has annoyed me for days. I've swerved round it and cursed the person who created the mess. It has irritated me that no one from the council has bothered to clean it up. Then I realized that I could easily sort it out. It takes a while for obvious stuff to dawn on me sometimes. I found a crushed Coke can, scooped the glass into an empty packet of Frazzles and found a bin to chuck it in. It took two minutes and I cycled on feeling better. It's the little things in life that teach me the biggest spiritual truths.

I met the former chairman of Railtrack who's agreed to head up Holy Trinity's development project. Speaking to John Robinson for 20 minutes made me believe that the project is absolutely possible and totally necessary. He has a confidence that creates confidence in others. We'll just need to raise about £4 million.

I've turned down an invitation to be 'team pastor' for a group of businessmen going out to Mozambique to do some charity work. I'd last ten minutes in that jungle.

Tuesday 24 January

I met my fellow curate buddy, Philip, in Costa this morning.

Apart from Philip's flamboyant, expensive coffee choices (something exotically frothy and skinny with soya milk), I like him. He's an absorbed listener. I shared my fears about starting the FULL service on Sunday. Just before we left – and this sounds made up – a lady in a lovely coat came up to me. She said: 'I heard you speak at Holy Trinity on Christmas Eve and it has really stayed with me. I just wanted to thank you. I think I might want to come to one of your FULL services at The Mission.' She'd seen the article in the paper. Maybe God speaks to me a bit more than I thought.

Wednesday 25 January

Quote of the day: 'A ship is safest in port but that's not what ships are made for.'

We launch the pub service this Sunday. I'm terrified.

Friday 27 January

I turned up at church to find a bikini-clad woman in a variety of revealing poses having her photo taken by the side door. To call it a bikini is perhaps being a bit generous. Her photographer looked comically seedy.

'Just one more, Tina,' I heard him say, clicking away furiously. 'Try to look a bit more cryptic.'

'I'm freezing, Tony!' she shouted back.

I took a deep breath and went over to introduce myself. They were very apologetic. Mumbled something about wanting to make the most out of Holy Trinity's wonderful backdrop. Tina quickly put her long coat on and they scurried away across the Old Town cobbles. I shouted after them that they were welcome at church on Sunday. You never know.

Saturday 28 January

I'm so relieved that Mum is our first guest speaker at FULL tomorrow. She calms me. She knows what to say whoever is in front of her. I know that if all else fails on the technical and logistical side she will nail it. I just hope someone turns up to hear her. I'm trying to articulate what to say at the start. I've come up with this so far:

> *I used to believe that to be a Christian you were signing up to a life of rules, boredom, joylessness and crap biscuits. I've mostly found it to be the opposite. The Christian life has been an adventure. A life of purpose and belonging, forgiveness, deep joy and inner peace. Not to mention sacrifice, struggle, hardship, mystery, pain and tears. I think this is something of the 'full' life that Jesus speaks of.*

Sunday 29 January

Nothing brings out more extremity of emotion and feeling in me than doing a new thing. It's terror and exhilaration entwined. I was so nervous and afraid at the thought of FULL starting at 4 p.m. With five minutes to go, I sat in a deserted corner of The Mission and quietly tried to keep the fear monster at bay. Well, I cried a bit actually. No one had turned up. Our team were all in place – but had no one to welcome or serve posh coffee and biscuits to. They all looked at me for inspiration. It was well awkward. Their expressions said: 'Where the hell is everyone??!!' As I sat round the corner, this massively unhelpful text bleeped in from one of my vicar pals: 'Don't rely on your own charismatic personality, Matt. Introduce people to Jesus, not yourself. I will decrease, He will increase. God's blessings for it.' I know he meant well, but come on! Not right at this moment! I texted back: 'I'll try not to be myself then.' Trying to muster some faith, I said a tearful, snotty, pleading prayer that all would be well. I got myself back out there.

In the end it wasn't a disaster. About 50 people turned up. Most of them wouldn't be seen dead in a conventional church. I'll never forget the sight of a burly bloke called Wayne and his family wandering in. How he ended up there is quite a story. He told me that his son Harry was born a few weeks ago. There were major complications and Harry was in an incubator for days fighting for his life. Kneeling with his head pressed against the incubator glass, Wayne said he prayed for the first time in his life. He made a deal with God: if Harry got better he promised to start going to church. 'Over the next few days Harry got loads better,' Wayne told me. 'Then I remembered my deal with God. I thought, "Oh crap, I've got to start going to church!" I noticed a *Hull Daily Mail* in the waiting room and I started reading it. The first story I read was your one about the FULL service. The headline said: "The church service for people who don't go to church". I knew I had to come, so here I am.' Unbelievable. We're meeting for coffee next week.

Mum spoke movingly about how she came to faith. The FULL band were a revelation. My instinct about them playing the Johnny Cash version of 'I Saw the Light' was a good one. It had people up clapping and dancing about. Ron the landlord and his wife said they watched the service from a TV screen in their upstairs office. The CCTV cameras were trained on us. I learnt so much today. In all our weaknesses and fears, God gives us all the strength we need. Onwards.

Monday 30 January

FULL dominated my thinking all day. Weighing up what did and didn't work. Figuring out who came and how best to follow them up.

Tuesday 31 January

I visited my uncle's friend Tivvy at his home in York today. Death is not far away now. He's skeletal. Every breath is a struggle. The asbestosis has taken hold. I was conscious that this would be the last time I'd see him alive. I put my hand on his shoulder and tried to offer words of prayer and comfort. Tivvy was too angry to receive prayers and platitudes, though. I don't blame him.

Wednesday 1 February

Neal has come round to the idea of appointing Ben as our youth worker. He sees how necessary it is. We met in Nero's to discuss his possible job spec. I think it was a bit ambitious. Looking down the list of Neal's expectations, it's as if he's expecting Ben to be the head of Tearfund or something. Does he have a vibrant faith? Yes. Is he good with kids? Yes. Is he prepared to live in the tiny church house in the middle of a challenging estate? Yes. Let's give him the job.

Thursday 2 February

A young lad in his twenties has gone missing in the parish. He was last seen on CCTV about to go across one of the Old Town bridges. The cameras don't pick him up at the other end. It doesn't look good. We offered prayers for him in the chapel.

Mum and Amy have had a healthy reconciliatory conversation. It's major progress.

Anna and I watched *Planes, Trains and Automobiles* again tonight. Few films make me laugh and cry as much. I want to live out my days like John Candy's character, Del Griffith. He's full of positivity, warm humour and goodness. 'Those aren't pillows!'

Friday 3 February

The Bishop of Hull has contacted Neal for his feedback about FULL. He probably wants to make sure I'm not bringing the Church of England into disrepute. Neal copied me in to his response. I was very encouraged. He makes me sound like a proper leader. As if I actually have a clue that I know what I'm doing.

Neal wrote:

I thought FULL was excellent. Matt put a huge amount of work into it – sorting publicity, building a team of Welcomers, refreshment providers and worship band, liaising with The Mission pub as well as planning and leading the service itself. That all this came from a standing start and having been here just seven months is an amazing achievement. There was a really friendly and relaxed atmosphere, yet the gospel was shared clearly and God honoured. There were times of lively and loud worship and times of prayerful and reverent silence. I know it's early days, but I felt very encouraged that everything had come together so well. Inevitably there were a few teething issues over the logistics of operating 'away from home' – moving a fair bit of kit etc – but we'll learn from that. I look forward to the next service at the end of the month.

It's not possible to have a better boss than Neal.

The debate over same sex marriage has become red hot again after the Bishop of Salisbury spoke out in support of it. He said:

We are living in a different society. If there's a gay couple in The Archers, *if there's that form of public recognition in popular soaps, we are dealing with something which has got common*

currency. All of us have friends, families, relatives, neighbours
who are, or who know somebody, in same-sex partnerships.

It's an interesting perspective. The tide seems to be turning. I'm just surprised the bishop thinks *The Archers* is one of the 'popular soaps'. Not in my world. Bishops seem to exist in an entirely different cultural zone to most ordinary people.

Saturday 4 February

I had the privilege of baptizing 85-year-old Edith and her 15-year-old great-grandson in Ward 28 of Castle Hill Hospital. God really met us in that place. Edith told me she'd been waiting over 40 years for it to happen. I don't think she was aware of me or anyone as I poured the water over her head in the name of the Father, Son and Holy Spirit. She was locked in a deep embrace with God. It was an intensely personal moment.

I read a lovely news story about the Queen today. The contents of her handbag were revealed. They included a £5 note – for the church collection. Lovely.

Sunday 5 February

We woke to a wonderful snow duvet covering the Old Town. It was the thick, crunchy kind that is perfect for throwing at someone's head. Before and after the services I found a few victims in the square. People took enormous delight in sticking snow surreptitiously down the back of my clergy shirt. The crisp, clear conditions made me feel so alive.

Church was comically cold. I tweeted: 'Bear Grylls wouldn't last two minutes at Holy Trinity this morning. Come along to our arctic-themed services at 9.30 a.m. and 11 a.m.' I was amazed that anyone would want to sit in there. It was coffee on the rocks after the service. Irene had fourteen layers on. Neal led the communion in fingerless gloves. I put on a comedy balaclava but was politely told to take it off. Homeless Larry told me that he and his pal actually slept rough in the snow last night. I couldn't believe it. We did our best to warm him back up.

Monday 6 February

A lad nibbling at the edges of faith came round for a talk tonight. Somehow we ended up jamming Elvis songs. He's obsessed with him. He showed me a massive tattoo of him on his stomach. As we thrashed through 'Suspicious Minds' and 'Crying in the Chapel' in the front room, I had a short moment of clarity about how bizarre my job is sometimes.

Tuesday 7 February

A day of prayer and quiet at the St Bede's Pastoral Centre with Sister Cecilia. She thinks I'm in a healthy place spiritually. She offered me some wise stuff to think about and a few reading options and then left me in her room for six hours. I found the candlelight helpful. I stared at the flame for a long time, thinking deep thoughts. I meditated on Psalm 62 and hoovered up Cecilia's art books. Painters I'd never heard of like Bruegel and Marc Chagall particularly struck a chord. Then I stumbled on a work by Matthias Grünewald. It hangs above an altar in Isenheim, a place that sounds like a destination for the hobbits in *The Lord of the Rings*. It depicts a pasty, white, tortured Christ covered in sores and ripped, damaged flesh. Apparently those suffering from terminal, excruciating skin diseases were laid before the piece in their last moments before death. It was said to bring them the comfort that the Son of God absolutely identified with their pain and suffering – and that he waited for them in death.

Wednesday 8 February

Uncle Mike texted to tell me that Tivvy had died overnight. The family want me to take the funeral.

I led a Valentine's Day-themed school assembly this morning. Just saying the word 'kiss' caused pandemonium among the kids. I didn't regain control after that. More death stares from the class teachers as they filed out.

Thursday 9 February

I met Luke Campbell at St Paul's Boxing Academy today. He trained and competed there as a young lad. Now he's one of the contenders for the bantamweight gold medal at the London Olympics. He was charming. An unassuming bloke who's totally focused on winning gold. I've asked St Paul's and Luke to attend a special service we are holding at Holy Trinity for the sports clubs in Hull. I'll interview him and hopefully raise a few quid for his training regime and equipment. Luke's life won't be the same again if he wins that medal.

Friday 10 February

Another day plagued with worries about something bad happening to the girls. I know it's not healthy. I wonder if this is a common trait among other IVF parents who struggled so much to conceive? We spent so long trying to have kids and now I seem to be spending my life worrying to death that we'll lose them. Today's concern was Heidi's chest infection. There's a chance she has asthma. Or in my head there is. She's pumped full of drugs and we had to put a nebulizer over her face which really distressed her.

Anna also told me that her parents took their eyes off Esther for a few seconds and she crawled to the top of the stairs. I didn't need to know that. For the rest of the day I had hideous daydreams of her falling down them.

I needed some fresh air. We pushed the girls into the Old Town. The sun was glorious, lazily melting the snow. I bought some cheap greetings cards, including the iconic one from the 1980s of the blonde tennis player scratching her behind. I'll send it to Grandma. It will make her laugh.

Sunday 12 February

Our one and only student, Danny, was baptized at Holy Trinity today. He's had a whirlwind faith journey since randomly walking in a few months ago. More holy water went on me than on him. My technique is all over the place. My robes got properly drenched. Neal and I led the service together, which was special. For all the frustrations, heartaches and massive disappointments of serving here, this made it all worth it. This is why we do what we do. To see new life and transformation. It's not a bad thing to get out of bed every morning for.

Monday 13 February

Noel Gallagher's solo gig in Manchester tonight felt sacred. Thousands of us sang as one to classics like 'Talk Tonight' and 'Supersonic'. I wept, arms aloft, during the 'Don't Look Back In Anger' encore. I think my friends Lee, Dave and Pete were close to tears too and they never cry. It seemed impossible not to. Those special songs elevated our humdrum lives for a short time. It was pure escapism. Without overstating it (well, maybe a touch), I think tonight's gig was a little taste of what heaven is going to be like. Unfortunately it wasn't long before we came crashing back down to earth. A group of young lads got into a massive brawl as we shuffled out of the venue. My bar for heaven is set very, very high.

Tuesday 14 February

I took Anna for a drink to The Buck for Valentine's Day. It's just round the corner from her parents' home in York. What an error. It was so grim and unromantic. I'm not a pub snob, but there's only so many ripped seats and 'Daz is a homo' graffiti scrawls on the tables that I can cope with. At least Anna liked the card I got her. My message said: 'Stop being so attractive – I can't get anything done!' I got a lovely kiss for that. We walked back and got an early night.

Wednesday 15 February

Ben has officially been appointed Holy Trinity's first youth worker in history. I'll be his line manager, Lord help him. I've never done it before. Working out targets and boundaries is part of it, apparently. All that stuff gives me a nosebleed. I'm hoping we can try being really honest, generous and loving towards one another as well. Let's see how we get on doing that.

I took Ben round the Old Town pubs tonight for his informal 'induction'. I introduced him to some of the area's more colourful characters. He shared some of the basic rudiments of bass playing with me. His skill on the instrument is ridiculous. It's a genuine thrill to watch him play. I sent a picture of us holding aloft two pints of Anglers Reward to his current boss and possible future father-in-law the Reverend John Lee – Ben's been loved-up with John's daughter, Bekah, for years. I texted: 'Poaching your youth worker is thirsty work!' As we wobbled home, something wonderful occurred to me: *We've finally got a babysitter!* Joy! I didn't think it was necessary to mention it to Ben at this stage. I'll let him settle in for a day or two.

Thursday 16 February

I'm quitting Facebook, Twitter and my mobile phone for at least a month. They have become unhelpful distractions. I'm an addict. I need to get clean.

Sunday 19 February

First proper meal out with Anna in ages without the girls, thanks to cousin Ben, our new babysitter. Where did the waiter decide to seat us? Next to a couple with two young kids. Noisy, demanding kids who liked to make drum sounds with their cutlery and plates. All the colour drained from our faces. We ate our prawn cocktails with faces like thunder.

Monday 20 February

I laid Tivvy to rest today. It was the busiest service the guy from the crem had seen in years. I felt fired-up to honour Tivvy and speak out on the scandal that killed him. In tribute to his love of the band Lynyrd Skynyrd, mourners filed in wearing cowboy hats, leather trousers and T-shirts emblazoned with the Confederate flag. His coffin arrived in a sidecar attached to one of his favourite Triumph motorbikes. Uncle Mike's tribute to his best friend was so funny and poignant. He listed the ten things that Tivvy hated the most in the world. They included (in no particular order), Osama bin Laden, Saddam Hussein and Margaret Thatcher. All the contributors said that it was an irony so many people had turned up to the funeral, because Tivvy hated people. His character was an odd mixture of openly hostile, ferociously grumpy and unwaveringly loyal.

In my eulogy, I referred to Tivvy's triple passions – motorbikes, rock music and karate. 'I don't know how he fit it all in – and manage to squeeze in all those f-words,' I said. I took a deep breath and went for it:

Tivvy suffered from mesothelioma which was a cancer caused by him being exposed to large quantities of asbestos during his many years at York Carriageworks. He lived with the constant fear that he was suffering with it. Tivvy is one of hundreds of men who have died because of exposure to asbestos dust at the carriageworks. It is an absolute scandal that the workers were never told of its dangers or given protection from it, when the powers that be knew full well how deadly it was. So it's no wonder that Tivvy was angry – he had every right to be.

I hope you take some kind of comfort from a line in one of Tivvy's favourite Lynyrd Skynyrd songs, 'Simple Man', which we'll hear later: 'And don't forget, son, there is someone up above.' And it is this someone – this Jesus Christ – who I believe stands with us in our grief and pain today, and offers us all the hope of eternal life.

May Tivvy rest in peace and rise in glory.

Tuesday 21 February

I woke up early with a sore throat. The inside of my mouth resembles a gunshot wound. I cycled to the NHS walk-in centre and was prescribed antibiotics.

Wednesday 22 February

Lent begins. No mobile phone, bread or sweets until Easter Sunday. It felt strange not to be able to call someone immediately. Or text one of those little poo emojis to Lee.

Being in Holy Trinity was grim this morning. Our new cleaner guy, Andy, has already handed his notice in after less than two weeks. I liked him. His music taste was impressively eclectic. He classes Billy Bragg as a friend. I invited him to FULL.

Neal was a bit flustered when he came in. A bloke involved in Hull's civic life – who is nothing to do with us – has sent out a press release calling on us to be given 'Minster' status. The *Hull Daily Mail* went big on it. I don't get it. It's more likely to be given 'Carpet Warehouse' status if we don't turn things around. Changing the name would do little in the short term. It's all about us finding the heart and soul of the place. Turning up the spiritual temperature.

Thursday 23 February

Esther has got chicken pox. It's a good thing, apparently. The hope is that Heidi gets it now. They can become immune together.

Neal, Irene and I took stock today. We think we've come a long way in quite a short space of time. When you're in the middle of the Holy Trinity maelstrom, you don't think much has changed. Yet we have changed, and we're still changing.

I met the beer festival guys to plan how we will welcome and accommodate hundreds of thirsty people. I'm trying not to worry too much about it yet. I have to space out my worries or my head will explode. What did Jesus say? 'Who by worrying can add a single hour to their life?' I seem to be constantly deleting hours.

Friday 24 February

One of my precious York friends, Dan the Tan, started his run on Deal or No Deal this afternoon. Questioned by Noel Edmonds on his possible strategy with the red boxes, he said: 'Fortune favours the brave, Noel.' I'm hoping he has a big win and then lavishly treats all his old friends to drinks and luxury items.

Saturday 25 February

Esther looks like a poor village wench from the Dark Ages. She's completely covered in grotesque spots and blisters. They are on her eyelids, head, fingers – everywhere! Bless her. I want to make it all OK for her again. She's in discomfort and crying constantly. Anna is being pushed to the limit because she can't go anywhere or see anyone in case other children catch it. I'm getting it in the neck because I'm out a lot. It's a busy time. 'Better that both of us don't suffer?' I said. In hindsight, just shutting up would have been a far better option.

Open mic night at Holy Apostles tonight. The sound was a car crash. Terry and I have no idea what we're doing. Numbers were down a bit and the estate guitar club didn't turn up to perform. Terry brought his boss from work along to sing 'Hallelujah'. He completely ballsed it up – and the next one – and the one after that. During his third song, I made the gesture of a revolver being slipped into my mouth to make Terry laugh.

Sunday 26 February

Our second FULL service at The Mission tonight. I interviewed the Reverend Matt Martinson about how he went from being a dangerous armed robber to becoming a vicar. He had the place transfixed. Matt described his younger self as a violent thug. He said his father was a nightmare – a violent drunk who wrecked his childhood. Matt became feral and wouldn't think twice about stabbing or punching someone. Sixty people rocked up and packed our little pub room. Where are they coming from? I find when I'm brave enough to push these doors, stuff happens. It must be God. It can't be me.

Tuesday 28 February

Visited Edith in her nursing home. She's very frail but said her recent baptism was one of her life's highlights. I got the impression she's ready to be with Jesus.

Thursday 1 March

My Christianity levels are severely tested working round here at times. A drunken man totally lost it with his girlfriend in Trinity Square this afternoon. He ranted and raved in her face between swigs of his can of Carlsberg Export and threatened to do awful things to her. Apparently he's well known for beating her senseless and prostituting her out to anyone who'll pay. The police were soon on the scene to calm him down. They issued a warning and sent him on his way. The woman didn't say a word. She shuffled hopelessly off behind him, head down, eyes glazed. Who knows what fresh hell she's faced with tonight? I felt so helpless just watching. A bloke next to me muttered that the guy's head should be cut off. 'No one would miss him.' I found myself nodding in agreement but later did a bit more thinking. I realized that God still loved that wretched man. He calls me not to give up hope for him. To believe that transformation and salvation is still possible. No part of my human self can muster that much grace, if I'm honest. Not for someone like that. He looked too far gone. Too corrupted. I have to draw on every last bit of Jesus within me to believe he could change. And even then I'm running on fumes.

I spent time on the Thornton Estate this morning. I became a bit despondent. Holy Apostles is in a desperate state. I'm out of moves. I don't know how we can grow it. I stood in the deserted church and shouted desperate prayers. I went out to walk the patch a bit. I bumped into a lovely lady called Sharon whose brother has just died. I offered a prayer and arranged to meet her. I also had a fruitful chat with the manager of the community-run shop. I felt better.

My landlord friend Lee took me out for a haddock and chips at tea time. He has an endless supply of funny stories about the Hull pub scene and rugby league.

Friday 2 March

I met up with Wayne for a coffee. Since he walked into the FULL service with his family a few months ago we've become an important part of his life. He wants to learn more about God. Faith seems to be making him happier.

Saturday 3 March

A former trawler captain has set up a display at Holy Trinity to coincide with our sailors' service next week. Ken was fascinating. One story he recounted particularly resonated with me. Two brothers were working on the same deep-sea shipping vessel. One night a violent storm erupted and one of the men was swept overboard. His brother instinctively dived in after him. The next day a Russian vessel found them floating on the surface of the water. They were locked in a haunting, frozen embrace. Inseparable in life and in death.

Ken said he was once swept off his ship's deck when nets became tangled around his ankles. Luckily he was wearing his friend's oversized boots and they slipped off in the water. He made it back onboard. When they reached port his friend demanded new wellies.

Tuesday 6 March

I met bodybuilder John in The Mission this afternoon. A chunk of his disability allowance has been taken away for no good reason. He's now struggling to pay his mortgage and petrified about becoming homeless. I tried to reassure him. We can't see John end up in a doorway. The benefits system has become so cruel and heartless. Faith-wise John is in a much stronger place. 'I do have love to give but I don't know where to put it,' he said.

I'm so frustrated about my sermon for this Sunday. I can't find that inspirational hook to hang it on.

We've been contacted by the city centre spiritualist group. They've asked if they can use Holy Trinity to do a fundraiser. They also want to make the church part of their ghost tour. As bare-faced cheek goes, this is off the scale. What next – requests for seances in the chancel? Free ouija board lessons in the nave? We gave them a polite but firm 'no'.

Wednesday 7 March

I had another terrible night's sleep. The wind was wild outside. At about 3 a.m., my sermon came to me. It poured out of me onto the back of an envelope. I never know when the inspiration will come.

We discussed spiritual gifts at Bible group tonight. I turned down their pleas for me to give a demonstration of 'speaking in tongues'. It's the special God language given to some Christians to pray and praise when their own dialect can't express how they're feeling. I've been able to speak in tongues since my early days as a new convert. It always feels a bit weird. I sound like that crazy baddie in *Indiana Jones and the Temple of Doom*. I usually only pray that way in private. I still remember the time we persuaded one of our youth leaders to do it on a coach ride to Harlech during a Christian summer camp. I don't know what language he was speaking in (if any), but I literally wet my Bermuda shorts laughing. The bus went into meltdown as he rocked and swayed down the aisle, babbling hilarious sentences. He soon started telling us off in English when we pelted his head with Tooty Frooties.

I'm actually going to an old school revival meeting at the City Hall tomorrow night with Neal and Danny. It will be full of people speaking and singing in tongues, I expect. I thought we could all do with a change of scene.

Thursday 8 March

I've seldom seen a man as uncomfortable as Neal at the revival meeting tonight. Mass hysteria was breaking out among the people in the seats around him. He just sat there like a reserved middle manager on his train commute home, trapped among frothing charismatic pentecostals. I was no less uncomfortable, to be fair. We'd gone to give Danny a flavour of a different type of worship. Within 20 minutes of the incendiary music kicking in, his arms were waving in the air. Before long he'd piled down to the front for prayer.

The preacher, who I'll call Daryl, was a piece of work. He wore a shiny suit and had an expensive haircut. Every so often he shouted 'Fire!' into the mic and made a sound effect like an actual roaring blaze. It was pure theatre. People he touched and prayed for fell down as if they'd been shot, except for one bloke who'd clearly been dragged to the meeting by his wife. She pushed him in front of Daryl as he prowled the first few rows looking for potential 'salvations'. The guy was completely immune to his 'fire' words and magic hands. I'll give Daryl points for perseverance. He went virtually nose-to-nose in one big final effort to get him to see the light. 'Will you accept Jesus as your Lord and Saviour, right now?' he asked. There was a dramatic pause. A sharp intake of breath from the audience. This was it, we thought, he was going to crack. He wasn't. The husband gave a ridiculously exaggerated shake of the head. It was beautiful comic timing. Daryl moved on to the next row.

I don't think Daryl and I would be friends. During his endless preach, he insisted that church leaders had become afraid to preach 'the truth'. That we pandered to the way of the world and refused to speak out against the 'evils' of homosexuality. It was the most surreal night I've had in years. It did little to cure my cynicism about the more extreme end of the charismatic tradition. I lost sight of Neal, too. I think he actually ran away. Fire!

Friday 9 March

I thought I'd heard the girls scream at full capacity. I was wrong. They found another level during their MMR injections today. I held Esther as the massive needle went in. I couldn't watch. There was a second of silence, an almost serene pause. Then she erupted. Anna held Heidi and the same thing happened. We rocked them back to quiet and took them round Asda.

Saturday, 10 March

Heidi now has chicken pox. It was inevitable, I suppose – but massively inconvenient. Another week of quarantine cabin fever looms. Anna looks crestfallen.

I handed cousin Ben the keys to his new flat on the estate this afternoon. I felt like George Bailey in *It's a Wonderful Life*. I suspect Ben won't ever live anywhere as tough as this again. High-rises surround the place. We'd cleaned the flat up for him a bit. Anna had filled the place with scented candles and other lovely homely touches. I'm full of admiration for Ben. He had his pick of the leafy suburbs to do youth work in. He chose this. I will look after him. He has given me fresh hope.

Sunday 11 March

Very encouraging numbers at the 9.30 a.m. service. For once a baptism family came back. The dad now wants to get confirmed. I just wish I could remember his name. Neal was tickled pink after a family he invited earlier in the week also turned up. He couldn't remember their names either. Our relentless focus on getting alongside people and building relationships seems to be working. We are so focused on growing this place. So desperate that it will no longer be lifeless and tragic. I preached my heart out and hoped it had hit the spot with people. Then a lady with paranoid schizophrenia gave me some feedback during coffee time. 'You were vague, Matt,' she said. 'Way too vague.'

Monday 12 March

I went in front of my curacy assessment panel this afternoon. It's designed to take stock and evaluate how we are doing as new reverends. I was honest but resisted the urge to overshare. I think they would struggle to relate to my unedited first months in Hull. All was well, I think. They seemed to appreciate the effort we were all making to turn things around at Holy Trinity.

I've volunteered to do some shifts at the community-run fruit and veg shop on the Thornton Estate. I don't know a Jersey Royal from a red cabbage, but I can't think of a better way to build relationships with people.

Poor Heidi will not go to sleep because of her pox spots. She's screaming as I write this. It's going to be a long night.

Tuesday 13 March

The debate about same sex marriage rumbles on among some of the church's top brass. A cathedral dean called Jeffrey John claimed that the Church of England's 'prejudice' over the issue was the major reason for the rise in UK secularism. I disagree. I'd argue it's more to do with our gradual retreat from the lives of real people – gay or otherwise.

I read an interesting interview with Archbishop Rowan Williams. He talked of a formative experience he had on a sink estate in Liverpool during his training. 'The vicar said to me something I've never forgotten,' he said. 'The people here have doors slammed in their faces every day of the week. I want to make sure they don't have another one slammed on the seventh.'

Thursday 15 March

It hit me like a slap in the face today how amazing Anna is. I spent the duration of a boring meeting counting my lucky stars. Reflecting on her qualities. So often I'm not around to help. So rarely do I sweep her up in my arms, shower her neck in kisses and tell her how much I appreciate her. I should be telling her daily what a phenomenal mum she is. I worry that she thinks of me with weary frustration. Or unleashes a heavy sigh or a pronounced tut whenever someone mentions my name or says 'You're Matt's wife, aren't you?'

I shared some of my reflections with Anna when I got home. We agreed that we are going through an unpleasant patch in our marriage, perhaps the hardest time since the kids came along. My job is a jealous lover. It too often takes everything. I can see why clergy marriages break down. We committed ourselves to one another afresh. I said sorry for when I wasn't there. Or when I am there but not really there. We held each other. All was well.

Friday 16 March

Rowan Williams has announced he's stepping down as Archbishop of Canterbury. He seemed so relieved at the press conference. I bet he was. He warned his successor that they would need the 'constitution of an ox and skin as thick as a rhino'. I have a lot to thank Rowan for. Without him, ordained pioneer ministers like me wouldn't exist and I'd have to be a proper vicar. No one would want that. I tweeted that – if asked – I'd consider replacing him. 'I'd make a few changes,' I wrote. Starting with all pews. They'd be sensitively ripped out immediately and put on a big bonfire in the grounds of Lambeth and Bishopthorpe Palaces.

I'm engrossed in the Old Testament book of Esther. It would make a fabulous musical. There are gloriously heroic goodies, terrible baddies and a great king. I'm amazed Lloyd Webber hasn't been all over it. You can almost hear the songs bursting off the page.

Saturday 17 March

I met Irene this morning. We have so many shared frustrations about the way clergy are selected and trained. The process virtually entirely excludes anyone who is uneducated or not academically-inclined. It drives us mad. It's little wonder that the Church of England has retreated so shamefully from the council estates and poorer areas. The Christians who live in these places – who speak the language and are immersed in that culture – are too often overlooked for being reverends, and seldom told that it could even be an option. I'm not being cruel, but one of our fellow curates in East Yorkshire is a virtual mute. He does not seem capable of actually talking to anyone in a remotely 'normal' way – unless he's had a glass of port. What on earth does he think our job involves? I'm sure he has a robust faith. He is intelligent. Bookish beyond belief. He has absorbed libraries of deep, complex theology. But as a priest called to serve the people? Words fail me. He told Irene that he was waiting for a cathedral to hire him to study. What are we doing?

One of our elderly church welcomers lambasted me for making a homeless bloke a cup of tea this morning. 'You'll only encourage them, Matt,' she said. Unbelievable!

I've sent a press release to the *Hull Daily Mail* about Ben's new youth and children's worker role. I didn't mention the fact that he went out on a pub crawl with an old friend last night and was violently sick. Not a great start. I guess it's all part of the maturing process.

Anna and I had a lovely walk with the girls to The Minerva for a quick half. The air was lovely and the Humber perfectly still. We got home and watched *Deal or No Deal*. We've become worryingly addicted since Dan the Tan has been on. We're hanging on Noel Edmonds' every word.

Sunday 18 March

I've written to Archbishop Rowan to thank him for being brave enough to start the Church of England's pioneer movement. All the articles being written about his retirement say that he had an impossible job and that his tenure was dominated by the issues of women bishops and homosexuality. I thought he could do with some encouragement. Archbishop Sentamu is in the running to succeed him, apparently. Selfishly, I'd hate to lose him as my diocesan boss but know what a significant leader he is. He'd be faced with an impossible task too. But at least the Church of England would be more fun, colourful and rooted in reality. He gets my vote.

Mother's Day has gone from being Anna's worst day to her favourite day, now we have the girls. We kept her snuggled under the covers and showered her with cards, gifts and a strong cuppa. A happier face I've not seen for a long time.

I had a revealing conversation with three homeless guys before the 9.30 a.m. service started this morning. They spoke so candidly with me about their heroin addictions. Apparently a bag of the stuff costs £10 and lasts most of the day. But the race is constantly on to find the money for the next one. Their days are spent wandering the streets, high, desperate or bored. The booze and the drugs keep them warm and numb to the desperate reality of their predicament. We kept them warm for a bit with Dot's refreshments. It was heartbreaking to see them shuffle out during the first hymn on a fresh quest to find the money for another bag. What's the answer? I wish I knew.

Monday 19 March

Mum is back from her trip to Australia with Barry. She's even more in love with him. She deserves every morsel of happiness that comes her way. If Barry makes her happy then I'm happy. Overly protective and wary of her heart being broken again, but happy.

Good chat with a lad called Stewart between press-ups and star jumps at boxing training. He's trying to get into the Navy. He wants me to pray that he does. I've added him to the list.

Tuesday 20 March

My press release about cousin Ben made it into the *Yorkshire Post*. 'Ben is going to bring a much more modern approach,' my quote says. 'If churches don't invest in youth work we may as well give up and go home – that's the reality.'

The girls played in the garden while I washed the car this afternoon. It was a rare scene of domestic bliss. I didn't get much washing done, to be honest. I was too busy soaking them to within an inch of their lives.

Wednesday 21 March

I visited Bodmin Road Church on the Bransholme estate today. I'd heard good things about their forward-thinking approach and wanted to steal ideas. Their church welcome leaflet is a thing of refreshing beauty. It blew me away. It's everything I would want to communicate to someone new. 'Chances are you're not a churchgoer,' it says. 'Churches are cold, out of touch and boring, aren't they? Chances are you're not religious. Religious people are old-fashioned and often judgemental, aren't they? They don't drink beer, don't follow rugby or football, don't ever shop at Primark and prefer *Songs of Praise* to *The X Factor*! Chances are you do believe there's something out there.' The leaflet goes on to list what to expect from Bodmin Road Church: '... a church with a 40-year record of community involvement ... a church with people you can relate to ... a church that looks after your kids if you bring them on a Sunday ... a church that isn't freezing or judgemental or boring. A church where the music is modern. A church that puts the ancient and unchanged message of Jesus into today's language.' As I said to the pastor: 'When can I start?!'

Thursday 22 March

My first talk in a synagogue tonight, to the Hull branch of the Council of Christians and Jews. I shared my experiences of visiting Auschwitz and what it meant for my faith. Few things have shaped me as much as those few hours numbly walking around. They presented me with a lovely plaque to mark the occasion.

Dan the Tan had his shot on *Deal or No Deal* this afternoon. He's an instantly likeable character. The crowd lapped him up and the women swooned. He's annoyingly good-looking and has a six-pack. He won £8,000 in the end but it could have been £20,000 if he'd had the guts to go one more round. To be fair, it could also have been 1p.

I've received a letter from a Lambeth Palace official to say that Archbishop Rowan is too busy to respond personally to my note of encouragement. Seems a bit unnecessary. Like receiving a card saying you've not been invited to a party.

Friday 23 March

I've received a personal letter from Archbishop Rowan! What a legend. He wrote:

> Dear Matt,
> a quick personal word of thanks for your card and message.
> I was very touched indeed to hear from you – as I look back on

the decade, I do thank God that pushing forward the Fresh Expressions agenda and Ordained Pioneer Minister model is one of the things I've been allowed to be part of. I wish you – and your pub congregation – every blessing and joy in Christ.

Lovely.

My new favourite place to think, watch and write is a window seat at Nero's overlooking Queen Victoria Square. It's people-watching heaven.

Saturday 24 March

My buddy Pete arrived at our Holy Apostles open mic night just in time to play the songs 'Mr Brightside' and 'Mardy Bum'. It gave the place a lift. I'd killed the atmosphere with my version of the Oasis B-side 'D'yer Wanna Be a Spaceman?' We got back to ours and reflected on life over a couple of single malts. I'm worried about my Pete. The human jukebox is singing a sad song right now. His relationship with his girlfriend, Rhiannon, isn't going well. I tried to comfort and counsel him as best I could. I'm still convinced those two are meant to be together. I've learnt that no one ever listens properly to relationship advice when they're madly in love. You just have to let things take their course. It either works out or their hearts break.

Sunday 25 March

Our pub service FULL continues to exceed my expectations. People poured in again this afternoon. The only downside is the set-up. It's a stressful nightmare. The drum kit is a pig to move. The pub only closes for drinks and food at 3 p.m. so we don't have long to get ready. People are often only just finishing up their Sunday dinners and pints of Heineken. Others come in for a drink to discover a service about to start and a man with a dog collar greeting them at the door. It messes with their heads. We must be mad.

I interviewed cousin Ben about what his role at Holy Trinity will be. He was a bit nervous and 'ummed' and 'ahhed' a lot. But this is part of his training. I believe in him. My challenge is to get him to be as comfortable speaking up-front and leading and ministering as he is playing his bass guitar. He's so joyful and natural plucking those strings. It's hypnotic watching him.

Monday 26 March

I interviewed Olympic boxing hopeful Luke Campbell at the 'Celebration of Sport' service at Holy Trinity tonight. Numbers were pretty tragic until all the St Paul's Boxing Academy gang turned up in their shiny blue tracksuits. What a relief. I met up with Luke earlier in the gym to go through what we'd talk about. He's a very impressive individual. Totally focused and confident without being arrogant. You have to have something about you when fast, strong, fit people are trying to hit you in the face really hard. Luke told me that when he was younger and first getting into boxing, he would go into church to pray. One day he felt he'd grown in confidence so much that he didn't need to do that any more. 'I knew God was with me,' he said. Interesting. I wore my St Paul's T-shirt over my clergy garb for the service and danced around shadow-boxing Luke in the interview. I claimed that I was the 'hardest vicar in Hull'. No one looked convinced. I prayed for Luke that he would stay healthy for the Olympics and do himself and the country proud. I think he can win the gold medal!

I'm knocking booze on the head until Easter Sunday. I want to approach the Passion story fresh and clear-headed.

Tuesday 27 March

Epic church council meeting tonight. Nearly three hours unfortunately. Entrenched views and fears of change surfaced. There's concern about the 11 a.m. traditional service. It needs to improve on every level. It's lacking joy, life and a sense of community. Choral-style worship should be full of awe, colour and a sense of the numinous. Neal longs to see it come to life. In a very pastoral, sensitive, kind way, he told the meeting that the choir needed to up their game. He made the fair point that we aren't a cathedral so should stop trying to act like one. On a brighter note, the council unanimously agreed to approve the Holy Trinity development project. It will cost a few million, they reckon. The plans include removing the pews and replacing them with chairs that are more bum-friendly. Praise the Lord.

Interesting conversation with a chap on a bench in Trinity Square. It began as a chat about Hull City but quickly went deeper. He opened up about leaving his wife and the pain he felt at the promiscuity of his daughter. I gave him my card and told him to call me if he wanted to continue the conversation. He seemed desperate to find some hope and purpose.

Wednesday 28 March

Heidi is making my hair turn greyer. It's scary how many of my character traits she has picked up. She is a little girl of extremes. She goes from absolute joy to absolute despair in the space of ten seconds.

The sun was shining today. It never makes me feel worse.

Friday 30 March

The checkout lady at Tesco looked so sad as she scanned my shopping (Doritos and a music magazine) today. 'What are you thinking about?' I asked her.

'Absolutely nothing,' she replied. I didn't pursue it.

Anna's mum cooked us a pasta, prawn and salmon dish tonight. I had thirds. I think her cooking has had a profound effect on my relationship with her and Paul. She makes mouthfuls of healing.

Saturday 31 March

Sermon writing takes me forever. I am a terrible procrastinator, and engage in all manner of endless tasks to distract me. Today it was doodling whirlwinds and tapping out the dramatic drum bit at the end of each *EastEnders* episode.

Sunday 1 April

I finished today's sermon with the 'pioneers' prayer', believed to have been written by the legendary mariner Sir Francis Drake. It stirs me to have a go. Be more courageous. I've stuck it on my office wall. It reads:

> *Disturb us, Lord, when*
> *we are too well pleased with ourselves,*
> *when our dreams have come true*
> *because we have dreamed too little,*
> *when we arrived safely*
> *because we sailed too close to the shore.*
>
> *Disturb us, Lord, when*
> *with the abundance of things we possess*
> *we have lost our thirst*
> *for the waters of life;*
> *having fallen in love with life,*
> *we have ceased to dream of eternity*
> *and in our efforts to build a new earth,*
> *we have allowed our vision*
> *of the new Heaven to dim.*
>
> *Disturb us, Lord, to dare more boldly,*
> *to venture on wider seas*
> *where storms will show your mastery;*
> *where losing sight of land,*

we shall find the stars.
We ask You to push back
the horizons of our hopes;
and to push into the future
in strength, courage, hope, and love.
Amen.

I listened back to my sermon when I got home. I'd recorded it on my phone. I want to get better. I spoke too loudly. I need to use the power of the hushed tone as much as the piercing shout to get my point across. One of my vicar heroes, the Reverend Derek Wooldridge, was a master at it. I can still picture him on that stool at our youth camp in Criccieth, North Wales, talking about Jesus to me and all my mates. He'd erupt with some point or other. And then bring it down to a whisper – as if he was sharing the most intimate secret. Somehow what he said seemed more important because of the way he said it. I want to learn how you speak like that.

Holy Trinity was low on April Fool's Day pranks. I thought about calling Neal to tell him frantically that the church was on fire. I bottled it. His heart wouldn't have coped.

Monday 2 April

Ben's first day as Holy Trinity's youth and children's worker. He told me he was excited and scared. The perfect combination, then. I took him to Hull Pie for a sausage stew. We then planned out what he would actually focus on in the coming weeks. He will get some youth and children's work going on a Sunday morning at Holy Trinity and Holy Apostles; start a midweek youth group; develop a young adults group with FULL people and make links with the schools and colleges in our patch. That should keep him busy for a bit.

I took Ben to the boxing club tonight to introduce him to the coaches and see what shape he's in. He was blowing after five minutes. I think he nearly threw up.

My friend from the Old Town has had a son. It doesn't seem long ago that I prayed for him in the church car park that this would happen. He was beaming. I was further encouraged when Luke Campbell tweeted me to ask if he could come to church on Sunday.

Ben and I shared a poignant moment before he went off to his flat on the estate tonight. He was worried. Strange house, strange city, strange job. I reassured him that he could call me at any time if he feels scared, anxious or threatened. I prayed for him and he limped off into the dark. Walking like he'd filled his trousers. He'll really feel it tomorrow. Another victim of the notorious St Paul's circuits.

Tuesday 3 April

I've decided to have the dodgy cross tattoo on my right arm redone. It's always looked as if I did it myself while riding a ski-lift in a strong gale after downing six cans of Special Brew. With hindsight, taking my inspiration from a clip art diagram was a mistake. It's been an embarrassment on my arm for about four years. Now the scary lady at Body Art Hull will make the cross bigger and bolder. And straight. Really important, that. I'll have the words 'Love never fails' from 1 Corinthians 13 above it in Anna's glorious handwriting. She's banned me from getting a massive hawk tattooed on my chest like the drummer from Foo Fighters.

I'm trying to follow Jesus's passion journey step by step this Holy Week, immersing myself in what he went through and seeing it through fresh eyes. Jesus confronted the Pharisees outside the synagogue today in Matthew 23. He gives them both barrels for their hypocrisy and judgementalism – 'You brood of vipers!' His line about their bowl being clean on the outside but dirty on the inside struck a chord. Jesus knows human beings. He sees us from the inside out. No part of us is hidden from him. I find that both terrifying and reassuring at the same time.

Dashed back to York to see Mum. She's poorly. Between hacking coughs, she sheepishly told me that Barry will be moving in soon. I'm determined to be happy for her. My attempts to wrap her in cotton wool are coming to an end.

Wednesday 4 April

Met Neal and Irene in Wetherspoons to sort out our baptism policy. We don't want to become a Christening factory – an assembly line of babies 'getting done' and their families disappearing into the sunset. We're going to ask them to attend a few services before the baptism. We want to try to build proper relationships. Get to know them and they us. Make it so everyone can say the baptism words with confidence and familiarity. After that, the sunset is available for them to head into if they so wish. We hope a few might stay with us.

I'm writing this in bed and Esther is next door screaming. The twins have come back from York unsettled and antsy. Esther's cries don't seem to be about anything in particular. It's the unknowable parts of parenthood that I struggle with. Now we face the parental dilemma that sends Anna's favourite mum forums into meltdown – do we leave her to scream herself out or go in to comfort her? Parents seem absolutely split on this. There's no consensus. You're left feeling like a terrible parent whichever decision you make.

Anna is really down today and struggling to cope with the girls. Her actual words were: 'I can't go on like this, Woody!' Unthinking hyperbole, I hope, but not good. We talked about putting the girls into nursery for a second afternoon a week to give her a bit of respite. As for Esther, I've made a decision: I'm going in to comfort her.

Thursday 5 April

I dreamt last night that I got married to the generously-beaked glamour model Jodie Marsh. I'd become a widower and met her at the swimming baths. Jodie seemed really nice in the dream. Godly, too. Weird.

I'm still worried about Anna. She's on the edge. I'm throwing myself into sharing the load. Being more present. Extra nursery time means spending extra cash but Anna's sanity is worth going into debt over.

At our weekly Wetherspoon's clergy meeting this morning, I insisted that we all share something positive about our work. We keep getting bogged down in all the negative stuff of church life. Having the *joie de vivre* of ministry being hoovered out of us by the naysayers and doom-mongers. Being resolute in our encouragement of each other stops us becoming like that ourselves. Lovely stories poured out of Irene and Neal. It's clear that the three of us come alive when we're engaged with real people. I don't care how much money is raised for the building project, that's what will turn around Holy Trinity in the end.

I had coffee with a young actor called Daniel later. He'd emailed out of the blue a few days ago to ask for spiritual guidance. He recently moved back to the area after being a resident actor with the Royal Shakespeare Company. Admittedly I was more impressed with his love of Oasis and knowledge of their B-sides than the fact he once performed in *The Merchant of Venice* with Patrick Stewart. I tried not to sound too keen or excited when Daniel said he now wants to be part of a church community. He told me his faith had lain dormant for years but lately seemed to be coming alive. Daniel's also keen on helping us develop Holy Trinity as an arts space. I could tell he regretted saying that. I suddenly thought he could do a dramatic mystery plays-style Holy Week reading out in Trinity Square tomorrow. He's tentatively up for it.

Neal played the flute at tonight's Last Supper re-enactment. It was heavenly. I used to have an issue with men and flutes. It didn't look right, somehow. Neal has changed my mind.

Friday 6 April

We were up at 4 a.m. with Esther. She wouldn't go back down no matter how much milk she consumed. I ended up in the spare room. Esther snuggled in next to Anna. I think this was her plan all along.

I've just finished watching *The Passion of the Christ*. It was necessary. It never fails to move, shock and remind me. I find the gory flogging scene when the Roman guards turn Jesus's back into something that looks like pizza topping unbearable. 'It is as it was,' Pope John Paul II said of the film. I'm staggered afresh at what Jesus went through.

Somehow Christ's journey to the cross on Good Friday always exposes me to myself. The broken bits of me can't hide today. I reflected on how different I can be at home compared to church. Holy Trinity Matt is usually lively, interested and friendly. Always there for everyone. Then there's the me inside the house. He's too often grumpy and tired. Impatient and smelly-nappy-averse. He's too often there for himself. I'm keen on sorting this out.

I'd give our worship and dramatic reading event out in Trinity Square a solid 6 out of 10. We were up against the Hull rugby league derby so the Old Town was deserted. Terry led the music in his usual 'this could be the last chorus I ever sing in my life so I'm going to burst a blood vessel doing it' kind of way. I persuaded my new actor friend Daniel to climb onto the Andrew Marvell statue to deliver his script. I respected him for having a go with a day's notice. It was fun and different – although the Shakespearean-style language was lost on most of us. I told the crowd: 'I've no idea what he's just said but it sounded brilliant!'

Saturday 7 April

I read an interesting blog about wearing the cross of Christ as decoration. The writer argues that 'we bear the cross, we take it up daily, we follow the way of the cross. Only then will we be worthy to wear it as a piece of jewellery. Does your life give honour to the one who died there for all?' I commented (aware of the massive cross tattooed to my right arm): 'For me, there can't be enough crosses on public display – tattoos, necklaces, ornaments, whatever. The more crosses around, the more reminders we have. I've got a dirty great big one on my arm and every day it reminds me – whether I want it to or not – just what I have to pick up and what I have to strive to live up to. It may be on my arm but unless it's engraved on my heart as well, I agree, it's just a rather unpleasant decoration.'

Easter Saturday always feels like a limbo day. I finished my Michael Ramsay book and made a Spotify mix to run to, rediscovering the song '66' by the Afghan Whigs. Neal led night prayers beautifully at Holy Trinity. The choir's vocal renaissance continues.

Sunday 8 April

Easter Sunday morning. Irene woke up to discover her house had been broken into while she and Ian slept. The thieves got away with hundreds of pounds. It was hard to feel a sense of resurrection joy and celebration after she told us that. Irene put on a brave face. 'It's only money, Matt!' she said. 'At least we weren't killed.' I know she'll be feeling it deep down, though. It's a terrifying thing to have happened. Her lovely home has been violated. She'll need loads of love and reassurance. I plan to give her plenty.

Despite being up through the night with Esther, I somehow made it to the 5.30 a.m. sunrise service. I wish I hadn't. It was led by a nearby church who like things formal – even on Easter Sunday. At no point in that hour or so did I get the impression that they were happy about death being defeated and the promise of eternal life. If you were ever going to make an effort not to be stern of face, stiff-lipped and stuffy, surely this was the time? Clearly they didn't get the memo. The service was word-heavy, dull, joyless and full of pious, unnecessary ritual. I felt embarrassed that I had invited some of our fringe families to come.

By total contrast, the 9.30 a.m. service at Holy Trinity was full of joy. Loads of young families turned up. Luke Campbell came with his mate. He held the comfort cross I'd sent to him last week. I posted it to his home with a little card and £50 to get himself some new boxing gloves. I wanted to encourage him before he went off to the Olympics. He must be bricking it. All that expectation about winning the gold medal will be weighing heavily on him.

I cycled like the clappers to the estate to lead the Holy Apostles service. It was pretty tragic at first. Very few in again. Then just as I began the opening welcome, a striking lady strolled in with her daughter. It turned out she was Latvian and from the Russian Orthodox tradition. Her daughter had dragged her along because of my open invitation to the children at the school assembly. Earlier this week I'd encouraged the kids to bring me chocolate. These lovely Latvians had baked me a cupcake covered with hundreds and thousands. They were soon shaking a tambourine with the rest of us. I pray that they come back.

I've turned my mobile phone back on now Lent is over. My life was significantly better without it.

Monday 9 April

Dan the Tan has got engaged! He proposed to Elli on top of a mountain while they were snowboarding. They've asked me to marry them. With Dan's TV game show experience, I'm going to have some fun with those vows.

Me: 'Dan, will you take Elli to be your wife? Will you love her, comfort her, honour and protect her and, forsaking all others, be faithful to her as long as you both shall live.'
Dan: 'I will'.
Me: 'Is that your final answer?'

Tuesday 10 April

My relationship with Anna was on the agenda during my spiritual direction with Sister Cecilia today. I was honest about how strained things have been. She can see right through me anyway. Not being straight with my nun is futile. I told her that being a dad, a husband and a reverend don't seem to be mixing too well. Cecilia suggested I do a dialogue exercise. Write a brief history of our relationship and the key factual stepping stones of Anna's life as I saw them. I then had to create a strange, 'twilight' section, documenting how I perceived her thoughts and feelings during those key moments. How she felt when the first love of her life dumped her – that kind of thing.

I wrote a letter telling Anna how I felt about all kinds of issues. Even the ones that would be difficult for her to read. In fact, especially those ones. The sting in the tale was that I then had to write Anna's reply back to me. The exercises were essentially Sister Cecilia's sure-fire steps towards teaching me to stop being a selfish sod. It was awkward at first but I got into it. It helped me imagine how Anna really felt about stuff. I realized that we've been trying to cling on to who we were – the way we did marriage and each other – before Esther and Heidi were born. Before the dog collar went on. We are in a new season and we need to embrace it. We need to let go of the past. So many people I know have become too dull and safe since having kids. They seem to live their entire lives for them and through them. I think there's a middle way. I don't want Esther and Heidi to grow up thinking that my life stopped when theirs started.

My letter to Anna – and her reply back to me – revealed something I've known for a long time. I need to step up at home. I wrote: 'Dear Anna ... I see how consumed I am with my world, my priorities, my issues. I've neglected you. I haven't given you enough head space and heart space. I've not taken enough interest.' And I wrote that she wrote: 'Dear Woody ... I see you doing this high-profile job and being everything to everyone and sometimes I just want to scream: *What about us?!*'

I visited Dan the Tan and Elli afterwards to talk about their wedding. He told me all the backstage gossip from *Deal or No Deal*. Apparently they record three shows a day. Contestants are holed up in a hotel for two weeks. He said there's a fair bit of drinking and a lot of dancing and late-night Noel Edmonds impressions.

Thursday 12 April

I think my line management style is doing Ben's head in. He keeps waiting to be told what to do. I'm trying to help him see that he's got to take the initiative. Decide for himself what he's going to do and how he's going to do it. I gave him some ideas about what that might look like. I reassured him that this first month is all about him building relationships. I have to remember that pioneering doesn't come naturally to everyone.

A regular at one of our new services came to see me today. She says she's ready to forgive her husband for running off with another woman. She said the anger had eaten her up inside and she wants to be free. 'I can't do it myself, Matt,' she said. 'I need God to help me.' It was a humbling encounter. I prayed that she'd find the strength to forgive and a deep peace.

Friday 13 April

I'm hopelessly addicted to *Game of Thrones* on Sky Atlantic. It's full of sex, power games and mindless violence. Not unlike the Old Testament, then.

I can't sleep for worrying about the beer festival in less than a week's time. It could end in disaster. A mess of drunken, bearded men throwing up in the choir aisle after too many pints of Trinity Ale. Have I gone too far this time?

Saturday 14 April

High drama out on my run this afternoon. I was jogging up South Bridge Road when I noticed a little girl of about two pushing a toy pram. She was on her own, looking lost and confused. The road was busy. I stopped and asked where her mummy and daddy were. No response. Just then a couple pulled up in their car. They'd also noticed the girl. They waited with her while I ran off to try to locate her family. All of a sudden I heard two girls screaming 'Daisy!' Apparently Daisy had escaped through a back door and taken off. Her grandad arrived on the scene looking as if he'd aged another ten years. All was well in the end but the incident has done little to ease my worries about Esther and Heidi. I made sure I checked all the doors and windows when I got home.

Endured a difficult site meeting with some of the CAMRA committee about the beer festival. They are anal about everything. I'm anal about nothing. It was a relief when our churchwarden Tim turned up to answer the questions I couldn't. Which were all of them, to be fair.

The girls' godparents Jonny and Anne came to stay tonight. Esther and Heidi crawled all over them. Jonny and I got a pass out to go on an educational tour of some of the Old Town's hostelries. Jonny is a raconteur extraordinaire. I've never known anyone talk so much crap so brilliantly. I made him tell me the poo sandwich story for the hundredth time as we strolled to The Lion and Key.

Sunday 15 April

I'm feeling a bit despondent about the FULL service. Half of the band have drifted away for one reason or another. The novelty of banging those drums and singing those choruses has worn off. They've all left politely with no dramas, but I can't help taking it personally. I used to think that leading a church for people who don't do church would be an effortless, glamorous endeavour. Not now. I can feel some of the momentum ebbing away. My confidence, too.

Monday 16 April

After yesterday's disappointment, tonight I saw the future at Holy Trinity. A little, encouraging sign of the progress we've made. I stood in the nave and looked down the church. There were Hull beer festival people erecting bars, attaching hand pumps and testing ale temperatures. In the chancel, there were actors rehearsing for a performance of *Everyman*. The old place was buzzing with new life and creativity. Hull people using the space for something other than Sunday worship and history tours. I found myself fighting the urge to cry. I felt stirred to do more. To take more risks. Push more boundaries. Have more faith. Hold Neal and Irene closer. See my wife and children occasionally.

Esther hasn't cried once tonight. Anna and I did a little dance of joy in the bedroom – quietly.

Tuesday 17 April

Woke up to discover a big double-page spread in the *Hull Daily Mail* about the beer festival. Their influential (and notoriously caustic and world-weary) feature writer, Ian Midgley, was really positive – bordering on excited. Real ale clearly brings out the delight in people.

I'm always fascinated by the conversations us priests have when we get together. I met up with one of my curate pals this afternoon. We went from our thoughts on transubstantiation – whether the bread and wine literally becomes the body and blood of Christ at Holy Communion – to whether we bought lingerie for our wives. Turns out my friend is something of a regular at Ann Summers on his wife's birthday and at Christmas. 'I'd recommend the styles and quality in there,' he told me. 'Just remember to take your dog collar off.'

Wednesday 18 April

Final preparations for the real ale festival. No going back now.

Thursday 19 April

Amazing first day of the beer festival. People poured in faster than the ale could be poured out. We were inundated. The CAMRA guys think we might run out before the last session on Saturday. More importantly, the atmosphere was incredible. Holy Trinity hummed with laughter and vibrant conversation. There was a healthy respect for the surroundings, too. No hint of trouble. Even the swearing and beery burps were kept to a minimum.

Landlord buddy Lee is doing well with the food. His pies are heavenly. On the downside, there's a bit of tension between some of the organizing committee. I think they're just a bit overwhelmed with the huge response. Also, one of our stalwarts has withdrawn her financial giving to Holy Trinity in protest at us staging the festival. I respect her opinion but I wish she could see the good that's coming out of it.

Photographers and journalists swarmed the place early doors. This was a story they all seemed keen on fully immersing themselves in. I told one feature writer that Jesus would be propping up the bar talking to people about what really matters in life. The comment went everywhere. It even generated a debate on BBC Radio 5 Live. My old colleague Arun texted in a comment to them: 'I think the Rev in Hull has it spot on about where Jesus would be. The Pharisees accused Jesus of being a drunkard and a glutton. The church should be among the people. Sounds like a brave and risky decision by the Rev. I hope he doesn't get kicked too much for it.'

I squeezed in a funeral visit between pint-pulling. It's a delicate one. There are big family issues. I always seem to get them. Death so often brings out the worst in people.

Finally home now. Body full of adrenaline and Anglers Reward. Heart full of joy. A great day.

Friday 20 April

I got to church early to help facilitate the clean-up operation. That's a lie, actually. I got in the way of the clean-up operation. I facilitated the banter in and around the clean-up operation. I can never understand why people aren't as energized as me first thing in the morning. A few of the hung-over CAMRA volunteers shot me murderous looks as I skipped past them riding my mop like a Grand National winner.

The ale festival has gone way beyond what any of us thought possible. People were queueing to get in this afternoon. Queueing to get into our church! The queue snaked right out into Trinity Square. I basked in the sight of it for ages. Who would have thought that six months ago?

It was pretty intense behind the scenes. The festival organizer walked out this afternoon. It's a real shame after all his hard work. Things became fractious between him and one or two of the committee. Even in the midst of a major triumph, conflict seems to be unavoidable. The row was over the dwindling beer supplies. It has just about run out. No one could agree on a solution. I tried to lift the tension in the middle of their heated discussions with a joke: 'You lot couldn't organize a p*** up in a church!' I said. Bit too early for that one, on reflection.

The media coverage has been off the scale. I was on the BBC's *Look North* and ITV's *Calendar* last night. They both featured footage of me, Neal and Irene at the official opening, raising our glasses in the air. I screamed 'Woo hoo!' like a maniac. We made the front of the *Hull Daily Mail* too. 'The Holy Gr-Ale!', the headline read.

I put a shift in today. My head is swimming with the numbers of people I spoke to about church, God and real ale. So many Hull people came into Holy Trinity for the first time. Despite the size of the building and its key geographical location, they had never thought to pop their head in until now. Let's hope they come back.

Manning the bar with the CAMRA volunteers was interesting and entertaining. They treat the different ales with all the passion, attention to detail and pernickety geekiness as philatelists with their Penny Blacks. Pulling a proper pint is an art. One of the grumpy volunteers kept telling me to 'Stop ****ing wasting it!' He'd apologize and then swear again two minutes later.

Saturday 21 April

We officially ran out of beer at 2 p.m. People were still trying to get in for hours afterwards. The Old Town pubs became full of our cast-offs. Uncle Mike's band The York Turnpike Trust played as the last few drops were drunk. I'm hoping we've made nearly £4,000 for church coffers. We need it. People have been really generous with their donations. I've been pleasantly surprised by the reaction of our stalwarts. The festival has won many of them over, I think. They've enjoyed watching hundreds of people pour into the church that they love. Growth is infectious. I got away to Caffè Nero to prepare for my sermon tomorrow.

Sunday 22 April

Ben has created a 'kids' zone' at the back of church for the 9.30 a.m. service. It's just a few tables with craft and a baby play area. We're hoping that it might morph into a Sunday school once we've grown a bit more and some kids start coming consistently. I preached on the healing of the lame beggar. I did a dramatic re-enactment with Ben as the beggar. He hammed it up in all the right places. It's lovely to have a sidekick. A comic foil. The service was well attended again. The congregation were in good spirits. The pungent beer fumes helped with that, I think.

The day was soured a bit when I had a frosty email exchange with one of my old friends. He was supposed to be coming to Hull tonight to introduce me to his wife but I couldn't face it. I had no conversation or bonhomie left in the tank. A dark bedroom was calling. I sent a polite apology but he wasn't happy. 'You may be a vicar, but you're still a *****,' he replied. Ouch.

Monday 23 April

I've decided to attend my secondary school year group's reunion. I'm fascinated to see how we've all changed. They really won't believe I'm a vicar. I expect it will be an evening of excruciating awkwardness on a grand scale. I can't wait.

Tuesday 24 April

A fellow priest has sent Neal a scathing email about the beer festival. 'I was angered and dismayed to see the coverage on *Look North* of the CAMRA festival showing the consumption of alcohol within Holy Trinity Church,' he wrote. 'I wish to suggest that there should be a considered debate at leadership level within the local church, as to what should be our socially-responsible public stance upon such matters, and how that should affect decisions re hosting events such as this.'

Neal's response was wise. Full of common sense, biblical literacy and Christ-likeness. He said the ethics of the festival had been debated by our church council. He wrote that good food and drink was 'of God' and:

> ... *during the festival itself, I saw nobody out of control, nor any hint of drunkenness. On the contrary, people were very respectful of the building and the atmosphere was good-natured and friendly ... many of the people who came in had never been inside Holy Trinity before and probably, rarely, if ever in a church. Yet they came, and from the conversations my colleagues and I had, were deeply impressed and moved by the venue. So who knows what seeds were sown with people who we as 'the church' would find it very difficult to reach? We as a church, need to give permission for people to come in on their terms and yes, to be able to ask questions of us about our faith. All I saw was people who simply wanted to enjoy a very tasty drink or two and friendly conversation. I cannot see any wrong in that. The fact that the beer festival happened in church I feel is entirely a good thing.*

Neal is far more pioneering than he thinks he is. He's not just giving half-hearted permission for me to try new things – he's fully entering into it all himself. Other more traditionally inclined clergy have so much to learn from his approach.

Wednesday 25 April

I had a fascinating conversation this morning. The encounter was like something from Ishiguro's *The Remains of the Day*. A lady told me that 50 years ago her husband went abroad for three months to work. During that time she had a short affair with a guy from her office. It soon ended and she travelled out to be with her husband. Racked with guilt, she confessed her infidelity to him. He seemed nonplussed at the time, content to sweep it under the carpet of 'keep calm and carry on' Englishness. Then a couple of years ago, completely out of the blue, her husband exploded with rage while they ate their usual tea at their usual time. 'Why did you sleep with him?!' he demanded. The lady said their marriage had been tense and strained ever since. She was beside herself, still weighed down with the most terrible guilt. 'I tried to bury it but it just won't go away,' she told me. 'I think about it every day.' Seldom have I met anyone so tormented, so in need of the beautiful touch of grace. I did my best. I prayed that she would find freedom. But I'm not sure it did much good. She thanked me and shuffled out into the Old Town with the saddest of faces.

What would have been my first wedding has been cancelled. Turns out the groom has run off with another woman.

I was in windswept Bridlington tonight for a training session about healing and deliverance ministry. There was a comedy moment when the speaker was talking about demons and things that go bump in the night. Just as he was winding up, there was a sudden, loud crash in the adjoining kitchen. A pan had inexplicably fallen to the floor. Creepy.

Thursday 26 April

Note to self: always read peoples' funeral tributes *before* the service. It was excruciating at the crematorium this morning. A close friend of the deceased (Marion, a lady in her eighties) was supposed to read out a tribute. She didn't have time to send it to me beforehand. Not a problem, I said. Schoolboy error. When it came to her moment, she couldn't do it, as she was too overcome with emotion. I stepped in – and quickly wished I hadn't. 'Marion liked to help me with my Ann Summers deliveries,' I read. 'She couldn't wait to get her hands on the latest battery-operated merchandise.' There was a collective gasp, followed by the most awkward of silences. Except for the sound of Marion's friend. She'd stopped crying now. She was laughing her head off.

Friday 27 April

Just about the perfect day off. I nearly managed to not think about church. I nervously accompanied Anna to twins' club. Her friends are lovely, but there was only one other bloke there. The worst kind of unhelpful dad bragger. His two-year-old twins were showing remarkable progress, he told me. Educationally, socially and behaviourally, their list of achievements sounded prodigy-like. How are you getting on with yours?' he asked, finally. 'It's horrendous – they just cry and poo all the time,' I said, before escaping to hide in the disabled toilet.

We packed the kids off to nursery this afternoon. I took Anna out for lunch. Her hormones are all over the place. I don't know why. She's either shouting at me at great volume or ripping my clothes off in a blaze of passion. She confessed to feeling broody. Hungry for more kids. *Nooooo!*

Saturday 28 April

I hosted another open mic night on the estate at Holy Apostles. Attendance was low, the music below average and the atmosphere stilted. One of the grandmas – 'scary Kath' – livened things up, mind you. She stormed out of the toilets, shouting: 'Some dirty b******'s done a big s*** on the floor!' The poor guy playing 'Mr Tambourine Man' totally lost it.

Sunday 29 April

Setting up for FULL is too stressful. It can't go on like this. I'm a nervous, sweaty mess by the time I get up to speak. Danny doesn't help. He keeps trying to have deep and meaningful conversations with me while I'm up to my armpits in leads and speakers.

My Morning Glory vicar college friend Jason was our interview guest. I didn't know he used to own a Rolls Royce in his high-flying days. That soon went when he became a Christian. Now he's a vicar and drives a second-hand Volvo. Neal was thrashed in our 'Beat the Vicar' game again. Jason and Neal share a steam-engine obsession, so I got them duelling over a series of spirit- crushing locomotive trivia questions. Jason won. He knew that the A4 Pacific 'Mallard' was built by Sir Nigel Gresley at Doncaster for the London & North Eastern Railway. I presented him with a 'I beat the vicar at FULL' T-shirt. Afterwards, Jason tried to engage me in a conversation about the life-affirming joys of a day on the Talyllyn Railway in Wales. When he mercifully paused for breath I jogged away to talk to someone else about anything else.

Tuesday 1 May

I was grilled by a load of Adelaide Primary School kids this morning in their RE lesson. I was armed and ready to tackle the big humdingers. Tough questions I've been bamboozled with in the past, like: 'Why aren't dinosaurs mentioned in the Bible?' 'How can God be three people at the same time?' and 'Why is there so much suffering in the world?' A little lad put his hand up and asked: 'Do you brush your teeth, Reverend?'

I found a bloke from Beverley on the internet who restores and sells bikes out of his front room. I need a sturdy one that won't get nicked. Tony is a proper enthusiast. He gave up the rat race a few years ago to immerse himself in this labour of love. His kitchen is like a wonder-bike emporium. They were hanging everywhere. All colours, shapes and sizes. I bought a functional road bike – a British Eagle in racing green. Wheeling it out of the kitchen I saw another one. A fantasy vision from my early teens. The bike I'd always wanted but never got on Christmas morning: the classic 1980s Raleigh racer. This one was a limited edition 1982 Raleigh Milk Race Special. White and blue with red tyres. Simple, aesthetically sublime and a seat so small and savage that it must have been designed with a tube of Anusol in mind. Tony had lovingly restored it from an original frame he'd found on eBay. So I left his kitchen with two bikes – a head buy and a heart buy. Anna wasn't happy when I got home. 'We're skint and you come back with two bikes!' she protested. It was worth the b*ll*cking, though. I've finally laid to rest the ghost of those 1980s Christmases.

Wednesday 2 May

I met the Bishop of Hull, Richard, at his house for a review of my first year. I say house – it's a flipping mansion. For an institution that always seems strapped for cash and that calls its churches to be imitators of Christ and defenders of the poor and downtrodden, we often do a very good job of looking pretty flush. It baffles me that we house our most senior God man in the area in one of the grandest properties in the area. All for one late-middle-aged couple to rattle around in. It's not Richard's fault, but it's obscene really. And it's the same for us less senior clergy. We're usually housed in a four-bedroomed property. Even if you're a 60-year-old reverend whose only housemate is a Border Collie. I don't get it. Increasingly loads more curates are single and not all the married ones breed like the Waltons.

I like Bishop Richard. He's approachable. Cuts out the fluffery and gives it to you straight. He seemed chuffed to bits with our progress at Holy Trinity and the rate it's happening. The conversation was going well until a sentence of mind-boggling arrogance slipped out of my mouth by accident. I'm cringing thinking about it. I was lamenting the fact that so many churches round here seem to be in death mode. Dwindling away to a light smattering of the elderly faithful. 'How would you deal with failure?' Richard asked me. This sentence actually popped out of my mouth: 'I don't really do failure, Bishop.' His bushy eyebrow lifted – and then the other one. I spluttered and backtracked. Tried to explain what I really meant. It was too late. I'd said it. The Reverend Matt Woodcock doesn't do failure. B*gger.

To my horror, I got home to realize I'd put the dates in wrong for our Holy Communion practice at York Minster. It's a three-line whip before we are ordained as priests. Unmissable unless we are dying or stuck in a lift. Anna and I have our trip to the Feversham Arms Hotel booked and paid for that night. It's all she's been talking about for weeks. The back massages, the posh meals, the candle-lit baths. I sent the most grovelling email to Bishop Richard to get out of it. It's up there with some of my best work.

I rode in to church on my classic Raleigh racer for the first time this morning. I hated getting the red wheels dirty. It pleases me just to look at it for long periods.

Friday 4 May

I'm reading my retired vicar friend John Young's book, *Lord … Help My Unbelief*. I like his easy, breezy style and turn of phrase. His section on sin is particularly good. 'Christians are not basically good people,' he writes. 'They are thoroughly dissatisfied people. They are dissatisfied with themselves. They know that they're selfish, or that they can't control their temper, or that they're jealous or greedy or lazy. It's because they know their own shortcomings and great needs that they've gone to the one person who can help them: Jesus Christ, the great physician.' I agree.

Saturday 5 May

Holy Trinity hosted the finale of a big fashion show organized by local businesses this afternoon. A massive catwalk was erected in the centre of the nave. Spray-tanned models strutted up and down on it. They made a striking contrast to our processing choir. Huge numbers packed the place. At one point a rumour filtered down to us that the Ann Summers models would be next on the catwalk – and that they wouldn't be wearing much. Stockings and thongs were mentioned. One week the church is full of beer, now it's scantily clad underwear models. I could already imagine the emails that would come in. After some wonderful diplomacy from Neal, the models stayed appropriately dressed – just about.

Sunday 6 May

Our faith-seeking actor Daniel is proving a bit unreliable. He didn't turn up again. I just wish he'd say if he's not interested in being involved at Holy Trinity. I feel like a loved-up teenybopper waiting by the phone to see if her older boyfriend will ring.

Tuesday 8 May

Another one of those days when my dissatisfaction with the way things are in the Church of England bubbled to the surface. Eight months in a dog collar has made me even more desperate for change. From my office armchair, I furiously scribbled down all the things that frustrated me in an effort to move to a more positive frame of mind. It was a long list.

My chief bugbear is the extent to which neglect and decline often seems to be allowed to flourish. Too many heads remain buried in the sand about the desperate truth of our situation. Entrenched and antiquated ways of doing and being church are still rife at a time when all the evidence and stats show that attendance is falling off a cliff and under-fifties at our Sunday services are becoming as rare as lesser spotted woodpeckers. I mean, how bad do things have to get before change – real, radical, tear-down-in-order-to-build-back-up kind of change – becomes normal?

Jesus teaches that if a branch isn't being fruitful it gets cut off so new life can emerge. The C of E seldom reaches for its secateurs. It too often lets things die slowly and painfully. I think that's the worst kind of death. Why shouldn't us clergy be held to account in a far more deliberate way? Bishops should have the authority to move us on. I want someone to be closely monitoring our progress at Holy Trinity. I want to know that we're growing and bearing fruit. Maybe I'm wrong, but I thought a key part of leading any kind of church community was doing everything you can to make sure it doesn't die.

I'd also radically overhaul how we select clergy. So many are academically intelligent and theologically adept, but socially awkward. Skilled and articulate in a discussion about the hermeneutics of Friedrich Schleiermacher, but with no idea (or interest) in how to engage the average man and woman on the street in conversation about the offside rule, the latest episode of *Game of Thrones* or a recent family holiday to Corfu. Ironically, in the church right now the introverted voice seems to be the loudest. I know there has to be a place for all personality types. We all have different ways of connecting to God and people. Lord knows, I have loads to learn from the quieter reflectors and more gentle spirits. But I do meet too many clergy who find the company of people an inconvenience to endure rather than something to embrace. Here's a thought for the assessors when they are selecting new clergy: choose someone who makes joy and laughter a strong goal in their life. I'd love to read a clergy recommendation that said something like this: 'Rachel is clearly a godly woman with a vibrant faith. It's encouraging that she is also a warm, interested person who likes normal conversations with ordinary members of the human race.

People seem to actually like Rachel and feel better about the world having been in her company for ten minutes.' Blessed are the warm and affable, I'm sure Jesus would say.

Furious scribblings done. Spleen vented. Chip on my shoulder put back in its case, I walked out to the Old Town to meet some people.

Wednesday 9 May

I endured an awkward massage at the Feversham Arms today. Weirdly, they actually stress me out. I get tense and self-conscious about my flabby bits and the potential for a nether-region malfunction. I'm still traumatized by that Turkish massage I had on holiday next to Lee. Our moustachioed masseurs stripped us naked for a back and frontal massage. They seemed very keen on checking the size of our penises. I fell over making my way to the cold bath. I seemed to go on sliding forever, right across the floor on my back like a baseball player trying to steal a base. A mess and tangle of glistening, bollock-naked white man on treacherous tiled floor. I can still hear the sound of those heavy-set Turkish men laughing hysterically with Lee. I can never return to Sultan Hamam's in Marmaris.

The Feversham is pure luxury – far too posh for us. A valet parked our knackered Hyundai. He looked horrified at the dried twins' snot covering the head rest and empty Quavers packets everywhere. I had my first ever glass of iced tea after our jacuzzi. It was so disappointing. Anna looked radiant. It was absolute bliss to retire to our room to read, listen to George Michael, drink champagne and graze on platefuls of olives and dry roasted nuts. No kids. Not a single cry. Just us. The song 'Fastlove' came on. Bingo.

We had a drink in the bar before our meal tonight. Two gin and tonics. All the colour drained from my face when the barman passed me the bill. He smiled sadistically. Twenty quid!

Thursday 10 May

I briefly turned my phone on while Anna slept early this morning. It went nuts. Frantic messages from my old press colleague Thom telling me his grandad had died. Would I do the funeral?

We had breakfast in bed. The works. Poached eggs, sausages, bacon, beans and toast. We didn't want to leave. Another week would have been lovely. We drove back through the awesome countryside of the Howardian Hills aflame with an inner joy. The atmosphere in the Hyundai was full of an easy, content love. No noise. No distractions. Just me and Anna, driving. Basking in our precious time at the Feversham. As a final treat I stopped at the Total garage to buy Revels. Love is ... letting your wife take out all the Maltesers and Minstrels while you get lumbered with the coffee ones.

Saturday 12 May

Ben's new youth group at Holy Trinity has annoyed the flower arrangers. They're making too much noise, apparently. Too giddy and riotous. If that's not progress I don't know what is. One of the flower team stormed into the session and told them all to pipe down. Excellent. I'd be worried if that wasn't the case. God is using Ben. He has a tremendous heart for these kids.

My prayer life is all over the place. I've got into the habit of fitting it in. Not good. My soul needs more of it. I hate it when I lose touch with Jesus. He's the only one who helps my mad life make sense.

Sunday 13 May

I'm trying to keep to my promise of getting the girls' breakfast when I can. I dread approaching their high chairs with bowls of mushed-up Weetabix. I get way more on me than in them.

Monday 14 May

I started another Christian basics course in our front room tonight. Ben is leading it with me. I don't think I can teach him anything more important. Finding time to help people find God – it's what we're here to do. For once everyone who said they would turned up. They're mostly people who've been coming to the pub service: Wayne, Louise, Beverley, Kirsty and Sammi. Lovely, all of them. They all seem keen to know if God exists. The hardest part of the session was hearing some of their first experiences of the Church of England. A few of them wanted to engage in their local parish church a few years ago but said they were left feeling intimidated, perplexed and confused by their experience of Sunday worship. Intimidated, perplexed, confused – not the first three reactions we are looking for really. I'm always interested to see how vividly people remember their first time in church. Let's hope we do better this time round.

Tuesday 15 May

Neal and I were interviewed today by a writer from *Ten Foot City*, Hull's popular but at times wildly inappropriate underground arts and culture magazine. This was a risky one to agree to, but lots of locals read it. The interviewer asked about our relationship and how the leadership dynamic works between us. I think I over-egged the analogy pudding. I likened Neal to Fidel Castro – the leader of the Holy Trinity revolution – and myself to Che Guevara – the one in the mountains spreading the word, breaking new ground, blowing stuff up and getting shot at. I couldn't think of who that made Irene. Probably the chief nurse in one of the field hospitals.

Church council meeting tonight. Another epic. We spent a long time talking about whether we should get CCTV cameras put over the church gates and the possible benefits of installing a new winding clock mechanism. *Viva la revolución!*

Wednesday 16 May

I met with Archbishop Sentamu so that he could assess whether I was fit to be ordained a priest after my rookie deacon year. It was very relaxed for a change. To be fair, I talked his face off for half an hour. He looked weary and bamboozled by the end, stifling episcopal yawns. I think he was prepared to make me a bishop if I'd shut up a bit. His first words to me were: 'You're a lager lout!' in reference to the article about the beer festival he'd seen in the *Church Times*. He seemed genuinely excited by our little revolution in Hull. He asked if we were making sure children and youth work was part of it. I told him we'd employed Ben.

After my verbal onslaught, he finished by encouraging me to slow down. He said I couldn't keep up this pace. I'd burn out. I needed to listen to God in the silence as well as in the frenetic people activity. Fair comment. He prayed for me, using the story of Elijah as an illustration. God didn't speak to him in the fire, the wind or the earthquake but in the 'still, small voice'. 'You are like a whirlwind, Woody – slow down!' I high-fived him and walked out, promising to do my best. Love that guy.

Thursday 17 May

Bodybuilder Jamie came back to our little Bible group tonight. We haven't seen him for ages. He dominated the session with tales of Herculean battles against medication, drink and depression. We were so happy to see him. We are a rag-tag bunch. I tweeted a picture of us all with the words: 'Our amazing Holy Trinity home group: student, bodybuilder, doorman, support worker, Rev. Growing together.'

I'm struggling with my sermon. Reading through it, I was bored and uninspired. It lacked spark, creativity and any sort of relevancy to peoples' ordinary lives. I binned it. Back to the drawing board.

Friday 18 May

Trying to get some morning quiet prayer and Bible time in our house is just not working. It's futile in the midst of all the noise and chaos created by Esther and Heidi. The rhythm of my God time is going to have to change.

Saturday 19 May

I've received official confirmation from Sentamu that he's happy to ordain me as a priest. I will get my wings and a shiny new Bible in the liturgical passing-out parade at York Minster next month. His letter said: 'I am grateful to God for the way your ministry is taking shape, particularly the way in which your incumbent Neal has been training you. May I encourage you to learn the lessons of his gentle and humble model of leadership and not feel that you must always be "on the go"!' I too love Neal's training approach. It boils down to this: 'Get out there, Matt, and go for it.' Legend. There's not an insecure, threatened bone in his wise body.

Sentamu's letter went on:

> *You are a person of great enthusiasm and energy, and these are strengths in your ministry. But you must also develop the habit of the heart which believes that all will be well. It will also be important for you to carve out some time for quiet and study, and I would encourage you to plan for this. I shall be glad to ordain you Priest on Trinity Sunday.*
>
> *+Sentamu*

That's fair enough, but the 'quiet study' will have to be done well away from our house. Esther and Heidi don't seem quite ready to allow it to happen.

Sunday 20 May

Lovely family time in Queen's Gardens this afternoon. There was live opera being blasted out on a big stage. I chased Esther and Heidi round pretending to be a child-eating monster to the sound of 'Ride of the Valkyries'. The weather was lousy but it didn't deter us. I banked today's memories. I'll draw on them next time I'm feeling blue. Beautiful, spontaneous joy.

York City are now back in the Football League after eight years. Dad was at Wembley to watch the play-off final with Anna's brothers Rob and Matty. He was in floods of tears when I phoned him. He was overcome. Fabulous to see that 50 years of watching rubbish provides the occasional moment of rapture.

Decent service this morning. I feel the 9.30 a.m. is getting close to what I'd hoped for when I started. It's livelier, younger and populated by more than 15 people. One of the stalwarts complained that I spoke too loudly in the service. Who? Moi?

Monday 21 May

Anna is livid with me. I'm an imbecile. I dived onto our lovely new super king size bed – Anna's pride and joy – like Superman to make the girls laugh. My actual words were, 'Is it a bird? Is it a plane? No – it's *Super-rev*!'. There was a horrible snap and the stupid thing broke in two. Nearly £1,000 worth of M&S bed ruined. We can't afford that to have happened. Anna shook with rage. It took all her restraint not to swear at me in front of the girls. I called Wayne to see if he might be able to fix it. He's a joiner by trade. Practical, kind-hearted men becoming Christians and joining our church has huge benefits. I'm praying he has healing hands. We're on the mattress tonight and I suspect I'll be in the dog house for quite some time.

Tuesday 22 May

Attended a compulsory clergy leadership training session tonight in the wilds of East Yorkshire. There was lots of group work and activities that involved making things out of spaghetti. I drew on fresh reserves of forbearance and one-to-ten counting.

Friday 25 May

Day off. Devoured pages of Hull's beloved poet Philip Larkin today. Cynical and world-weary, yes, but what a truth speaker. What startling insights he had into the desperation of the human condition. I'm convinced Larkin was searching for deeper meaning in his life. I see him reaching out for hope in among his caustic verse. I don't think any poet I've read articulates loneliness better than he does. This line from 'Toads Revisited' struck a chord: 'Nowhere to go but indoors,/No friends but empty chairs.' I'm meeting people for which that is a daily reality.

Anna and I cycled to East Park this afternoon after dropping the girls at nursery. Broken bed forgotten, the sun poured onto our faces as we laid in the grass to read, snooze, giggle and suck on iced lollies. I discovered that if Anna could only eat one meal for the rest of her life it would be her mum's lasagne.

Saturday 26 May

I always learn something when I cross swords with our church secretary Chris Fenwick. Our tear-ups are spiritually helpful in the long run. I was in a foul mood when I found my 'office' like a bomb site after a student event. There was gear everywhere. Chris explained why they needed to use the space. I muttered something grumpily and walked out. He was right, though. I was filled with remorse. I emailed an apology, writing: 'Technically "my" shouldn't exist in a church context – only "our".' He emailed back a thanks for my apology. Saying sorry is so liberating. My respect for Chris grows by the week.

Sunday 27 May

Student Danny was confirmed tonight by the Bishop of Hull. He's come a long way since he randomly turned up to the 9.30 a.m. service that cold morning. His family came to support him. He was beaming as I presented him to the bishop. He said his life had been transformed. His lovely girlfriend Kirsty is now getting interested in faith. On nights like this, this is the best job in the world.

Monday 28 May

Cousin Ben delivered his first practice sermon to me in the quiet of Holy Apostles this morning. It was a good first effort. He drew me in, taught me something and then applied it to real life. 'Just one thing, Ben,' I said.

'You might want to mention God next time.'

Thursday 31 May

These next few days preparing for my ordination as a priest will be silent. Archbishop Sentamu has instructed us all to shut up until at least Saturday night. I had an interesting discussion with a fellow candidate over a quick pint beforehand, cramming in as many words as I could. He's getting ordained in his own church because of his theological stance on women priests. He can't be 'tainted' by being ordained alongside them in the Minster during the vows. It's absolutely bonkers. The idea that anyone could be 'tainted' by beautiful Irene. He needs to spend a week with her and see if his views change.

I read some Mother Teresa reflections to get my head right. I stumbled on this beauty:

> *Jesus wants me to tell you again how much is the love he has for each one of you – beyond all what you can imagine. Not only does he love you – even more – he longs for you. He misses*

you when you don't come close. He thirsts for you. He loves you always, even when you don't feel worthy.

It was said of Mother Teresa that 'Through her humble service she endeavoured to bring souls to God – and God to souls.' As priests, that's surely what he called us to do? I'll continue trying very hard not to complicate it.

Esther barfed all over the back seat on the drive to York. I drove down the A1079 with my head out of the window like Jim Carrey in *Ace Ventura: Pet Detective.* The smell was unbearable.

Friday 1 June

We are in the middle of nowhere at the beautiful Wydale Hall retreat house for our pre-ordination retreat. I sneaked off for a game of footy with some of my fellow curates. We needed to stop praying and start playing for a bit.

Still loving my book about the life of Mother Teresa. She was relentless, impatient and tenacious. A true pioneer. 'I fear all things from my weakness – but I trust blindly in His greatness,' she wrote. 'If the inspiration comes from God, and I am convinced it does, there could be no question of failure.' Mother Teresa believes Jesus told her this: 'You are afraid. How your fear hurts me. Fear not. Even if the whole world is against you, laughs at you, your companions and superiors look down on you, fear not – it is I in you, with you, for you.'

I'm enjoying this retreat. I'd rather read more Mother Teresa and be still than listen to the talks, mind you. They're all fine, but just a bit dull and earnest for me. Nothing personal. I relate to the depth and soulfulness of the Catholic tradition much more when I'm on things like this. Too much of the modern evangelical way is just too wordy, neat and humourless. They always unintentionally make me feel like I'm not doing it right. Or that

I'm not good enough. We were described as being like 'butlers in God's house' in one of the sessions. It doesn't work for me. Butlers are too organized, prim and snooty. 'Wayward scullery maid' would be a more apt description for me.

Saturday 2 June

The trouble with reading an inspirational book about Mother Teresa, is that I quickly realize that I'm nothing like Mother Teresa.

I'll be a priest by this time tomorrow. In practical terms, it basically means that I'll be able to consecrate the bread and wine at Holy Communion, bless in the name of the Lord and absolve people of their sins. It is a special privilege. A high calling. The silence has now ended. We can talk again. Thank heavens for that.

Sunday 3 June

Moments before Archbishop Sentamu ordained me a priest at York Minster I had a funny turn. I thought I was going to collapse. I was drenched in sweat. The colour drained from my face and my vision became blurry. I became conscious that I couldn't swallow. In terms of places you'd never want to faint in, the middle of a packed York Minster, standing in front of Archbishop Sentamu wearing flowing robes, is right up there. The more I worried about falling over, the more I panicked. I could see Archdeacon Richard gesturing at me to see if I was OK. I sucked in deep breaths, hopped from one leg to the other and generally just tried to empty my mind. Always the drama. Was it a panic attack? Something I ate? A spiritual sign that God didn't want me to be a priest? Who knows. It didn't help that the Wydale Hall fire alarm had gone off at 4 a.m. We had to congregate outside in our nightwear and dressing gowns, shivering and muttering un-Christian things under our breath.

The usual family crew came to support me for the service. It was long, word-heavy and offered no discernible evidence that we were in the twenty-first century. Why can't they mix it up a bit for once? I understand the Minster likes to do things a certain way. Ramp up the pomp. Show off the rich beauty of the choir. Revel in the depth and gravitas of the liturgy. I just wish they'd dial down the numinosity vibe a tiny bit and strive for some humanity. It would be lovely if all our visitors could see a different side to the Church of England too. Learn that joy and laughter is actually allowed. That sometimes it happens in our churches. That we actively encourage it.

I was surprised and delighted to see my Morning Glory friend Aidan turn up to support me. He has grown a massive black beard. He looks like a skinny Brian Blessed. After the service Mum took us for a posh coffee and then we went to a family Queen's Diamond Jubilee party in York. It slung it down so we made the best of it under a gazebo. The girls are not the best respecters of confined spaces at the moment so we left quite early.

Monday 4 June

The country has caught Diamond Jubilee fever. I'm full of admiration for Her Majesty the Queen. Despite all the chaos, conflict, divisions, modernizations and radical changes to British life, she has remained our constant. Our one unflinching figure of calm, sober authority and service in a scandal-driven world. On a purely human level, I don't know how she's kept her sanity in the face of all that meeting and greeting, hand-shaking and cutting of red ribbons at new power stations and revamped art galleries.

It was niece Phoebe's third birthday party this afternoon. Nephew Joel now officially supports York City. He's smitten with a very average player called Matty Blair. If Joel is committed to following the Minstermen, he's going to need a *lot* of prayer.

Tuesday 5 June

Watched a bit of the Queen's celebration service at St Paul's Cathedral. I can never work out if the Royal Family are bored on such occasions or if they have a living faith or not. Prince Harry always looks like he can't wait to get to the pub.

Wednesday 6 June

A night of firsts at Holy Trinity. The first time I've ever presided at Holy Communion. The first time some of our new people, Ken, Mark, Tracey, Dan, Jamie and Josh, have ever received it. It was a special kind of joy to place the bread in their palms, look them in the eye and say, 'The body of Christ keep you in eternal life.' I know on the surface level they're just words, but in that setting they are elevated into so much more. They come alive. I shared a reflection on Caravaggio's painting 'The Supper at Emmaus'. I said that receiving the Eucharist was like having that 'moment of recognition' of the risen Christ – like the characters in the picture. There was a holy atmosphere in Holy Trinity's little Broadley Chapel. Something important passed between us all. I think Heidi woke up on Anna's knee and stared at me intently as I said the sacred words behind the altar. Mum led the prayers in that special way of hers. She seems to know where people are at and gently leads them into a God encounter.

Anna and I got home and opened a nice bottle of her favourite Pinot Grigio to celebrate breaking my communion duck without dropping or spilling Jesus everywhere. I love the little touches Anna makes to make our home feel nice. She is my queen of the scented candle.

Thursday 7 June

Being a priest became very real today. A distressed lady called to say that her house was haunted and that strange things were happening. Libby and her partner said they both felt a strange presence – as if someone was watching them. Doors apparently opened without explanation. Bright-coloured orbs could be seen floating around them on family photographs. Libby also claimed she felt an 'icy cold hand' grip her arm while she slept. Now the family all sleep with the lights on and have little pictures of Jesus dotted round the house. This all sounded like a case for Peter Venkman from *Ghostbusters*, not me. I still leave the landing light on when Anna and the girls are back in York.

I later contacted the diocese's designated 'exorcist' – nowadays known as our adviser for deliverance ministry – to get his wisdom and advice. He's dealt with thousands of these cases.

Filling slots for our 24-hour prayer marathon at Holy Trinity is proving tricky. And that's being polite. I've not had a single person offer to do one of the half-hour sessions. I've had to cut it down to a 12-hour prayer jog. Looks like it will be a long day for me and Ben.

I visited my first wedding couple tonight. They were open to talking about faith. Unfortunately it sounds like their families are not open to talking to each other. This poor couple are focused more on keeping the peace than what vows they'll be saying.

Friday 8 June

I received a lovely letter from my old Rome pen pal, Ronnie. He's lost none of his writing flair or ridiculous hyperbole. 'Dear Reverend Father Matt, *sempre benedetto*!', he wrote. 'If I were to be offered your bread and wine at Holy Communion, at your altar and by your hands, it would be for me the happiest moment of my Christian life, the apex, the vertex of all hopes.' Ronnie has a distorted view of me. I can never live up to it.

Saturday 9 June

I did my first house blessing and exorcism today with Neal and Irene. No heads did a 360-degree turn. No one spewed green vomit. It was all fairly calm – if a bit surreal. We hope and pray that peace will now be restored to Libby's family home. I didn't 'feel' anything particularly paranormal when we entered their house. I smelt plenty. Cigarettes, wet dog and pooey toddler, mostly. Neal reminded us in the car outside that we must walk in with complete confidence because Jesus is Lord and no powers, spirits or principalities can stand against him. I was ready to wrestle snarling demons to the floor by the time we got to the front door.

We all sat with Libby at first to hear her story. We were shown some family camcorder footage taken in the home of some of the strange goings on. It was a bit weird but the camera looked like something Del Boy would flog at Peckham market, so I still wasn't convinced I was seeing genuine scenes from the spirit world.

Irene kept giving me 'the look'. I think it said: 'Do you believe a word of this, Matt? Can you believe we're here doing this stuff?' I gave her a look right back. I'm not sure what Irene thought it said, but she gave me a little half smile and nodded knowingly.

We conducted a little house blessing service in the front room, which Libby seemed to appreciate. It included this lovely prayer from the Church of England's Night Prayer service:

Visit this place, O Lord, we pray,
and drive far from it the snares of the enemy;
may your holy angels dwell with us and guard us in peace,
and may your blessing be always upon us;
through Jesus Christ our Lord.
Amen.

Neal blessed a bowl of water and made the sign of the cross on the family's heads. Even the dog. We then went round the house with the water, making the sign of the cross on every door and wall. We prayed in the name of Christ that anything haunting the place would leave immediately. The most dramatic moment was on the landing. Without warning, Neal suddenly blurted out: 'Spirit, name yourself!' Nobody replied. Eerie few seconds, though. Irene gave me another look. Let's hope Libby and her family hear no more bumps in the night.

I got home and took the girls for a walk in the rain.

Sunday 10 June

Neal sent an encouraging email about yesterday. Apparently Libby and her family turned up to the 11 a.m. service in a very animated state. 'Apparently the house was completely different last night!' Neal wrote. 'They all had a good night's sleep and are amazed at the difference. So praise God! Apparently a neighbour went round yesterday afternoon and, without knowledge of what had happened, commented that the house seemed "lighter". They all said that they would be coming to church again next week.' Result.

Blown away by Psalm 52 tonight: 'But I am like an olive tree flourishing in the house of God; I trust in God's unfailing love for ever and ever. I will praise you for ever for what you have done; in your name I will hope, for your name is good. I will praise you in the presence of your saints.'

A happy morning at church. I caught sight of Esther and Heidi strutting around the place as if they were having the time of their lives. I hope they're still doing that when they're 15. Irene presided at her first communion. It was beautiful. I was so proud. The 9.30 a.m. was busy with young families again. New ones keep turning up. We keep growing.

Ben preached at Holy Apostles for the first time. It was good considering the technical problems and the fact his laptop fell on the floor in the first minute. Terry and Sharon presented me with a special joke tambourine before the first song. It doesn't actually make a noise. They'd stuffed the little pellet bells and jingles with foam. Apparently I keep knocking Terry out of time on his guitar with my exuberant shaking. I won't be silenced. Maracas next week.

Monday 11 June

I stopped in at the Ferens Art Gallery to see the new Andy Warhol exhibition. He's massively overrated. Maybe that was his intention? 'Art is what you can get away with,' he once said. Well, he got away with this stuff. I find his quotes more palatable than his art. I'm all over this one: 'They always say time changes things, but you actually have to change them yourself.'

Ben and I have set up the space in Holy Trinity for tomorrow's 12-hour prayer vigil. I think it needs a second opinion. It's a bit austere. It needs a woman's touch – if I'm still allowed to say that.

I'm unhappy about my weight. My stomach is grotesque. I refuse to descend into middle-aged flabbiness. So many of the lads back home have let themselves slide. No more bread, pain au raisins or late-night Topics from now on.

Tuesday 12 June

So what did I learn from 12 hours of prayer and a 24-hour fast? Well, I certainly need to do it more. And some of our flock should try it sometime. The turnout was woeful. I don't know why I bother. Ben and I were a bit irritable with each other through the day. I think we were 'hangry' – an unpleasant by-product of fasting. Our breath wasn't great, either.

We led the prayers in the chancel. I was holed up in there most of the day. Neal and Irene popped in and out occasionally. Ben lost interest at about 2 p.m. I told him to go home for a bit to rediscover his mojo. I played relaxing Taizé music and lit candles. A few people came in to ask for prayer. The evening session was better. At one point there were eight ruddy-faced blokes in a circle praying awkwardly. I wonder if this could be the start of a men's group? We finished with a lovely informal communion and night prayers. Worth doing, then, but room for improvement. Holy Trinity needs to learn how to pray. We need to heat up the spiritual temperature.

Wednesday 13 June

I'm feeling a lovely afterglow after yesterday's prayer session. The new toddler group at Holy Apostles also went well. Our main volunteer Sarah Glenton has a huge heart. Only two mums came, but it will grow.

Thursday 14 June

I was reminded today that a big part of this job is to be a pain carrier. I was finishing up in the church office dungeon when Barbara the cleaner came in to say there was a distressed couple in the choir vestry wanting a word. Our wonderful welcomer Veronica had seen them crying and offered them a cup of tea. I walked in to find the lady sobbing and being comforted by her husband. They'd just been told that their daughter had been diagnosed with cancer. It was the latest in a catalogue of family tragedies. Between guttural cries, the lady kept repeating that parents should not outlive their children. I felt woefully inadequate. I didn't know what to say or pray. I just let them talk and cry. I'm a typical bloke. I want to fix everything there and then. Make it all OK. Clearly I couldn't. So I just sat there listening. After a while they asked me to pray. I didn't really have adequate words but I did my best. I'll remember this encounter.

Friday 15 June

Wayne has been round to fix our bed – and hopefully our marriage. What a legend. I won't miss sleeping on the floor. Wayne is becoming one of my favourite people. His practical skills are extraordinary. He said the bed just needed the right sized beam or something. My eyes glazed over as he tried to explain it. He's up for helping me start a men's group. He wants something appropriate to invite his mates to. He tells me they wouldn't be seen dead in church on a Sunday morning. I get it.

Libby called to say the ghosts have come back.

Saturday 16 June

Mum came through from York to see us all today. I took her to the Ferens Art Gallery. Esther and Heidi did their best to destroy Warhol's priceless works. I think they'd have improved some of them. I could tell Mum was a bit agitated, as if she wanted to get something off her chest. It came out over lasagne and a bottle of Malbec tonight. Turns out Mum wanted my opinion on cohabitation from a Christian perspective. The rights and wrongs of her moving in with Barry. I avoided the subject a bit. Dodged and swerved. I don't really want this conversation with her. I simply made the point that she's known and loved Jesus for years. 'Ask him what he thinks,' I said. 'Maybe he can make an exception for you?' Understandably, she said my sarcasm wasn't helpful. To be fair, I love that Mum's in love again. Barry seems to adore her and that's all any son can ask for. I just don't want her to get hurt again. After a few awkward minutes, I recharged our glasses and we were soon back to good-natured debating, belly laughing and bouts of outrageous indiscretion.

Sunday 17 June

I used to think that Father's Day was a pointless commercial racket. And then I got bounced on by Esther and Heidi this morning and opened their card and presents (twelve first class stamps and some hand cream, bizarrely). I was a teary mess and now think it's the greatest day ever.

I spontaneously dragged the Holy Apostles congregation – mid service – onto the grass outside to picture what the community picnic could be like next week. Some of them are really worried about it. They think that people on the estate will dismiss them as cheesy Bible bashers and cause havoc. I prayed simply that God would bless the event and grow our church through it. Everyone then scurried back in before I could get my tambourine out.

Monday 18 June

I spent the day in Teesside drawing wisdom from my pioneer priest pals Dan and Ben. They do what I do in their neck of the woods. Dan is the most hippy-like skinhead I've ever met. He is trying to forego modern conventions and do family life based around conversation and music. I know one thing – he needs a bigger telly. His postage stamp-sized screen made watching the footy pretty much impossible. Earlier, he took me to see his church. It's a modern building and the worship fairly Anglo-Catholic in style. I was interested by their church tagline: 'Promoting positive emotional health and wellbeing in the community.' It could easily be the motto for an NHS mental health unit or care home. I got the impression it was a church where they found mentioning the 'God' word a bit difficult.

I then visited Reverend Ben – a former hairdresser – in his patch in Colby Newham. He volunteers at a hair salon one afternoon a week so he can build proper relationships with the locals. He said the perms and crew cuts very often turned into God chats.

Tuesday 19 June

Neal and I have been sent the *Ten Foot City* article about Holy Trinity. It's accurate but I sound like a right arrogant clown. It reads:

Arriving at the vestry, I knock on its ancient oak door and am greeted by Hull's own Paul Whicker: Matt Woodcock. He's not very tall but – as curate and pioneer minister – he most certainly is trendy, at least by the Church of England's standards. He's 36, with a proper cheeky chappie smile, and he actually looks a bit like Frank Lampard, but that doesn't stop him from being instantly likeable, and we are soon exchanging banter and anecdotes over a cuppa. At this point his boss, the Reverend Dr Neal Barnes, walks in. Like Matt, he is smiley and friendly, but clearly not as trendy: 'Neal is Fidel Castro to my Che Guevara,' Matt asserts, to which his superior is happy to agree.

Cringe.

Thursday 21 June

Niggles with Anna tonight. She's started using the phrase, 'I couldn't think of anything worse,' when I suggest something she doesn't want to do. She says it in a really annoying voice. Not unlike her dad, actually. I descended into sarcasm. 'Really? You couldn't think of anything worse?' I said (in an even more annoying voice). 'How about the conflict in Syria? Or the financial crisis in Greece? Or the massive gulf between the rich and the poor?' We avoided each other after that comment. We know when to be on our own. It never fails to amaze me that two such different people are joined in holy matrimony.

Friday 22 June

Anna and I had a heated debate in the early hours. Esther wouldn't stop crying. Anna wanted to lie next to her on the futon until she went off. I was in favour of letting her cry it out and Anna coming back to bed. We had a Mexican standoff on the landing – both convinced that our way was the right way. Anna ended up on the futon. I silently seethed my way to bed. I honestly can't remember the last time anyone listened to or agreed with anything I said in our house. Wives, grandmas, one-year-olds – my words seem entirely obsolete.

Going to twins' club helped thaw the atmosphere between us. When you hear the trials of some of the other parents it helps put things in perspective. Brummie mummy Alison always cheers us up. She regaled us with hilarious tales of a recent night out with her mum. They downed six pints of Guinness and black.

Monday 25 June

I'm always surprised by the power of a group of people sat in a room talking about stuff that matters. How quickly deep friendships form, how honest the sharing is and how often the inner light goes on to the possibility that 1. God might be real. 2. That he's actually knowable and 3. That we've only just scratched the surface when it comes to his love and our capacity to receive it and live it out in the midst of our daily lives. I'm always a bit melancholy at the end of a Christian inquirers' course. This group was special. Keen to delve deeper. We've discussed profound, important things, laughed a lot and eaten far too many Tunnock's Teacakes. I sent them all into the night with a final prayer and encouragement. It feels like saying goodbye to treasured family members at a train station. I'm excited about where they'll travel to next. Ben said he enjoyed leading the course with me. 'I was interested to see how much you were winging it every week.' Rude.

Tuesday 26 June

I don't know why I doubt God. I can see him at work so tangibly in people.

Wednesday 27 June

Cousin Ben had a wobble tonight. Between unnecessarily loud slurps of his tea, he expressed doubts about the work he's doing. Wonders whether the youth he's ministering to actually give a flying fiddle. His job is so often a thankless task. I reassured him that wobbles and doubts are healthy. They make us stronger. More robust. Ben said the kids at his youth club on the estate caused havoc during the God slot tonight. 'They're only interested in pissing about and playing sardines and Wii tennis,' he said. Perfectly normal, I reassured him. 'They've stopped swearing at you – that's progress! Keep going, Ben. You're making a difference.' I took him to Ye Olde Black Boy for a quick pint. That seemed to cheer him up.

Thursday 28 June

This morning Neal gave Irene and me a practical lesson in how to conduct a wedding service. It descended into chaos. Of course it did. He walked us through the whole process, starting with the bride's arrival at Holy Trinity's door and ending with the happy couple's final procession out. There's loads to remember, but the key thing seems to be maintaining an air of confidence and authority (however much your innards feel like jelly). 'Keep the couple relaxed at all times,' Neal urged.

We roped in some of the Holy Trinity team to take the wedding party roles. Initially, Neal 'married' Irene and Ben. I played the father of the bride. Our handyman David Howden was the best man. We went through the words and choreography. I found it impossible not to make Irene laugh as she committed the rest of her life to Ben. The only bone of contention we had with Neal's approach was that he always offers the bride the chance to say that they will obey their husband. Irene and I wouldn't be massively comfortable with offering that as an option. It feels ridiculously outdated and inappropriate.

Friday 29 June

Psyched myself up for a 10-mile run this morning but lost interest after 16 minutes and turned back. I think I overdid the preparation. Burnt myself out applying the Vaseline between my thighs, eating bananas and meticulously crafting a Spotify playlist. I'd nothing left for the run itself.

I'm seeing The Stone Roses tomorrow!

Saturday 30 June

I stood in Heaton Park with 75,000 people for eleven hours today to witness the resurrection of The Stone Roses. What a gig. The muddy, beer-can-strewn field felt like holy ground. It was sheer euphoria when Ian, John, Reni and Mani walked on stage. Their reunion, after such an acrimonious split, shows the power of redemption. Or, if I'm being cynical, the lure of a million quid each.

Luckily I bought a poncho on the way in for £3. I needed it. The rain was torrential. Bad even for Manchester. My companions Jonny and Pete got soaked. The atmosphere and sense of anticipation was like nothing else. I've never seen so many beanie hats, Adidas Originals and blokes strutting like primates. Drugs were everywhere. In just one stroll to the toilet, I was offered cocaine and ecstasy. I asked one dealer if he had any Paracetamol. I had a banging headache. Drugs weren't needed tonight. We had songs like 'Love Spreads', 'Waterfall', 'Fools Gold' and 'I Am the Resurrection' to take us to a higher plane. A massive firework display finished the show to the sound of Bob Marley's

'Redemption Song'. It was perfect. We all left as one. High as kites. Even those of us not off our skulls on Colombian marching powder.

Tuesday 3 July

Daniel the actor came to see me today to say he wanted to become a Christian – a 'proper one', as he put it. We read some words of Jesus together and discussed what being a 'new creation' might look like. I prayed that Daniel would know the rejuvenating love of God in a special way. My dungeon-like 'office' was a terrible setting for such a moment of spiritual awakening. David's filthy mops everywhere. Bits peeling off the wall. The lingering smell of dead rat. Maybe all that makes it even more poignant. A moment of light, beauty and holiness in among the mess and brown apple cores. I reflected later that all this came about because Daniel found our dated website and watched those cheesy YouTube videos I made on the camcorder. It was God working in that mysterious way of his again. He was at work long before I got involved in Daniel's journey. I'm saying that a lot in Hull.

Encounters like that make me wonder why the existence of God becomes so apparent, so obvious to certain people and not others. Are some hearts just more faith-inclined or what? Do some of us simply have more of a natural propensity to recognize the presence of the divine? The mystery of faith – it's maddening. One thing I am sure of more than ever is the authenticity of my calling to the priesthood. And the simplicity of it, too. I'm increasingly convinced that it mainly consists of finding out if someone is even mildly interested in faith – has an inkling that God might be real – and then helping them explore it and plumb the depths of the way, the truth and the life.

I visited bodybuilder John at the dialysis clinic this afternoon. A young woman approached me outside the hospital as I was locking up my bike. She shouted: 'Are you a priest?!' 'Yes, I am.' 'Pray for me, then!' So I did. She then stormed wordlessly back inside. At least John seemed pleased to see me.

Friday 6 July

Best friend Lee is presenting Prince Andrew with one of his award-winning pork pies during a royal visit to York tomorrow. I love the *Press* headline: 'The Duke of Pork!'

Saturday 7 July

I did a wedding preparation visit at the home of a lovely couple called Jayne and Scott. What could be more beautiful and stirring than listening to the story of two people in love? I read out the classic wedding 'love' passage from 1 Corinthians 13. They'd never heard it before. It was a Spirit-filled, eye-moistening moment.

I've encouraged Jayne and Scott to be as creative as possible with the service. The more bespoke touches the better. Admittedly, I wasn't expecting poetry from Scott. I'd unfairly judged him. I was prejudiced by his shaven head, tattooed arms and blokey banter. Yet there he was in his living room, reciting heartfelt verse he'd penned about Jayne. It described the way she looked, and how she made him feel. Seldom have I heard such simple rhyming couplets sound so beautiful.

'Will you read one of these out during the service, Scott?' I asked.

'You're ****ing joking, Matt – the lads would crucify me!'

Shame.

Sunday 8 July

I think I came close to a cardiac arrest this morning. Old Elsie – a member of Holy Trinity for the last 120 years at least – complimented my sermon as she was wheeled out after the service by her carer. Words of affirmation actually came out of her mouth! I gasped. Couldn't believe it. She'll be smiling next.

I baptized baby Isabella this afternoon. I used a football analogy in the sermon – with live action demonstrations. 'I'm going to catch the ball on the back of my neck, flick it up and volley it into the balcony,' I announced. The people in the front pews looked terrified.

I took cousin Ben out for a pub crawl tonight. He confessed to being an occasional secret smoker. A snaffler of Silk Cut on the sly. I promised not to tell his mum.

Monday 9 July

Lee's Minster FM interview this morning about him presenting the pork pie to Prince Andrew was unintentionally hilarious. Pure Alan Partridge. The presenter's opening question was this cringeworthy beauty: 'Aren't butchers supposed to be big, fat guys?' He then made the mistake of biting into a pie. It rendered him virtually speechless as the jelly, meat and pastry did its work. Wonderful car crash radio.

I need to be on my theological toes as well as my physical ones at boxing training these days. One of the more inquisitive lads asked me if Taoism was compatible with Christianity during the warm-up.

Tuesday 10 July

Anna looked really sheepish tonight when I walked in on her reading. She unsubtly tried to stuff the book down the side of the sofa. I looked later. *Fifty Shades of Grey.* Busted!

Just when I thought we were making progress with our culture of welcome at Holy Trinity, I hear something cringeworthy. Apparently a demanding lady was in a reserved pew at the recent veteran's service. One of our volunteers got into a heated debate with her when she refused to move. 'Who do you think this church belongs to?!' he was heard to shout. Then at church council meeting tonight there was a discussion about whether the choir kids should go out for their usual groups during a civic service. One lady piped up: 'They should be made to stay in – it's their duty!' Some days I feel like I've been transported back to 1912.

I remembered one of my Christian heroes Archbishop Óscar Romero today. Legend. I said a prayer of thanks for his life and legacy. I drew on this little nugget of a quote. It felt relevant to our work here: 'We know that every effort to improve society, above all when society is so full of injustice and sin, is an effort that God blesses; that God wants; that God demands of us.'

Wednesday 11 July

Daniel says he's had a tough week. It always seems to be the way with those newest to faith. Spiritual highs come down to earth eventually. Daniel says he's full of doubt. Uncertain about what worship style or tradition to embrace. Confused about what God is calling him to do. I encouraged him to calm down, give himself a break and remember the words of Jesus – that God's yoke is easy and his burden is light. As for doubting? I don't think doubts ever go away. Not mine, anyway. I lent Daniel Henri Nouwen's book *The Return of the Prodigal Son*. I think it might help with some of his inner niggles. Nouwen writes that God never gives up searching for us, no matter how many times we doubt or walk away from him. 'He begs me to let myself be embraced by arms that will carry me to the place where I will find the life I most desire.'

I was very conscious of my own mortality today. Time is passing too quickly. I've got too much I want to do. Too many adventures to embark on. I hope I don't die for a very long time.

Thursday 12 July

Another night out for Anna and me. Cousin Ben's babysitting is singlehandedly keeping our marriage healthy. We kept him well supplied with cans of Carling and meat feast pizza. We took Wayne and his wife Louise to Stanley's Brasserie as a thank you for fixing our bed. Wayne is a big character in every sense. We battled to hold court. I think he won on penalties.

I ate sea bass fillets and tiger prawns. Wayne ordered rivers of fizz. We toasted the fixed bed every few minutes to the annoyance of our fellow diners. I clocked Anna looking at me happily and knowingly at one point. I think it was a face remembering that this is what our life used to be like before Esther and Heidi. It was nice to dip into it again but we wouldn't change anything. We looked in at the girls sleeping when we got home. Their quiet breaths are such a magical sound, and their serene faces such a glorious sight.

Friday 13 July

Anna had some choice words for me tonight. I won't repeat them. I probably deserved it. She was up to her neck in babies, nappies and mess. So it wasn't the best moment for me to ask what time tea would be ready. I'm still finding marriage to be a steep learning curve. She's doing an amazing job with the girls. Esther and Heidi adore her. I can't get enough of watching them snuggle into her.

I asked Anna tonight if she wanted any more children. If she'd be prepared to go through IVF again. 'I'd love the experience of being pregnant again,' she said. 'I just feel grateful and content with the gifts we've been given. I don't want to be greedy.' Fair enough. I agree. I cooked her favourite pasta and chorizo dish, melting the cheese on top just how she likes it. We put the girls to bed and I tried to recreate their snuggle and nestling technique in the warmth of Anna's embrace.

Holy Trinity's transformation project is gathering pace. The plans look amazing. They involve sensitively taking out the nave pews and the installation of a cafe, tourist centre and space to make it a top music and arts venue. We might have an opportunity to do a few worship services in there sometimes, too.

I attended compulsory school governor training this afternoon in the ugliest looking building in the Northern Hemisphere: Kingston House. It's a late 1960s monstrosity that needs tearing down piece by piece. The session was OK. We were all in the same boat: no idea what we were doing and not understanding any of the acronyms the modern education system seems to love so much. We all stayed quiet and didn't ask any questions in order to get out of there as quickly as possible.

Saturday 14 July

Anna rushed out to buy the *Fifty Shades of Grey* sequel today. She's hooked.

I thought we were losing student Danny to the big, shiny charismatic church up the road. He's been spending a bit of time there. I wouldn't blame him, really. There's loads of people his own age and they all wear skinny jeans. They also boast of witnessing 'multiple healings' with 'dozens saved' every week. We must be doing it wrong. We only seem to have 'multiple issues' and 'dozens hacked off' every week. But then I walked into Holy Trinity this morning and found Danny hoovering the chancel with Gordon's 'holy dusters' volunteers. One of them told me he'd been doing it on the quiet for weeks now. How wonderful.

We had a barbecue for our little Bible group tonight. One of them, Obed, took me aside to say he wants to step back for a bit. It was an excruciating conversation. I was disappointed but we're not the Moonies. People can come and go as they please. I'll miss the sound of Obed's laugh and his smart, ironed trousers.

Sunday 15 July

It was our outdoor service and picnic on the Thornton Estate this afternoon. The weather forecast was terrible but the sun blazed. The grassy area outside Holy Apostles soon filled up with local families. I kept the service fun, accessible and short but it was hard work getting peoples' attention, particularly the blokes swigging from their cans of Fosters. Their looks of hostility when I encouraged them to join in the actions for 'Jesus Is the Rock and He Rolls My Blues Away' were something else.

Luke Campbell's friend turned up at the picnic to see me with his family. Apparently Luke was set to leave for the Olympic Village later that day. Luke's friend got me to write an encouraging message in a book he'd compiled for him. I was touched. I noticed he'd packed the holding cross too. I wrote that I'd be praying hard for him and that he'd inspired many people. I think he can win the gold.

Thursday 19 July

I had an interesting conversation with a lapsed Mormon who was wandering round Holy Trinity with his girlfriend. He told me he'd struggled to adhere to the strict lifestyle the religion demanded. 'Particularly the sex before marriage,' he said, looking suggestively at his ponytailed partner. The guy seemed full of anxiety. Worried that he wouldn't make it to heaven because of past sins. I tried to encourage him that the God I believed in was full of grace, not condemnation. I wondered if he'd ever find peace as they strolled back out into the Old Town, his hand proudly clamped to his girlfriend's right buttock.

Friday 20 July

There's trouble brewing over our desire to cut down the massive rotten tree in Holy Trinity's car park. We can't transform the square until it's felled. The tree's roots have pulled all the flagstones up and caused a right mess. Cutting trees down is never popular, though. The fell is being blocked by the council after complaints from green campaigners. The last thing we want is people chaining themselves to pew ends over this. Delicacy and diplomacy are needed – which is why I'm staying well out of it.

Saturday 21 July

The sun actually came out today. It makes such a difference to our lives. People just seem happier and chirpier. More positive. There was plenty going on in Trinity Square for once. The council had arranged for a basketball and table tennis club to give free lessons. I was still a bit disappointed with the footfall. There's just no culture of Saturday shoppers coming this way any more. It needs to be an unmissable part of a city centre visit.

Neal has been made a Canon of York Minster in recognition of all his awesome work over the past few years. The top brass probably feel bad about all the hair he's losing. Neal now has three titles before his name – Reverend, Canon and Doctor. That's nearly as many as the Pope. I'm so pleased for him. His lovely face was flushed and his neck went bright red when he told Irene and me. Always a tell-tale sign that he feels proud and happy.

I did the final bits of organizing for our church bike ride to Hornsea after the service tomorrow. The forecast is spectacular.

Sunday 22 July

Saddle sore but happy of heart after our church bike ride to Hornsea. I wish the girls didn't have to go back to York today. Life felt beautiful out in the countryside with brilliant people and the hot sun blistering my nose. We cycled along a disused railway track after gathering in a layby on the A165 (a well-known 'dogging' site, one of the group unhelpfully blurted out). About 20 of us turned up to cycle the 6 miles to the sea. Another couple of carloads met us on the beach in Hornsea. Some of the group took the cycling very seriously. Deputy churchwarden Andy wore some eye-wateringly tight blue Lycra. I couldn't look at him as he stood there.

Arriving at the sun-kissed, busy seafront, I got a flavour of what the Hornseas of England were like during their boom years, before everyone cleared off to Spain for their holidays. The beach was fabulous. We all stripped down to our swimming costumes and lay on the sand. One of our flock, Larry, hadn't brought his trunks but this didn't deter him. He stripped down to his Y-fronts and ran into the sea with a whoop and a holler. Many of us followed. Larry then splashed around and lifted kids onto his shoulders before launching them into the swell. Some of them he actually knew. I looked round at our group – young and old – eating their ice cream and fish and chips and savoured the moment. It dawned on me how much we'd grown. How alive we'd become. How far we'd come as a church and where we needed to go. I was filled with a special joy and optimism. Larry then thought it was hilarious to pour a bucket of sea water down my Bermudas. Git.

Monday 23 July

Student Danny's girlfriend, Kirsty, came alive at our little God group tonight. She said something had clicked inside her. A light had gone on. Up until now she's engaged with it because it means so much to Danny. She likes the gang and hanging out with Ben. Something changed tonight. She summed it up in a text to me later: 'After last week's session I decided I was done with merely dipping my toe in. So from now on I'm going to try to dive straight in. I have never felt happier at the moment. Thanks Rev. I wouldn't be here if it wasn't for you, Ben and Dan.' Faith in Jesus seems to actually make people feel happier.

The rest of the group seem to be making good spiritual progress, too. A couple of them said they now pray before going to sleep. It brings them real comfort. Another said he prays while driving to work. Interestingly – but not unsurprisingly – they're all struggling to read the Bible. They find it too daunting. Incomprehensible, even. I've encouraged them to read little passages from Mark's Gospel as a starting point.

Tuesday 24 July

We put on Sweaty Church in Trinity Square this afternoon. It's basically a load of sports and fun games and a bit of God. Its brainchild, Ian Mayhew, came to help. We put up a five-a-side goal, coconut shy and table tennis table. Ben set up a music system, booming out his beloved 1970s disco tunes. I looked ridiculous. Black clergy shirt, shorts, flip flops and goalie gloves. Families steadily drifted in. 'Beat the Vicar' at penalties went down well. Punters got three goes against me and won a free lolly if they got two in. I let the littlies score, but no one else. I felt like Neville Southall diving about. We raised about £500 for the boxing club. I'm covered in scrapes and bruises.

Ian is the most sober, sensible and creative man I know. He stayed over and was up at 6 a.m. reading his Bible. We had a lovely interlude in the morning sunshine riding our bikes around the marina. We cycled along the waterfront and watched the ferry from Rotterdam come in to port, imagining all the stoned and hung-over people inside. We raced and laughed and stopped to pray at the end of the pier. We got back and he showed me how to fill out my first ever risk assessment for Sweaty Church over tea and crumpets. He suggested I rephrase this line: 'Staff will be on hand at all times to handle balls.' Sensible.

Wednesday 25 July

Esther trapped her little finger in the baby gate this morning. She screamed in pain. Big cuddles and kisses helped. She was soon crawling about trying to find other things to do herself damage with.

I woke myself up crying with laughter in the early hours. I don't know why.

Thursday 26 July

Boxing coach Paul has encouraged me to start sparring properly. The members won't fully accept me until I've stepped up, he said. It's a fair point. I just prefer hitting bags to people. I'm worried about my nose being rearranged in ways I'm not happy with.

The *Hull Daily Mail* ran a double page feature on this weekend's Hull Trinity Festival. It shows how far it has come in the space of a year. They published a little something about Leroy Vickers being the guest at FULL on Sunday. It said:

> *Leroy Vickers will be performing some heavenly songs at Holy Trinity Church's FULL service in The Mission pub on Sunday at 4 p.m. The event will bring a spiritual element to the Hull Trinity Festival. It will include music from Leroy and the house band, plus a short reflection and prayers for Hull's Olympic boxing gold medal hopeful Luke Campbell. Reverend Matt Woodcock, who leads the service said: 'I'm not an opera expert but Leroy is an incredible singer – like Pavarotti, only slimmer and better looking. Music is a great way to connect with God.' Reverend Woodcock will also host an open mic night in the Kingston pub tomorrow from 7.15 p.m.*

I love the way God's church is part of this weekend. There's no separation between the sacred and the secular. It's all intermingled.

As it should be. For too long we've allowed ourselves to be marginalized.

Pete has arrived from Manchester, thank goodness. He never lets me down. I can't do this on my own. We practised our set for the open mic session: 'Suspicious Minds', 'I Am the Resurrection' and 'Fade Away'.

Friday 27 July

What started as a disappointing day ended in a euphoric mass singalong. Despite our best efforts, Trinity Square was pretty dead all day. I felt really sorry for all the market traders and landlord Lee who had erected a bar next to the stage in our car park. He took about £22 all day. The fact he has a gorgeous new girlfriend called Charlotte softened the blow a bit. He's smitten and already talking about marriage. I wandered round the square a lot trying to keep people's spirits up. Where was everyone? So frustrating. Pete and I performed a few songs on the Trinity stage. The light smattering of watchers seemed to appreciate it.

Compering the open mic night in The Kingston for the second year running was outrageous fun. Terry, Danny and Ben did a set together as the church band, followed by a long-haired Bon Jovi nut called 'DC Cowboy'. A cross-dressing stag party came in at that point. I interviewed the stag on stage about how he was feeling and the horrors that probably awaited him as the night unfolded. The whole place erupted at the end of 'Suspicious Minds'. A major love-in. My voice is in bits. I spilt kebab juice all over my clergy shirt on the way home.

I missed the opening ceremony of the London Olympics. They're going to be epic!

Saturday 28 July

I heard my first personal confession before things got started this morning. The guy had quite a big list. I hope he left feeling unburdened. Freer. It was a special privilege to listen and offer words of absolution. I am simply a flawed, human channel to the God of love and mercy.

I've never seen anyone work a crowd like the Hull opera singer Leroy Vickers. He had Trinity Square eating out of his hands today. His singing is so effortless. His onstage banter was so natural and funny. The turnout was much more healthy in Trinity Square. I think Lee broke even in the end. Record numbers poured into Holy Trinity. About 500, we reckon. Pete didn't want to leave after last night. We debriefed in Nero's and vowed to do more things together like this. Something special seems to happen.

The square got busy in the afternoon with the proud family and friends of those musicians taking part in the buskers competition. The pressure was on me, Lee and Leroy as the judges. A lovely local girl won it. Her dad wept when we announced the results. I think he was a bit worse for wear. During Leroy's set he took his top off and danced round the square, egged on by the crowd.

I later helped some of the organizers with the clear-up and Lee rewarded us with a cool Tiger beer outside The Kingston. I stood with the throng, the sun feeling lovely on my face. Few things in life feel more wonderful and civilized than a cold beer after a long day. It was spoilt a bit when a dishevelled bloke in a threadbare suit and string belt marched up to me and shouted and swore in my face. He ranted that there weren't any Bibles being handed out at the festival. 'Why aren't you evangelizing?!' he demanded. 'I am, brother,' I replied, picking my bottle up. 'Cheers!' He called me something unpleasant and stormed off. Christians!

Monday 30 July

So many Hull people told us over the festival weekend that the 'sleeping giant' Holy Trinity had woken up. Neal, Irene and I are determined that he doesn't go back to sleep. The *Hull Daily Mail* ran a prominent story about the festival's success. The headline said: 'Record crowds for the reverend and the festival music-makers.'

Tuesday 31 July

I spent a quiet day at the St Bede's Pastoral Centre. Sister Cecilia looked radiant and tanned. I jokingly asked if she'd been at the sun bed again. She noticed straight away how knackered I was. Running on spiritual fumes. She encouraged me to be kinder to myself. Tasked me with writing down the positives of the year using the words of Jesus from the parable of the sower as a guide. What has produced a crop? What fell on the path, on rocky places or among thorns?

Scavenging through Cecilia's library of God tomes, poetry and art books, I stumbled on two works by Caspar David Friedrich a German painter I'd never heard of. Both paintings were called 'Winter Landscape' and evoked the sense of desolation and consolation of the Christian experience. In the first, a crippled man looks out at a scene of black, snowy wasteland. He's leaning on a cane. Driving sleet is hitting his face. Dead tree stumps are all around him. It's bleak. He seems engulfed in despair. Like Dad used to be when York City lost.

In the second picture, the same man is sitting serenely against a snow-flecked rock gazing up at Jesus on the cross. He's flanked by two giant, fertile fir trees. The book commentator writes: 'Suddenly the eyes of his soul are opened. Friedrich invites us, in the still intimacy of this moment, to transcend human reason and contemplate the perfect harmony between creator and created.'

I identify with those two scenes. Consumed in the darkness and at the foot of Christ the light. I know where I feel happier.

Wednesday 1 August

The Trinity Music Festival raised about £450 for the St Paul's Boxing Academy. Head coach Mick Bromby was well happy. He was driving down to London when I told him – on his way to see Luke's first Olympic fight against an Italian called Vittorio Parrinello. It was a messy one but he beat him. People are getting right behind him in Hull. The Barracuda bar in town showed it live. I tweeted from the Holy Trinity account: 'We said our prayers for Luke Campbell today. Now we are biting our fingernails. Bring it home champ!'

Productive meeting with Neal and Irene this morning. We vowed to try to make sure things were a bit more relaxed at Holy Trinity over August. Less intense and frenetic. I've noticed that Neal's favourite phrase is 'Let's get all our ducks in line.' I've not worked a day with him yet when he hasn't said it.

Opera singer Leroy came in to see me, buzzing after singing 'Nessun dorma' at our pub service. He said he reconnected to God and dusted off his old cross when he got home.

Thursday 2 August

I visited Dewsbury Minster with Neal and Irene to get some ideas and see how they do things. I felt like we were really putting out their man on the door just by walking in. Being cold and slightly irritated seems to be a prerequisite for volunteering in these places. I can just imagine the Minster panel discussing the merits of a prospective volunteer after an interview. 'Mmm, I'm not sure about Clive. He just seems a bit, well, happy. Jolly. Laughs a bit too easily, don't you think? Too much like he's pleased to see people. I don't think this is the role for him. All in agreement?'

Friday 3 August

We got Esther and Heidi acquainted with peacocks, parrots, goats, reptiles and hens at East Park this morning. One of the birds squawked in Esther's face and made her cry. I got it on camera. A £250 *You've Been Framed* cheque right there. As we strolled round the animal sanctuary, Anna and I discussed the nature and nurture debate. It interests me. How much of our parenting is impacting how the girls will be as adults? How are we affecting their characters, hates, passions and idiosyncrasies? So far, whatever I do, the girls seem deeply uninterested in footy or anything that I might remotely enjoy taking them to when they're eight. I'll persevere.

I spotted a Roma lady giving donkey rides on our way out. An idea came to me. I asked if she'd be up for bringing Blossom to Trinity Square over Christmas. I'm thinking we could tell the nativity story out on the streets with real animals and characters from the Old Town community. She seemed interested. If we kept the event really small and manageable I think it could work. I'll make enquiries.

Saturday 4 August

A ginger bloke from Milton Keynes called Greg has won the Olympic long jump gold. Never has one bloke looked less like a top athlete in the history of the modern Olympiad. I love that.

I made a few YouTube videos this morning to publicize a bit more of our people-centred, spiritual endeavours at Holy Trinity. Remind the world that we are actually a church who believe in God and they can come in to get married, baptized, laid to rest, worship or – heaven forbid – find God themselves. They'd had two views by the end of the day. Mum and Grandma, bless them.

We've set up a space in the Broadley Chapel to offer prayers for Luke Campbell and his Olympic endeavours. Neal wrote a special one that people could go in and recite. The chapel door blurb says, 'Please pray for Luke Campbell, our Olympic boxer from the St Paul's Boxing Club next to Holy Trinity. We thank God for his years of training, dedication and sacrifice to gain a place in Team GB and pray that he will have the physical and mental strength to compete to the very best of his abilities.'

Sunday 5 August

I made a schoolboy error at the 9.30 a.m. service. I stupidly told the congregation: 'We are very relaxed here. Feel free to let your kids make as much noise as they want.' We say that as vicars, but obviously we don't mean it literally. One mum let her three-year-old smash his little fist into a tambourine during my entire sermon. I couldn't hear myself preach. I was articulating words of love and compassion while I fantasized about smashing the wretched noisy thing to bits. Bodybuilders John and Jamie also had to be stopped from confronting a guy who was talking loudly during the prayers. They were fuming about his lack of respect. John dropped the f-bomb under his breath. Jamie seethed: 'I come here to ****ing pray, not to listen to him talking about *EastEnders*!'

I've now come away with Dad to Lincoln for a few days for our annual bonding trip. We watched Luke Campbell narrowly beat a tough Bulgarian to progress into the Olympic semis. He'll get a bronze medal now, whatever happens! Lincoln is lovely. The cathedral is everything you want from such a building. It stands almost boastfully on top of a hill, casting a shadow over everything around it. I love the local accent. They say 'pound' like 'paaand'. There was a surreal moment when we walked through the city centre to get a pizza. A guy adorned in a Union Jack suit with a brolly on his head walked up to us clutching a box of Kleenex. 'Big tissues?!' he shouted.

Monday 6 August

Dad does reading the papers in a coffee shop better than anyone else I know. I left him to it while I went to Lincoln Cathedral for lunchtime communion. It's a great space. No pews to clutter it up. I made the mistake of telling one of the clergy that I was ordained. He was on placement from another church. It turned into an unwanted pastoral encounter as he unloaded about how much he was hating his church back home. How they were 'theological imbeciles'. I nodded sympathetically for a bit before making a quick escape and hiding in a side chapel to read the Bible and pray.

It was a relief to meet back up with Dad. He'd been scouring an Oxfam bookshop to find a Maigret book for his partner Maggie. We went for our customary chicken vindaloo after a few ales in an atmospheric pub.

Tuesday 7 August

Our hotel room should have been cordoned off this morning. Last night's vindaloo was in vengeful mood. We wearily staggered to a Costa to caffeinate. Thank heavens for their disabled toilet. I was in there so long the automatic lights went off. I texted Dad: 'Call Dyno-Rod. Quickly.'

Friday 10 August

Luke Campbell has made it to the Olympic final!! He absolutely destroyed a Japanese lad in the semis. He'll now fight an Irishman called John Joe Nevin for the gold medal. I can't believe it. Hull is going nuts about it. Luke is trending number one on Twitter and celebs like Dizzee Rascal and Chris Moyles have been in touch with him. To think I was buying him boxing gloves last month. A civic reception at City Hall is already planned for him next week. There was a lovely moment on the commentary when the pundit said: 'Luke comes from St Paul's ABC in Hull where the great Mick

Bromby coaches.' Wonderful. Fully deserved.

Saturday 11 August

Luke has flipping well done it! He's a gold medal winner! Once a skinny little kid from West Hull, tonight he's king of the world! I keep thinking about the investment Mick Bromby has put into him since he was 13. Luke will, I'm sure, end up going pro, but Mick helped get him there. The club needs to hoover up all the good publicity that comes their way and invest for the future. It's such a happy day for our city.

I didn't actually get to see the fight due to my school reunion. Wayne texted me constant updates while I gently confronted Sally Timpson about her cutting my heart out with a spoon and stamping all over it in the third year. 'But I just wanted to be friends!' she laughed. Still too early, Sally.

Sunday 12 August

I'm suffering from post-Olympics blues. I don't know how I'll cope without watching sailing at lunchtime.

Monday 13 August

I played golf with best friend Lee in York this evening. I don't know why. We always fall out. We both secretly cheat and constantly overexaggerate the length of our drives. He brought along a guy who's struggling with his mental health. I'm not sure we did him any good.

Wednesday 15 August

We used our voucher for a family photo shoot today. Esther cried and frowned all the way through it. The Addams Family portrait looks cheerier.

Thursday 16 August

I cycled into town to buy a nose and ear hair trimmer this afternoon. The impending doom of middle age creeps ever closer.

I'm reading a lovely book on prayer by Sister Wendy – the art-loving, hermit nun with the memorable teeth. It's full of helpful nuggets and is challenging my view of prayer. She writes: 'the simplicity of prayer, its sheer, terrifying uncomplicatedness, seems to be the last thing most of us either know or want to know. Feeling or non-feeling are equally unimportant. What matters is to stay at rest in the boat, down below sight level, while the wind that is the Holy Spirit bears us over to the still waters where the Father waits for us.'

Sister Wendy's central point resonates with me. That prayer is actually very simple. We make it too complicated, blabber too many words at God and don't dedicate enough time listening to him.

Esther has sleep issues again. Her new wake-up time is 5 a.m. She screams when we put her down at 7 p.m. Anna is discouraged and blames herself. We had a lovely cuddle before turning in tonight. I reassured her that she's a brilliant mum and things will get easier.

Sunday 19 August

I got to Holy Trinity well before the service to think and pray. It didn't last long. One of our elderly volunteers was soon storming in with a face like thunder, kicking off about the disruption at the Ralph McTell gig in church last night. I counted to ten. Breathed in. Gently told him that he'd have a heart attack if he didn't learn to hold some things a little lighter. I then sang the chorus to 'Streets of London'. He didn't laugh.

Monday 20 August

I felt a bit melancholy today. Everything and everyone felt a bit wearying. Listening to 'Some Riot' by Elbow didn't help. I think it's about a friend going off the rails. Guy Garvey is one of the great northern poets. He writes: 'I think when he's drinking he's drowning some riot./What is my friend trying to hide?/And it's breaking my heart to pour like the rain ... /When will my friend start singing again?'

Tuesday 21 August

I led lunchtime prayers and then drove back to York for my little birthday shindig. I got to Mum's house and realized what an ungrateful, miserable git I am sometimes. Anna and the girls, Mum, Grandma, Amy and her three were all there waiting to sing 'Happy Birthday'. Esther and Heidi adore their cousins. Nephew Joely is into flags at the moment. We all chose our favourites. I like Somalia's.

Wednesday 22 August

My Sunday sermon is about Christians falling out. Conflict in churches. I included the story of the two old guys at my friend's church who came to blows over the flower arranging.

Visited a local mum on the estate this morning to talk about her daughter's baptism. She was worried about my reaction to her children having different dads. She needn't have been. I'm beginning to understand the essence of my job: to leave people in no doubt that they are loved and accepted.

Thursday 23 August

I was rendered a helpless, blubbering wreck after coming to the end of *A Monster Calls*. It's an unforgettable read – full of pain and truth. It's a children's book every adult should read. The process Conor goes through with the monster in order to handle his mum's cancer is pure psychotherapy. The blame children put on themselves when traumatic stuff happens has lasting effects if left undealt with.

'It's my fault,' Conor said. 'I let her go. It's my fault.'

'It's not your fault,' the monster said, its voice floating in the air around him like a breeze. 'You were merely wishing for the end of pain,' the monster said. 'Your most human wish of all.'

Conor held tightly onto his monster. And by doing so, he would finally let her go.

Letting go. It's the hardest thing of all to do – but the most important.

I conducted my first wedding today. I united Michael Edward Roehampton and Sally Jane Brockhurst in holy matrimony. It was some experience. A lady with an outrageous pink hat was a bit the worse for wear before we even started. Michael and his two best men kept disappearing outside for a nervous smoke. Sally was 20 minutes early. I forced myself to speak slowly and calmly during the vows. It's a surreal, special moment when you ask the couple if they will commit to spending the rest of their lives together – whatever might happen. I still think it's the purest gesture of love there is. An extraordinary commitment. The highest of callings. Well, that's the theory, anyway. Sally was a ball of nervous agitation. She kept muttering that she wanted it all to be over. When I asked, 'Does anyone know any legal impediment why this couple may not be married?' the air was filled with a tense silence. Sally then blurted out: 'At least I know he's not gay then!' So awkward.

At the end, I lined Michael and Sally up, ready for them to parade down the aisle. 'Ladies and gentlemen, may I present to you the bride and groom, Mr and Mrs Sampson!' I boomed. Awkward pause, a few nervous coughs, a frantic look down at my notes … 'Sorry Mr and Mrs *Roehampton*!' Big, relieved claps and happy cheers.

Friday 24 August

Michael and Sally got in touch to say I'd written her dad's surname incorrectly on their marriage certificate.

Saturday 25 August

Holy Trinity veterans Dave and Julia presented me with a Bible written in Pitman's shorthand. I love it. They thought I'd appreciate it because of my journalistic background. It's actually how so many people see the Bible anyway – incomprehensible and totally baffling. I guess my job is to help them interpret it.

I can't imagine a happier sight than seeing your children jumping in puddles. I could have watched Esther and Heidi for hours on our walk this afternoon.

Sunday 26 August

The 9.30 a.m. service was a shambles again. The sound, feel, general organization and delivery were all terrible. I was fuming. I got home and had a Jerry Maguire moment. I thought everything could be solved if I wrote down all my frustrations and possible solutions in a long 'state of the nation' email to the team. Thank goodness I paused before pressing send. I let Anna check it over. Her sharp intake of breath was all I needed to know. She gently encouraged me to smooth some of the harder edges. Be less personal in my critique. Take out the swear words.

My basic point is that we've all become a bit flippant at Holy Trinity. The worship band looked like they'd rather be anywhere else. Ben said at least twice before beginning a song: 'I don't really know this one.' It hardly inspired confidence. He could always learn it. Would that be unreasonable? The toddler noise levels have become so cacophonous that a few people walked out on Sunday. I know I sound like a grumpy sod. I know we've longed for families to join us since we started. But we have to find a balance between peace and chaos. I phoned up a regular to ask him to sum up the 9.30 a.m. worship experience. 'Nerve-shredding,' he said.

Monday 27 August

My first sparring session at the boxing club tonight. Never again. I took on this pleasant lad who'd also never done it before. He was big. His arms looked as if they were moulded out of steel. My technique was all over the place and my punches ineffectual and weak. 'Like wet farts,' was how coach Paul described them. My opponent accidentally (so he said) smashed his fist into my nose. The shock and violence of it left me reeling. I wanted to start crying. My nose is now plum-coloured. The guy was very apologetic. One of the pros said he would now burn in hell for knocking out the vicar. No more sparring for me.

I've started listening to Maria Callas. Her voice feels like warm honey being poured into my ears.

Tuesday 28 August

I think it's time to move the FULL service out of The Mission. We've outgrown it. All the team agree. Next month's service will be the last one in there. I'm excited about what we can do with FULL in Holy Trinity.

Wednesday 29 August

Fruitful meeting with Irene this morning. She's never less than honest. She's not sure about moving FULL. Thinks it might be too soon. We talked a bit about Christmas. Irene and Neal are up for trying a Live Nativity. I jokingly said that it could be a game-changer if we walked real camels through the city centre as part of it. Who wouldn't want to see that? Thousands would come. They both laughed as if I'd lost my mind. Yet the more I think about it, the more I think it's possible. Someone must have a camel somewhere in East Yorkshire I could hire? Neal at least gave me permission to pursue the idea. I tweeted this out from the Holy Trinity account: 'Crazy request but does anyone know where we can hire a couple of camels?' It got loads of retweets and comments. Let's see what happens.

Thursday 30 August

Camel fever is sweeping through the Old Town since my tweet appeal. I was interviewed on Radio Humberside's lunchtime show. It seems to have caught people's imagination. They got a zookeeper from Bridlington on to talk about some of the practicalities. They reckon llamas might be a bit more realistic.

Friday 31 August

An outdoor market has come back to Trinity Square for the first time in years. A local trader called Julie Buffet has made it happen. The market used to be a huge draw to the area and people hope this will breathe new life into it. I pretended not to notice the dark magic stall selling tarot cards and pentangles. Radio Humberside presenter David Burns (or Burnsy, as everyone calls him) officially opened it. He's a right laugh. A big character in every sense. He loves rock bands and beer. His finger is on the pulse locally. He did a roving interview with traders and the public and then asked me about the Live Nativity. I said we were struggling to find real camels – and pregnant virgins. A bloke who used to be in the band The Christians played live at the opening. Nice version of 'Harvest for the World'.

Saturday 1 September

It's the start of our holidays. We're pretty much staying at home or with family in York and travelling about to visit various places and people. I've taken my email and Twitter accounts off my phone in an effort to be fully present. No distractions from loving my three girls with everything I can muster.

Sunday 2 September

To the countryside this morning to surprise and annoy my old vicar college comrade, Paul Bromley, at his church. All the colour drained from his face when he processed in to find me beaming at him on the front pew. He led beautifully. His flock consisted of a few respectable gents in suits and shiny brogues and some elderly ladies in flowery dresses. What I expected, really. I wonder if this is what God intended for his church? I had one of my usual, 'This can't be it' moments. But Paul's bright eyes and comforting, shiny head softened me. I tried to turn my whirring mind off. Stop deconstructing everything and let the peace of Christ wash over me. Not easy with the guy next to me coughing. It was one of those deep, guttural ones that went right through me. Someone pointedly thrust a Locket into his hand during the intercessions. I held Paul tightly during the Peace. I miss hearing his snores at 3 a.m. and raiding his secret fiery Doritos stash.

Monday 3 September

I played footy alongside former Welsh international forward Lee Nogan in a friendly tonight for my friend's team, Total Sports United. He was slower and creakier but stopped the ball stone dead whenever it went near him. A few of the lads berated him as 'No Goals' Nogan after his luckless stint at York City. I had more respect. He played in the same team as Ian Rush and Mark Hughes. Now I was tearing up the wing screaming at him to pass to me. He seldom did, but that was OK. It was a genuine thrill. In the bar afterwards, Lee shared some wonderfully indiscreet stories about some of the greats like Neville Southall and Paul Merson.

My appeal for Christmas camels featured in the *Hull Daily Mail* today. "'I'm very determined that this will happen," Reverend Woodcock said. "Even if I have to fly over to Egypt and bring some back on the plane myself."' Cheese. I think I'm losing the plot.

Tuesday 4 September

One of my baptism mums has found me some camels! She did some research and found a family farm in the East Midlands. They specialize in providing animals to TV and film crews. It costs £2,500 to hire three camels. No idea where that will come from, but we have hope. I'm just a bit worried that the Live Nativity could be on a far bigger scale than I first thought. I don't think I have the necessary skills to organize such a big city-wide event. I'm in danger of creating a monster. A camel-shaped one.

Anna and I ambitiously planned a relaxed and carefree day of fun family time. Twenty minutes in the soft play mecca that is Creepy Crawlies obliterated that fantasy. The height and sudden death potential of some of the apparatus that the kids were happily throwing themselves over, under and into sent my neuroses into the red zone. I darted around like a maniac trying to save the girls' lives every time they went up a slide. The day's stresses hit boiling point between Anna and me as we unhappily trudged round the centre's animal sanctuary. A couple of tired-looking donkeys eyed us curiously as we muttered at each other under our breath. Having children has brought into sharper focus how very different we both are. We get on each other's nerves far more quickly than we used to. 'What have we actually got in common?' Anna asked on the tense drive home.

'Our love of wine?' I suggested.

Wednesday 5 September

We lazily said goodbye to the afternoon in Grandma's garden in York. I did keepie-uppies with a tennis ball while the girls chased butterflies and wasps. Grandad's shed still looked exactly the same. I could picture him on his knees fixing my bike – inadvertently teaching me new swear words when he couldn't get the wheel off.

Thursday 6 September

A happy day in Scarborough. We found ourselves eating fish and chips at 11 a.m. outside the Harbour Bar. Our waitress offered the condiments in the most wonderfully reassuring East Coast accent.

I've contributed to a 'Faith Stories' video project Archbishop Sentamu is masterminding. One of my quotes sounds so wrong in hindsight: 'We tried furiously to have children.' 'Tried furiously.' A verbal image no one needed.

Friday 7 September

The camel story rumbles on. I'll look like a right idiot if I don't pull the Live Nativity off now. Finding the money to do it is still an issue. The *Church Times* used a picture of some bored-looking camels and the headline: 'Hull priest has "crazy idea" of using camels for Live Nativity.'

Sunday 9 September

It was good to be back at Holy Trinity. Within minutes Wayne had told me I looked old and hung-over (I wasn't) and Margaret collared me to say she'd received a complaint. An elderly regular is upset that I always apparently rush past her before the service and don't have time to talk. Then a troubled homeless woman completely lost it with her boyfriend in the cafe area. Her F-bombs and C-bombs echoed down the north choir aisle as Mark practised 'The Lord Is My Shepherd' on the organ. Yep, I've missed this place.

Monday 10 September

I've made good progress with the Live Nativity. I spoke to the top man at the Animal Company. He's quoted me just over £3,000 for three huge camels and their handlers (who dress as Wise Men), a donkey and three sheep. He assured me it would be safe to walk them through Hull city centre on the busiest shopping day before Christmas. I'll take his word for it. I also spoke to a helpful guy on Hull City Council who might be able to get us someone to pay for it. They have just forked out £250,000 on a very average ice rink, so we have hope.

Tuesday 11 September

I went to a really disheartening meeting of local clergy this morning. Never have I heard such despondency, cynicism and lack of faith in a roomful of people wearing dog collars. I was under the impression that joy and zest for life was a pretty high priority for Christian leaders. I'll file that away as another example of staggering naivety on my part. The final straw was when one of the priests questioned the resurrection of Jesus and the very notion that our job might include helping people to find God. Another said mission and evangelism was a 'pointless waste of time'. I wish I'd said something. Spoken out. Upended my coffee cup, smashed my custard cream against the wall and stormed out. I didn't. I stayed quiet. Kept my head down like a pathetic weakling. Quietly seething isn't going to change anything. Next time.

My maths hasn't improved. It turns out that I've miscalculated the Live Nativity budget. We're still short by nearly £1,000.

Wednesday 12 September

Yesterday I went to a clergy meeting that made me want to leave the Church of England immediately. Today I went to five church meetings that made me want to be an archbishop. They were life-affirming, joyful, inspiring – I want to change the world again!

Later I helped cousin Ben and Sarah out at the Play and Pray toddler group on the estate. One of the mums told me her son was being bullied. Apparently a gang of lads pulled his pants down in the street the other day. Another mum has just broken up with the father of her kids. She was tearful and angry. So many kids are growing up without dads round here.

Thursday 13 September

With Neal's blessing, I have officially booked camels, sheep and a donkey for Saturday 22 December. I've paid the deposit. No going back now. I'm praying like mad that I can raise the rest of the cash. I feel a bit sick about it. I've had one more idea to add a cherry on top of the spectacle. A cherry picker, actually. I want to fix a massive, twinkly star onto Wayne's cherry picker and manoeuvre it high above the outdoor stable. It would make a striking visual focal point. I just need to persuade someone to build the stable. Doubts and regret have plagued me all night.

Ben has challenged me over being more organized. Having clearer rotas. Well, having rotas. My spontaneous approach is doing his head in.

Popped round to see an interesting couple who want their son baptized. The dad was wary. He still bore the scars of a very conservative church he used to attend. He walked away when the minister told him that his granddad was probably not in heaven. This is the guy's first step back into church since hearing that. Let's see if I can do a better job.

Friday 14 September

Things were going too well. Whenever I try to do a new thing somebody somewhere gets very unhappy. An animal rights group has got in touch about the Live Nativity. I received an email from Animal Defenders International. They've got the hump (sorry) about us using camels. They claim it will be cruel and have urged us to cancel the event. 'Strange sights, sounds, touches or odours, and changes in temperature can cause stress in camels,' the email said. Forget the camels, my nerves are on a knife edge.

Paul Bromley forwarded me an email from Thapelo, our Lesotho friend who studied with us at vicar school. He wrote to Paul: 'Thank you for the lovely photograph of yourself on your ordination day together with mad Matt. I can't believe it that Matt made it to the priesthood when I recall the hopeless clown he was!' That's one for my headstone: 'Here lieth Reverend Matt Woodcock. A hopeless clown.'

Saturday 15 September

Bumped into one of the boxing coaches in church. I was surprised and delighted to hear he often came into Holy Trinity to find a sense of peace and calmness. He said he walks out feeling better than when he walks in. 'Don't come on a Sunday morning, then, whatever you do,' I joked.

Sunday 16 September

Anna walked out of Holy Trinity with the girls half way through the service this morning. She was weary of sprinting round the place trying to stop them screaming or becoming impaled on sharp pew ends. It's ironic that I'm up in the pulpit preaching about peace and my wife is below me feeling anything but.

Monday 17 September

I cycled to my usual early morning spot by the marina this morning to pray. A strange-looking man with wild, bloodshot eyes approached me. White froth circled his mouth. He mumbled something aggressively and looked pretty keen on throwing me into the Humber or worse. I sped away on my Raleigh racer. Visions of him eating my liver with a nice bottle of Chianti plagued me all the way home.

Thursday 20 September

Hallelujah! Hull City Council love the Live Nativity idea. Neal and I had a brilliant meeting with their events team. They've agreed to stump up most of the cash. They had a few concerns about the logistics of walking camels down a busy shopping street but they think it can be done without killing anyone. They've tasked me with compiling a detailed risk assessment for the event. My face lost a bit of colour at that point but I nodded as if it would be the most effortless thing in the world. Neal laughed nervously. How hard can it be?

Sunday 23 September

We've created a little gated area at the back of the chancel so the babies and tots have a safe space to crawl and throw things at each other during the services. Our families are loving it. Aside from a minor scuffle between two toddlers over a squeaky giraffe this morning, the worship atmosphere was far less manic. You could actually hear most of the sermon, too, which shocked everyone.

A retired priest has sent me a patronizing email after seeing the camels article in the *Church Times*. He encouraged me to read the Gospels and discover that camels aren't mentioned. He asked me to brush up on my knowledge of the major and minor Christian festivals too – particularly Epiphany. I should have let it go. Been the better priest and humoured him.

'Thanks for your interest,' I wrote back. 'I have been reading my Gospels and for that reason I forgive you for your patronizing and discouraging comments.'

I've decided to start a Holy Trinity football team. We'll practise on Saturday mornings and play the odd friendly. There's some decent interest. It should be a good relationship-builder with some of the dads who won't come near us on a Sunday.

Monday 24 September

I've come away to Spain with five of my oldest friends to play golf for a few days. Anna and the girls are staying in York with her parents so she's well happy. We were like giddy schoolboys getting on the plane at Leeds Bradford Airport. I sat next to a proper Yorkshireman who said he'd travelled the world but refuses to eat anything except roast dinners and fish and chips.

Our apartment is lovely with a pool out the back. We went straight to the beach. I spent five euros on some ridiculous white shades. I look like Kanye West with a burnt nose. Tonight we ate steak, drank cold beer and disagreed furiously about football, politics and the existence of God.

Tuesday 25 September

Crying with laughter is the best feeling in the world. I'm convinced it has healing qualities. It happened to me several times today. The only downside of this trip is the golf. I hate it and I'm terrible. We went to a karaoke bar tonight. The crowd booed me off before I could finish my heartfelt rendition of U2's 'With or Without You'. Ollie's 'Suspicious Minds' was annoyingly good, but brother-in-law Matty stole the show with 'Cracklin' Rosie'. I later got into an unnecessary debate about the ethics of money with Lee and Ollie. I piously and slurrily accused them of being 'greedy businessmen' who didn't do enough for the poor. They didn't like it. I shouldn't have said it.

A Colombian guy called Paco who we met at the bar offered to drive Lee and I back to the complex. We accepted warily, convincing ourselves he was a local gangster. Lee thought we'd end up in a ditch, stripped of our cash, passports and – heaven forbid – our underwear. We got back unscathed and unsullied.

Wednesday 26 September

It turns out Lee and I had unfairly judged Paco. Massively so. He served us our paella tonight. He's actually a waiter in a local restaurant and not the cold-blooded drug dealer for the local mob we'd imagined. Last night's lift was simply a genuine gesture of kindness. We tipped him generously to make us feel better.

Conversation topics varied wildly tonight: dads, boxing, girls from our school days we would restart the human race with if we had to in the event of a nuclear blast and whether Lee had a speech impediment. Amid the bonhomie, Ben, one of my oldest friends, received a sad phone call from his wife Ruth. Her mum Ann is riddled with cancer and has only been given a few weeks to live. Very sobering.

Thursday 27 September

I'm reading a book about the genocide in Rwanda written by the general in charge of the UN peacekeepers. The laugh count is fairly low.

I phoned home tonight and Heidi said, 'Hello, Daddy!' My two favourite words. Bursting to see them all tomorrow.

Friday 28 September

We endured a terrifying flight home. I thought we were going to die. The jet lurched violently from side to side. It did nothing for brother-in-law Rob's fear of flying. He had his head between his knees as we came into land, shouting '****! ****! ****!' over and over again.

Saturday 29 September

Back to reality. One of the clergy serving on a big north Hull estate is thinking of introducing boxing to their youth centre. She asked me if I thought it was ethical. Good question. I think it depends on the club. I trust the St Paul's coaches. They focus on discipline and positive values. Young lives are being transformed. Aggression has somewhere appropriate to go in that gym. Yet for all that, is it ethically right to hit someone in the face for sport? I'm still not sure.

Sunday 30 September

Our last FULL service at The Mission tonight. I think it's the right time to move on. We've outgrown the space and the effort to create a church in there has wearied everyone. Lots of new people came again. I'm up for the next chapter in Holy Trinity. I never thought making progress would mean moving into the church.

Monday 1 October

I met Anna for lunch at Nero's. She looked beautiful. I love the way she holds her coffee cup. Nurses it with both hands like it's giving her great comfort. She gives the coffee a soft, cute little blow before her lips take the plunge. I slurped mine exaggeratedly to make her laugh.

Tuesday 2 October

I keep waking up totally convinced that I've swallowed something. I make a choking sound and rouse Anna to help me dislodge it. The other night I thought I had a child's toy stuck and last night it was some sheeted plastic with holes in it. I'm sure a therapist would have a field day. My visit to Sister Cecilia was timely, then. We touched on some areas that I feel happier to avoid. Chiefly the fact that I live in constant fear that something bad will happen to Esther and Heidi. Cecilia encouraged me to list those things that scare me in relation to the girls and what I was doing spiritually to remedy them. After long periods of quiet and meditation I took out photos of the girls and prayed for them. I prayed about my fear. I prayed for God's protection on them. I felt a wonderful sense of release. Cecilia said that Anna and I must continually give them over to God. She sent me off into the quiet with two lovely Bible passages. One from Hosea 11.4 – 'I led them with cords of human kindness, with ties of love. To them I was like one who lifts a little child to the cheek, and I bent down to feed them.' The second was from Isaiah 43.2: 'When you pass through the waters, I will be with you; and when you pass through the rivers, they will not sweep over you.'

Wednesday 3 October

Serving God in this place felt so effortless today. I was touched with the tangible sense that special things are happening in and around Holy Trinity. The atmosphere felt more positive. Lighter. A good night's sleep helped. I said one of Sister Cecilia's special prayers before lights out and it worked. No hideous choking night terrors. No creeping fear. I didn't just sleep – I hibernated.

The God slot at the mums and tots group at Holy Apostles is a thing of messy beauty. It feels like a triumph just to persuade any of the adults not to walk out for a Lambert & Butler. I'm often struck by little moments of sacredness in among the noise and apathy. One of the grandmas shared how weary she feels constantly looking after her daughter's kids. It's affecting her health and yet she does it unwaveringly. She's full of an unrelenting love for her family. One of the dads told the group he'd lost his job yesterday. He's now applied to be a debt collector.

Someone likened me to St Francis of Assisi today. Apparently he did a Live Nativity in a cave back in the thirteenth century. There's no record of him using real camels, though. He wasn't that stupid.

Thursday 4 October

I've made a YouTube video about the pioneer ministry going on at Holy Trinity. Maybe it will inspire a few more people to get involved. Some more Christians with a sense of humour and the ability to engage with people would be lovely. The video is pretty cheesy to be honest. The tagline reads: 'Pioneer Ministry at Holy Trinity, Hull. On a mission. Be part of it.' In truth, this would be more accurate: 'Pioneer Ministry at Holy Trinity, Hull. Absolutely winging it.'

Friday 5 October

Irene was a bit grumpy with me about the pioneer video. She messaged to say I made it look as if she didn't exist and wasn't contributing anything. 'Who is this?!' I replied.

Saturday 6 October

I struggled to swallow again at the start of Dave and Leah's wedding today. It was just like being back in York Minster during my ordination. Panicked thoughts about fainting during the vows filled my mind. Mum reckons it's stress-related. Neal says I should go and see my GP. Irene thinks I need to go and see a shrink (although, to be fair, she's always saying that). The feeling passed quickly, thank goodness. The rest of the wedding was a joy. Leah arrived in a classic open-backed Humber car. Her beaming dad waved like the Queen at the little crowd watching outside church. Escorting the car were ten Vespa scooters from the Hull and District Scooter Club.

Organist Mark and I had a reviving pint after the wedding outside the sun-kissed Kingston. We laugh easily together. He's become a proper kindred spirit. We've started leaving kisses to each other at the end of our texts. I love finding friends in touch with their sensitive side. I always leave Mark's company a bit more educated about things like octaves and perfect pitch. He also has a limitless arsenal of inappropriate anecdotes.

Sunday 7 October

I noticed bodybuilder John was puffy-eyed and distraught-looking before the family service. Turns out his dad has died. I invited him into the chapel to pray.

I probably went too far at Wayne's son's baptism service. In my enthusiasm to get people to engage, I overdid the informality and fun. The sense of the sacred and that necessary touch of holiness got lost a bit, if I'm honest. Dragging Wayne and Louise and Harry's godparents up to start a Mexican wave was one thing. Dribbling a football up the nave and round the font while giving a John Motson-style commentary was too much. Lesson learnt.

I received a gutting email from Sammi when I got home. She's been coming to church loads and seemed to love the Christian basics course at our house. She wrote to tell me that she won't be coming back. She expressed heartfelt thanks, but said her burgeoning faith had gone. She doesn't believe. I can't help feeling like I've failed somehow. I'll miss Sammi. Huge respect for her, though. She's come to a definite decision about God – so few people are even willing to go there. I emailed back to say we'll still be there if she needs us. I sat in a dark room to let the disappointment wash over me tonight. Tomorrow's a new day. Onwards.

Monday 8 October

I was randomly reunited with my nursery school sweetheart, Chloe Greenwood, this afternoon. The last time I saw her properly was in a sandpit. Her opening line was a good one: 'What's happened to your curly hair and pot belly, Matt?' Then she accused me of running off with Sarah Jamieson. 'You broke my heart!' she laughed. Life as a four-year-old was complicated.

Wednesday 10 October

Embarrassing mums and tots session at Holy Apostles this morning. The mums were in a revealing mood about home life in the high-rises. I had to take refuge in the kitchen at one point. There are just some intimate female conversations that no vicar should ever be in earshot of.

Anna has been watching Jo Frost – the 'Supernanny' – for some inspiration. She's determined to follow her lead, starting with the 'naughty step'. We hope it might hold the key to Esther and Heidi doing as they're told moving forward. I fear they could be spending half their lives sitting on it.

One of my oldest friends, Ruth, has asked me to visit her mum Ann in York Hospital before she dies. She hasn't been given long.

Thursday 11 October

A hugely significant day. Anna and I sang and danced round the front room like wild banshees. Heidi's done her first potty poo! We never thought she'd get there. The stool was small but perfectly formed. We made girls who can actually poo on their own. So happy!

Friday 12 October

I forced myself to take a whole day off. It was a conscious effort not to think about the people on my radar and the things I had to do. Running helped. It sweated out all the negative tension and knotty bits. I felt like a new penny. Anna engaged with me as if I was her husband again – not just some irritating, distant bloke living in her house. We watched a few episodes of *Modern Family*. It has that knack of making us laugh, cry and feel fluffy about the world for half an hour. I don't want much more from a TV show.

Saturday 13 October

There was a surprisingly good turnout at Holy Trinity United's first football practice this morning. Some of the lads came from church, others from invitations round the Old Town. A few saw my social media posts. It reaffirmed to me how much blokes like to belong and gather – particularly in a footy context. I'm hoping this will lay the foundation for a men's group. We need some fitter players, mind you. This lot were dead after 15 minutes. Major heart surgery waiting to happen. Ability levels were fairly low, too. Student Danny actually admitted that he's never played before. How could he be 21 and never have knowingly played football? It's just not possible, is it? And then the practice started. Yep, Danny hasn't played before. He was like a drunk having his first go on stilts. An Irish guy called Brian Gilliland was also bad. He made up for it with his hollering and swearing, though. The lads were keen at least and want me to organize some friendly games. I need to find teams with broad minds and a sense of humour. Anna encouraged me to tone down my competitive spirit and see this as a fun, relationship-building opportunity. A time to change blokes' perceptions about faith and church. I certainly need to shout at everyone a lot less next week.

Sunday 14 October

I had a beautiful encounter with Ruth's mum, Ann Cluderay, this afternoon in her York Hospital ward. I came away feeling inspired and determined to make every day count. Ann is close to death, yet still so full of life. She savours every breath. Belly laughs more than anyone in her condition has a right to. She told me about her remarkable life. Doctors told her 13 years ago that she didn't have long to live because of a huge growth. Her health improved a bit – but her perspective on life changed forever. Ann decided to go for it. To set fire to caution and live as fully as she could. She bought a round-the-world ticket on a cruise liner. As the ship pulled into the harbour at Singapore, Ann bumped into a guy called David. That was it. They fell in love. They've been inseparable ever since. Ann has visited Hawaii, Vietnam and Tahiti. She's ridden elephants and cuddled pandas. Seen her daughters Ruth and Laura get married and got to hold and love four grandchildren. Ann told me she now has absolutely no regrets. I believed her. She has wrung life dry. Drained every drop. Who can say that with total confidence?

It felt weirdly normal to plan Ann's celebration of life service. Before I left, in the quiet of that bare hospital ward, Ann and I shared a solemn moment. I think God met her in a powerful, tangible way. I gave her my comfort cross and encouraged her to hold it in the tough days ahead. To ask God for strength and peace. Her eyes filled with tears as I laid my hands on her head to pray. I want to live more like Ann.

At Holy Trinity this morning one of the HT United lads brought in a distressed work colleague. She genuinely thought she'd burst into flames if she walked in. With no spontaneous combustion evident, she relaxed a bit and asked me to pray for her in the chapel. I hope she'll be back.

Monday 15 October

I'm anxious about speaking at the 'Leading Your Church Into Growth' (LYCIG) conference in Leeds tomorrow. I'm cursing myself for agreeing to do it. My mentor and LYCIG leader, Robin, is constantly pushing me to do things I don't want to do. No part of me wants to stand in front of 70 battle-hardened vicars to suggest how they might want to grow their churches. They might laugh me out of the place. I keep picking up the phone to call Robin to pull out.

Neal sent me the most wonderful, encouraging email at just the right time. The guy has pastoral bones. He just knows what to say to make you feel better. He wrote:

I realize it's a big deal speaking to a large audience of clergy, but then God's given you wonderful gifts of communication and an ability to inspire others. So I am sure that all the prep and prayer will be honoured by him. Perhaps it's when we feel weakest and most vulnerable that the Holy Spirit finds us at our most pliable and workable – a bit like the clay – and he's able to use us most powerfully? And it's worth remembering too that all the experienced clergy will be carrying all sorts of burdens and anxieties. Who knows who may be coming feeling exhausted and dry and searching for fresh impetus and focus in their ministries? They have been hacking away at the coal face for years and seen little coal. So what you have to say, while both challenging and encouraging, I am sure could well be just what they need.

I didn't pick up the phone again to cancel after reading that.

Tuesday 16 October

I've survived one of the most daunting experiences of my ministerial life. Massive funerals, complicated pastoral situations, beer festivals, I can handle. Speaking to other vicars about how they can grow their churches? Terrifying. I hate it. I was badly briefed by Robin. Unsure of what he wanted me to say. My mouth emptied of moisture as I got up to speak. My armpits were dripping. Robin said words of encouragement to me but I didn't really hear him.

I began with a few badly timed stories about my week. The delegates were confused rather than amused. I was making them nervous. Somehow I got through it. I had a go. I got a flavour for how Anna feels with her anxiety. The 'creeping terror', I think they call it. I need to seriously get a grip and put stuff in perspective. I should try being an aid worker in South Sudan. Or a childminder.

Wednesday 17 October

Another first today: anointing people with oil. The LYCIG conference delegates lined up at the end of a beautiful service tonight. As a team, we dipped our fingers in oil, made the sign of the cross on their head and hands and said: 'I anoint you in the name of the Father, the Son and Holy Spirit.' I was too overzealous at the dipping stage, lathering oil onto their foreheads like a panto dame's make-up. Oil dripped down one guy's face like thick yellowy tears. His cream cardigan was covered in it.

Thursday 18 October

I got the dreaded 'Can I have a quick word, Matt?' just before I left the LYCIG conference. A priest ministering on a tough estate wasn't happy with me. Felt my humour went too far. Fair enough. I forced myself to thank her for the feedback without sounding defensive or irritated. It's all part of my journey to being a more appropriate human being.

Saturday 20 October

Sixteen lads turned up to the HT United training session this morning. I think I've hit on something. We play my old church, St Paul's, Holgate, in York next weekend. I'll need to find some ringers to prevent a total massacre.

I took Esther to Anna's favourite cut-price shop, Heron's, this afternoon to buy bread, milk and Caramacs. It made us both very happy.

Sunday 21 October

There were two moments of ground-swallowing cringe at the two services I led this morning. I need to choose my words more carefully. During my sermon at Holy Apostles, in an effort to encourage more prayer I handed everyone a humbug. For the time it took them to finish it we'd sit in silent prayer, I said. Channel our inner St Augustine. 'So I want you to pop it into your mouth and give it a slow, gentle suck.' Cue a raucous lady unleashing the most deafening, filthy, inappropriate laugh. It was awful. I didn't know what to do. It set off the whole congregation into laughter convulsions. Someone shouted, 'fnarr fnarr!' It was the longest, most uncomfortable silent prayer time of my life. Seldom have I crunched into a humbug so quickly.

Then there was my sermon at the Holy Trinity service. I can barely bring myself to write down what happened. I asked the congregation to shout out the top five reasons why they thought people stay awake at night. '*Sex!*' big John shouted with annoyingly brilliant timing. There was a full second of stillness. The word echoed around the 700-year-old walls as if they were revelling in having it bounce into them. Then all hell broke loose. Cheers and gasps of horror erupted. And they were just from Neal and Irene. I didn't dare ask for any more reasons. Our services are getting out of hand. I've unwittingly created a stag-do culture in the house of God.

Tuesday 23 October

Cousin Ben and I went to the Pave bar in Princes Avenue for the jazz night. I'm trying to encourage him to meet some musicians and start performing on his bass. He's on another level. Jazz passes me by a bit. I don't feel cool enough or up my own backside enough to fully understand or appreciate it.

Wednesday 24 October

I was told that one of the mums brought a spiritualist medium to our service last week. I hope she hasn't put a hex on me. Neal and Irene agreed that we've let things get a bit out of hand in an effort to welcome and embrace everybody. I'm still not sure where the line is, but I think I did a little dance over it last Sunday morning.

Ben needed a confidence boost today. Youth work can be a thankless task. You rarely actually get to see the fruit of your labours. I mean, if my old youth worker, Peter Froggatt – tormented and forced to endure Job-like trials at my teenage hands – knew I was a priest now, I think he would need CPR. Or some paracetamol and an early night at the very least. I reminded Ben of all the young people he'd impacted already. Of the healing words and actions he'd poured into broken lives and desperate situations. Probing a bit deeper, I got the real reason for Ben's ire. He says he's ready to ask Bekah to marry him – but can't afford a ring. We laughed at the brutal piece of advice I allegedly offered him on the drive home from the church weekend where they first met. He claims I said: 'Bekah's not just out of your league, Ben, she's out of your solar system. I'd leave her well alone or you'll get your heart stamped on.' Thank the Lord he didn't take a blind bit of notice of me and listened to Anna instead. That was seven years ago. It took one date for them to become smitten with each other.

I met something of a lost soul in Wetherspoons later on. Alan's been coming along to HT United training. Overweight and low on self-esteem, he spends all his spare time playing computer games in his bedroom. He says he wants to explore faith with me and also craves community. 'I just want some friends, Matt,' he said between sips of his Grolsch. It breaks my heart when people say that. I'm determined to help him make plenty more of them.

Thursday 25 October

We have a real baby Jesus for the Live Nativity! He's a two-week-old called Sidney from East Hull. I hit it off with his welder dad Gareth and barmaid mum Lyndsey at our church baptism evening tonight. They're dead keen on being Mary and Joseph. I can tell they want to know a bit more about God too. Result.

Friday 26 October

Neal was the most irritated I've ever seen him this morning. He'd got the unwanted news that the church finances are still in a right mess. Biblically bad. Neal looked as if he had the weight of the world on his shoulders. I prayed for him in the chapel that his spirits would be lifted. A few million quid would help, admittedly. Neal's hair needs replenishing too. It's disappearing rapidly. I'm faring no better. My hair looks as if someone has sprinkled Johnsons baby talc all over it. The average life expectancy of Holy Trinity clergy is plummeting.

Saturday 27 October

HT United's first ever game this morning. We were massacred by my old St Paul's pals. I played like an old donkey but shouted and encouraged my heart out. Most importantly, there was a lovely camaraderie. We awoke to driving sleet. I got the classic morning call from our Nigerian secret weapon, Obed (in a brilliantly acted croaky voice): 'Eeugh, hello Matt [*coughing fit*]. I don't feel too good and I've just had some friends turn up from London ... blah, blah, blah.' It was a BAFTA-winning performance. I admired him for it.

I took Anna to a St Paul's Boxing Academy show at the KC Stadium tonight. She looked knockout in her red dress and sparkly earrings. I felt like a gangster arm in arm with my glamorous moll.

Sunday 28 October

We reflected on Jesus as the Great Physician at the FULL service tonight. The medical and the spiritual. I got Deputy Churchwarden Andy to talk about his experiences as a front-line nurse and jumping in to help victims of the Clapham rail disaster. Irene gave a moving testimony about the road crash that nearly killed her. She still walks with a cane. She spoke so honestly about how she felt God was with her through it all.

There were a few issues tonight. Our welcome team didn't turn up so I ran around too much. A little kid ran riot throughout the whole thing. I think his mum was so tired and stressed that she didn't hear or care that her child was single-handedly destroying the sacred, holy space we'd created. I didn't mention it. Suffer the little children.

Monday 29 October

A few tense words with Mum today. She keeps asking what I think about her moving in with Barry. I don't have an opinion. Not one I want to share with her anyway. It's none of my business. She was a bit dismissive of marriage which annoyed me. I know she doesn't believe that. After a few starchy words, we just about left the conversation as friends. I wish Mum knew how much she means to me. She's the most inspirational, flamboyant and spiritual human being in my life. I need to tell her that more.

Tuesday 30 October

I feel wretched. I forgot our wedding anniversary. Eight years married today. The worst thing is that it never even crossed my mind. I collected the girls from York as usual. After about ten minutes, Anna, quietly and icily, said: 'Happy anniversary, Woody.' *Nooo!* I couldn't believe it. I was only praying for Anna this morning and giving thanks for our life together. The worst thing was how

Anna took my oversight. It would have been easier if she'd ranted and raved, but no, she just sighed and wearily accepted it. She said she was waiting all day for the postman to arrive at her office with a bunch of flowers. Heartbreaking. Anna got me a funny card and a special pen I'm now writing this with. I will make it up to her – big time. Starting with the biggest bunch of flowers I can find tomorrow.

Wednesday 31 October

Anna appreciated her flowers and my efforts to atone for forgetting our anniversary. Thank goodness for that.

I had cross words with the jazz night organizer at the Pave bar tonight. Ben and I waited all night for his promised turn on the bass. It never happened. They sniffily ignored us. Ben looked crestfallen. I approached the guy at the end to protest – perhaps a little too vociferously. I was gutted for Ben. The keyboard player was so dismissive and haughty that I could have stuck his pork pie hat somewhere unpleasant. I walked away after saying my piece. We won't be going back. Ben was so embarrassed. At least we won the raffle. That showed them.

I blessed Wayne's new house with holy water and prayed for him this morning. It descended into a water fight. My stole got soaked.

Thursday 1 November

All the colour drained from my face during our clergy meeting in The William Wilberforce – and not just because we were sorting the rotas. My insides were all over the place and I was forced to leg it to bed. It's terrible timing. I don't have time to be ill. As I lay there dying, I saw some interesting Facebook posts about prayer. One said that statistically Christians weren't any more likely to recover from cancer than anyone else – despite all our praying. Interesting.

We need an honest conversation about Holy Apostles as a clergy team. Despite our best efforts, the service just isn't growing. People on the estate just don't seem to do Sunday mornings.

However, the growth rate of Esther and Heidi is remarkable. I really noticed it today. They can now string little sentences together – mostly about Peppa Pig and 'poo poo'.

Friday 2 November

I'm rediscovering the art of proper conversation with Anna this week. Last night in bed we just talked about this and that. Nothing earth-shattering. Things like her planned trip to Heron's for a small shop, theories about why Heidi's hair wasn't growing as fast as Esther's, the annoyance of our threadbare carpet. It was lovely. It crossed my mind how horrible it would be if I wasn't married to Anna.

Saturday 3 November

I'm at Wydale Hall retreat centre for an intense day of curates' training. The topics included dementia, psychosis, hearing impairment and infant death. The speaker on 'deaf church' was funny. She told a story about signing during a dull sermon by some bishop or other. She noticed that all the deaf people in the congregation had stopped taking any notice. They were all signing to each other about their holidays, *EastEnders* and what they'd had for breakfast. The bishop burbled on, oblivious.

Another engaging speaker shared how we could minister effectively to people suffering from mental illness. She categorized the different stages of psychosis. One stage was 'a constant state of euphoria'. My friend Paul Bromley nudged me to say I was a definite sufferer. I replied that being near him was definitely curing me of it. We fled the polite bar conversation tonight to watch the film *300* in Paul's room and eat Skips and Starbars.

Sunday 4 November

I'm speaking at the Leading Your Church Into Growth national conference in Swanwick tomorrow. Another three days away from home. God gets way too much of my time.

Tuesday 6 November

Presided at the Eucharist in front of about 150 clergy this morning at the LYCIG conference at Swanwick. I was overcome with the bowel-curdling fear that I'd drop the chalice or not be able to get my words out. I sat in the chapel for ages beforehand sucking in calming breaths. By the time I strode out awkwardly in my robe and green chasuble and said the opening words behind the altar, the whole thing became something of an out-of-body experience. I was lost in it. Lifting the bread – the body of Christ – was an extraordinary moment. I felt so close to God. A few stray tears dripped onto the altar cloth. I think this was my first real experience of what colleagues call 'the holy mysteries'. That unexplainable connection to the divine in the sacraments. One of the lecturers at vicar school used to weep as he presided at the altar. I understand why now. I bowed in front of the altar, too, without feeling like a complete tool.

Some of the delegates from the Anglo-Catholic end of the Church of England spectrum cornered me at the bar tonight to give me some feedback about the communion. 'It was heartfelt, Matt,' one of them (an obese chap with hair like John Travolta in *Saturday Night Fever*), said: 'But you've got to do something about your hands. They were all over the place!' Fellow LYCIG team member Anna Norman-Walker said it looked as if I was one of those airport runway guys in the hi-vis jackets guiding out a 747.

Wednesday 7 November

I led the main conference teaching session this morning with Anna N-W. She's refined, articulate, a brilliant communicator and talks like Felicity Kendal. Watching her in action reaffirmed my belief that anyone who thinks God doesn't want women to be ordained are at best misguided and at worst absolutely bonkers. Anna and I couldn't have been a more different double act. I'm sure my accent following hers was something of a jarring experience for the delegates. I spoke about my experience of putting on church mission events like the men's health nights, and the fact that after my urologist buddy, Graeme, had spoken about malfunctioning testicles, prostates and erectile malfunction for half an hour, men were much more receptive to the spiritual. As a guy told me at one of our health events once: 'I've just spent half an hour discussing my balls – I'm sure 20 minutes of Jesus won't do me any harm.'

Thursday 8 November

Anna N-W shared a lovely story about the Easter Sunday service at her village church a few years ago. During her sermon, her husband came running out dressed as a huge, white Easter bunny. After a comedy debate about the meaning of Easter, Anna then sent him out to a chorus of 'awwwws'. The church's elderly organist failed to see the funny side. As the bunny was escorted away, the guy climbed out of his organ booth and stormed out, shouting 'This is an absolute disgrace!' The congregation thought it was part of the act and accompanied his walk out with cheers, whistles and slow hand claps. He never went back.

Friday 9 November

Encouraging to find out today that two of the HT United lads told me they want to start coming to church. I think they've been impacted by the welcome and sense of community.

Saturday 10 November

I've been reflecting on a mysterious photograph I stumbled across while reading about 9/11. A delivery man is walking down a New York street holding a package. He's entirely oblivious – or perhaps not – of the carnage unfolding in the distance behind him. The twin towers are ablaze, spewing out billows of thick, grey smoke. The image can be taken one of two ways. Either the guy knows what's happened to the towers but carries on as normal anyway. He refuses to deal with or accept the destructive reality going on behind him. Or he is somehow delivering in ignorance of what's going on. I'd love to know which one it was. Of course, he could just have been ridiculously conscientious.

I've been preparing for Remembrance Sunday tomorrow. Holy Trinity is a constant reminder of the horrors and sacrifice of war. The names of the dead are everywhere. I spent some time reflecting on this Seamus Heaney poem called 'The Summer of Lost Rachel': 'So let the downpours flood/Our memory's riverbed ... And recollects our need.' And this from Wilfred Owen: 'What passing-bells for these who die as cattle?/Only the monstrous anger of the guns.'

Anna and I will be reliving our honeymoon in Sandsend by this time tomorrow. I can't wait.

Sunday 11 November

Great to see a few of the HT United lads turn up to the Remembrance service this morning. I read names from a roll of honour and we gathered round the poppy display. A brilliant light cascaded through the stained glass window above, illuminating the suffering Christ. It spoke more sacred words than I did.

Anna and I have escaped to Raithwaite Hall, close to our honeymoon destination in Sandsend. We lounged around in bed sipping fizz and eating grapes. As we got ready to go out, I saw myself in the full-length mirror – untowelled. I wasn't happy with the view. My love handles have turned into love shelves. I have work to do.

Monday 12 November

It was a strange feeling not to be wrenched awake by cries, incessant demands or the thwack of a stuffed toy against my temple. Anna looked wonderfully dishevelled this morning. Curly hair all over the shop and make-up skew-whiff. Beautiful.

At breakfast the waiter forgot to bring our poached eggs. We sat there for ages like proper lemons – too English to mention it. Later on, we befriended a lovely couple, Leon and Jasper, in the jacuzzi. I noticed they were well trimmed and had glowing tans. I'm yet to meet a poorly-groomed gay guy.

We got to Whitby at twilight. It might be my favourite time of day. On a par with sunrise, certainly. We lost ourselves in the arcades for a bit. Anna lost a fortune on the 2p slots while I machine-gunned flesh-eating zombies. I bought *Oliver Twist* and the complete Father Brown mysteries from a bookshop. As I was walking out, I lost my footing and rolled over the cobbles. The whole street seemed to notice. I bowed and hobbled away to the sound of barely stifled laughs.

Tuesday 13 November

I'll never tire of walking from Whitby to Sandsend. This coastline restores me. A couple of optimistic surfers were bobbing in the water looking well hacked off. It was like a mill pond. The workforce of Sandsend seemed to be having a bad day. A waitress in the cafe we ended up in seemed spectacularly indifferent to the presence of customers. A bejewelled woman in a gift shop was also bad-mannered. She didn't bother to look up from her crossword when we went in to browse the snow globes and Beatrix Potter thimbles. My hearty 'Good morning!' was met with an indifferent nod. It pleased me to notice that she had four down wrong. It was 'ebony'. Our hope in humanity and the power of cheeriness was restored when we got back to our hotel. 'Welcome home!' the hotel porter gushed.

Wednesday 14 November

There's no gentle easing back into this job after a few days away. Firmly back to reality today. I popped in to see one of the estate mums near Holy Apostles. She's been having a tough time. Her mum has been threatening to take her own life because things have got too much.

Thursday 15 November

There was a special moment just as Irene was about to start her lovely praise service this morning. Suddenly the main door swept open and a busload of elderly residents were wheeled in from the nearby Raleigh Court Care Home. It was like that scene from *Flash Gordon* when Brian Blessed's Hawkmen swooped in. They filled the place. Irene's face was a picture of grateful joy. At the end of the service we all joined hands to say the words of the grace in a big circle. I turned it into a mass Hokey Cokey – wheelchairs and all. Then we ate buttered scones and drank tea in china cups. Perfect.

Friday 16 November

One of the HT United lads, Matthew, asked to take me for a coffee today. I thought he wanted to talk about offside traps and Hull City's promotion chances. No. He shared a story of such heartbreaking family tragedy that I feel numb. It's straight from the pages of a tragic novel. Matthew and his brother had a relatively happy, normal childhood. His parents loved each other and lived in easy contentment. Then everything changed when his dad's colleagues played a practical joke on him. They wrote a fictitious love letter from a lover who didn't exist and planted it in his jacket pocket. Nothing was ever the same after that. Matthew's mum found the note and refused to believe it was a joke. She kicked him out and over the following days and weeks became consumed by alcohol to numb the pain. Within a couple of years she'd died of liver disease. Matthew said he was overcome with sadness. He described lying down at his mum's graveside every day, nestling his head against the headstone, sick with grief and the unfairness of it all. 'I've been that way for a long time, Matt,' he said. 'It's such a lonely feeling. I'm ready to move on and be happy.' I offered what words of consolation I could after hearing such a sad story and arranged to meet up again. I think church life would be of real benefit to Matthew.

Mum and Grandma came to see us this afternoon from York. I held them both tightly. I'm so lucky to have their love in my life. Matthew's story has taught me that a few random events here and there and things could have been so different. I've just read Philip Larkin's 'An Arundel Tomb' again. It ends: 'What will survive of us is love.' That's got to be the hope for any family, surely? What will survive of us is love.

Sunday 18 November

I woke up feeling cock-a-hoop. Giddy and blessed to be alive. I ran into the girls' bedroom with a towel on my head singing 'Master of the House' from *Les Misérables*. Of course, there's things that have me nibbling my fingernails like carrot ends. Our congregation numbers are up and down which worries me. My pastoral load is unrelenting and I sometimes worry that people see a bit too much of Matt Woodcock and not enough of Jesus. But I'm so happy in Hull. We all are. I'm more convinced than ever that God has called us here. There's no city like it. I cycled to church with a huge smile on my face and hope in my heart. That's all you want on a freezing Sunday November morning, I suppose.

I bumped into a guy coming out of the chapel before the 9.30 a.m. service. He told me that he was nearly sent down last year. I didn't ask why. He said he'd used our chapel to pray before the court case. Since then, he's been quietly coming back to pray and feeling determined to make something positive come out of the experience. He's longing to resist the rage he feels welling up inside when things don't go his way. I gave him my number and encouraged him to get in touch if he wanted someone to pray with or talk to. I was reminded afresh how important Holy Trinity is to the city. It's home to an anonymous congregation. Quiet chapel dwellers seeking peace, reassurance and forgiveness at difficult times. What a precious free gift we offer. It's what drives us to keep Holy Trinity flourishing.

We took the girls for a drive out to Market Weighton after lunch. I had romantic notions of us finding interest, fulfilment and refreshment in this small market town. We left after 20 minutes. Another crushing disappointment. It seems Market Weighton has one claim to fame: 'Giant' William Bradley, who was born there in 1787. He was the tallest British man ever recorded, measuring 7 feet 9 inches. A street was named after him and a statue erected in his honour. We eked out six of the 20 minutes looking at that. I've added 'family outing organizer' to my list of fathering failures.

Tuesday 20 November

Another dark day in the history of the Church of England. The General Synod – our national decision-making body – has voted down the legislation allowing women to be bishops. What the hell are they thinking? We are a national laughing stock. Unsurprisingly, Irene is devastated. I'm ashamed to be an Anglican today.

The homeless guys at Francis Street car park had other things on their mind tonight as we dished out hot soup and chocolate bars to them. One of the blokes has a court case tomorrow. Another was a nervous wreck after a knife attack. It did me good to be among them. To listen to their stories. One of the guys was the absolute double of Lando Calrissian from *Star Wars*. I couldn't stop staring at him.

Before picking Anna and the girls up from her parents' house, I popped in to see cousin Becky and Matt. He'd promised to donate me some of his hand-me-downs. I snaffled some of Matt's expensive shirts and tight, garish tops that made me look like Julian Clary. I messed around with Becky, taking selfies on the bonnet of Matt's red Porsche. He's got more money than sense.

I checked in with the Overton family tonight. Jess emailed me a picture of Molly's headstone. It reads: 'Just six hours old. Beautiful and brave. Cherished. Safe in Jesus's arms. Forever loved. Forever missed.'

Wednesday 21 November

I woke up still angry and confused about the women bishops vote. I tweeted: 'Off to find my amazing colleague, Rev Irene, to plant a big smacker on her cheek. She is proper bishop material. #oneday #hope.'

I organized a church social tonight at a local curry house. It's one of those places where you have a hunch you'll be saying hello to the food again the next morning in one form or another. There was a decent atmosphere among the gang. Wayne has grown a moustache for Movember. He looks like a camp Bond villain. Our massive centre half from HT United turned up. Between forkfuls of chicken biryani he told us that he had recently finished a performing arts degree. He had to squeeze his massive frame into a leotard – regularly. We demanded to see pictures.

Thursday 22 November

Legendary kid's TV presenters the Chuckle Brothers came into church tonight before turning Hull's Christmas lights on. They're doing the panto here again. Their happy, moustachioed faces are even more pleasing to look at in the flesh.

Friday 23 November

I've reluctantly agreed to be Santa for the twins' club Christmas party. One of the mums, Ali – a gloriously indiscreet Brummie and former 18–30 holiday rep – will be my elf. 'I'm going to help Santa empty his sack!' she squealed to roars of laughter. Awkward.

Saturday 24 November

I'm now the St Paul's Boxing Academy chaplain. I put a poster up at the club. It says: 'Need advice? Need support? Need someone to talk to? Need someone to pray for you? Don't hesitate to contact St Paul's Boxing Academy chaplain Rev Matt Woodcock, from Holy Trinity Church.'

We put the massive Christmas tree up in church this morning. Neal's life hung in the balance climbing up the ladder.

Monday 26 November

I received an encouraging message from a local bloke who randomly came to the FULL service last night. He wrote: 'Thanks for yesterday. It really helped me out. I prayed with Father Neal in the chapel. A prayer so edifying that I was "up and at 'em" today – not the "man in the wilderness". You lot are a smashing bunch and reaffirm my faith.' So that was nice.

Tuesday 27 November

My landlord friend Lee has taken on yet another pub. I'm thrilled – it's one of my favourites – The Minerva at the end of Hull

Marina. He'll do wonders with it. Lee asked me to bless the pub and said we can have our staff Christmas party there.

Wednesday 28 November

Human dramas are never far away cycling through the Thornton Estate. As I was riding past a block of flats, a couple spilled out onto the street. 'I loved you!' a dishevelled bloke shouted at a striking woman with peroxide blonde hair. He stormed away from her up the road. 'Come back, Eddie!' the lady screamed after him. There were mattresses, clothes and other domestic bits and bobs strewn everywhere. A hairy, fierce-looking neighbour then appeared at his window. 'Keep the ****ing noise down!' he yelled. The woman unloaded a string of expletives back at him. I cycled past. Head firmly down.

One of the boxing club dads has asked me to pray for his son. It's his first fight on Saturday.

Thursday 29 November

I finally met up with Dad today. We go through these strange periods of impasse for no particular reason. I was honest and told him how disappointed I was that he didn't feature more in Esther and Heidi's lives. 'They need you, Dad,' I said. He nodded ruefully. I suggested that he, Mum, Amy and I could meet up and have a meal together or something. The first time in decades. It's an opportunity not to fight or blame but to be reconciled a bit. We might even enjoy it. Dad was animated by the idea – after three pints of Sovereign, admittedly. The problem is I just don't think Amy would come. She'd think it was too cringey and painful. I'll ask. We went onto The Three-Legged Mare and the York Arms. A girl in my year at secondary school served us. She looked sad and world-weary. If she recognized me, she didn't show it.

Friday 30 November

My head had the ache of Dad all over it this morning. I remembered that hangover cure advert we always laugh at from the 1980s. A dishevelled guy looks at the bathroom mirror with bloodshot eyes. He takes a couple of Alka-Seltzers and the narrator says this killer line: 'Alka-Seltzer – so at least you know you're going to live.' I know exactly what he means.

I walked past my former *York Evening Press* offices this afternoon in Walmgate. My old hairdresser popped her head out to say hello. Somehow she'd heard about the camels. I also saw my old deskmate, Steve. Still ambitious as ever. Now looking for a job in horse racing or golf. He said he missed me as I walked off. I felt really touched.

I read an inspirational story in *The Times* as I slurped an Americano in Nero's. An NYPD cop had noticed a homeless guy in a shop doorway on a cold night. He went to a shop and bought him shoes and socks. There's a lovely picture – taken by a tourist – of the cop kneeling at the homeless guy's feet to put them on. I love the fact that there's millions of unseen acts going on like that all over the world right now.

Mum isn't keen on meeting Dad for a family reunion meal. It's not happening. I'm disappointed but I understand.

Saturday 1 December

HT United training this morning. Sharpy turned up with an unforgivable tash. More Movember horrors. We finished with a penalty shoot-out. I invited them all to our Christmas services and socials. They all promised to come, which is always a bad sign. They never do.

I got one of those dreaded phone calls after lunch. Mum needs a scan. It's something to do with her ovaries. I can't help but fear the worst. She was a bit cagey when she told me. It would be a horrible cruelty if it's something serious or terminal, just at the point where she has found love and happiness again. This can't happen. I couldn't sleep. Every shift and creak the house made was like a symphony of fear. It closed in on me. I pulled the covers over my head and lay there for a long time.

Sunday 2 December

I had a really difficult conversation with Anna tonight. She spoke some truths about our marriage that were hard to hear. Hard, because I knew she was right. 'I've had enough, Woody,' she said between tears and blowing her nose into her tissue. 'We see so little of you that I may as well be a single parent. You need to decide what you want. You give that church everything and we're left with the dregs. I won't go on like this.' I just listened. I've been so oblivious to Anna's feelings. So selfish with my time. I'm making my wife deeply unhappy and unloved. She's gone to bed now. I'm filled with dread that she'll leave me. I don't know what I'd do. My life doesn't make sense without her.

This diary isn't helping. I'm sick of writing it. I can't stop thinking about all the huge things coming up these next few weeks. All that weight and stress and things that could go wrong. The camels might make an incredible spectacle but they're terrible for married life. My wife feels unloved and unwanted. What could be sadder than that? Why do I never learn? I'm determined to fix this. Tomorrow is a new day. God's mercies are new every morning. Let's hope Anna's are.

Monday 3 December

I made time for some serious reflection about last night's conversation with Anna. I can't go on compromising family life but I don't know how I can get through this month without being full-on at church. My mind is a constant whirr of noise and buzz.

I went through the Live Nativity script with actor Daniel tonight. He's agreed to help me direct it. We have a long way to go. It's too dry at the moment. Lacks any sense of humour or imagination. It's not 'Hull' enough yet. Our shepherds are some of the coaches from the boxing club. They're refusing to wear their boxing gloves as they lead the sheep in the procession because – wait for it – they think they'll look silly! I've got no time for divas. My fingernails are just stubs now. My blood pressure is approaching the red zone.

In other news, Daniel told me he's considering leaving us and joining the Catholic church, Wayne wants to get confirmed and Ann Cluderay has been moved into a hospice to see out her final days.

Things were still a bit frosty with Anna when I got in tonight but we had a constructive conversation. I think she's just happy and relieved that we're now naming the elephant in the room and trying to do something about it.

Tuesday 4 December

We're all feeling the pressure at Holy Trinity. Irene and I had an unpleasant clash at our clergy Wetherspoons meeting. We were grumpy anyway, but took it out on each other. We said things we didn't mean. Irene had put me down to help with the school Christingle service, but I'm now going to visit Ann in the hospice. She wasn't happy. Said I should honour my commitment and not just do what I want when I want. We were like school kids trying to score points in the playground. We each appealed to Neal to take our side. He wouldn't. Always the quiet diplomat. The bar staff seemed very entertained. Two priests, collared up, going at it. My pay-off line as I stormed to the toilets was out of order: 'I'll try and get Ann to hold off dying until after your service, then!' I felt terrible. The irony that we're in the season of peace, joy and goodwill to all people is not lost on me.

A smattering of snow dropped today. Heidi came back in from the garden with hands as cold as ice pops. Esther is more cat-like. Happy to nestle in the warmth.

Anna and I held each other tonight. We cleared the air a bit. Thawed the ice. Things are better between us. Every day – no matter how busy I am or preoccupied I feel – I'm just trying to be more present with her and the girls. It's helping. Underneath all her stresses and frustrated outbursts, Anna is such a gentle and understanding spirit. It's why I love her.

I've just read 'Emerging' by R. S. Thomas. I think it articulates the mystery of how I'm feeling about God right now. 'in everyday life/it is the plain facts and natural happenings/that conceal God and reveal him to us/little by little under the mind's tooling.'

Thursday 6 December

Ann Cluderay died today. Died with no regrets. Left this world with nothing that she'd wished she'd done or said that she didn't get the chance to do or say. The last time I visited Ann, her face lit up and she stopped me as I was walking out. 'Haven't I done well?!' she said.

It was a cold day. I noticed one of the homeless guys who comes to us for tea and toast on Sundays walking shivering through Trinity Square in a thin jacket. I took him into Wetherspoons with me for a hot coffee. He wasn't in the mood to talk.

Neal and I had a fruitful meeting. I apologized for the bust-up with Irene. I'd called her to sort out our differences and say sorry for saying the things I did. Staying mad with Irene is impossible. We love each other really. I revealed my latest fundraising plan: a sponsored 10-mile run inside the church dressed as our favourite Bible characters. His eyes rolled spectacularly.

Friday 7 December

Esther and Heidi are two today. They let us know it in fine style – bouncing up and down on our heads with wild excitement. Most of their presents were pink and Peppa Pig related. I led a singsong at twins' club for them on my guitar. A punk pop version of 'Wind the Bobbin Up'. The girls wore their new pink all-in-one hooded rain suits. They look like extras from an East 17 Christmas video.

One of the HT United lads broke down in tears at our social at The Minerva tonight. Ian is a brilliant man and professionally successful, but his life is a bit of a mess. Between sobs in the backroom he told me about feeling a sense of crippling loneliness. He goes away on lavish holidays to try to numb the pain. When Ian left his high-profile job last year he was shocked by how many people walked away from him. He said they only wanted him for what they could get. His phone stopped ringing. It's left him deeply angry and sad. This is why I started HT United. I felt Ian unburdened himself tonight. Had an outlet for his pain. Rediscovered friendship based not on what he's worth, but who he is. It wasn't until I became a reverend that I realized the extent of the loneliness disease, often among those who look so outwardly happy and successful. It's little wonder that male suicide rates are so high. I'm convinced we can improve men's mental health by creating opportunities for a bit of simple friendship.

Lee the landlord is freaked out after finding a ouija board in his cellar at The Minerva. He wants me to get rid of it and pray around the pub.

Saturday 8 December

Amy and Mum are finally reconciled. They made peace with tears and Cava. Esther successfully pooed in the potty for the first time. It's a happy day.

Sunday 9 December

We've reached crisis point at Holy Apostles. There were nine of us at worship this morning. The mood was so despondent. It's not sustainable. I've tried everything I can think of. We need a serious talk after Christmas about the future. I think there's a better way to do and be church round here and it's not on Sunday mornings.

Monday 10 December

Holy Trinity featured on Archbishop Sentamu's online Advent calendar today. Every day reveals a nugget of spiritual wisdom and something encouraging that the church is doing. I thought Sentamu summed up the Live Nativity rather well. He wrote:

> *There are so many ways we can get the Good News out to people – we're not meant to keep the message to ourselves. Nothing beats meeting people in person. One of our priests up here in Yorkshire has had a fantastic idea to get the Christmas message out in a new way this year. On 22 December thousands of people are expected to descend on the city centre in Hull as Mary, Joseph, baby Jesus and a procession of animals, wise men, shepherds and angels (all played by local residents) will walk through the streets bringing the old story to people in a fresh way.*

> *Following God is often an adventure. It's rarely dull. Why not get out there and do something different? The joy of God's love is contagious – once you release it, there is no stopping it!*

Tuesday 11 December

My old friend Luke Smith has been diagnosed with cancer. He's only 32 and has a wife and two young sons. He sent out this group email to friends and family: 'The results have come back and shown that it is bowel cancer … I will start a six-month course of chemotherapy in January. We are beginning a new life stage of confronting the cancer that may have spread throughout my body.' Never less than brutally matter-of-fact, Luke. I've always admired him for that. I messaged him that I was gutted, angry, but full of hope. He texted back: 'I don't feel afraid. God is undeniably good. Thanks for standing with me.' I recently stopped my monthly giving to help fund his church work among students. Great timing as always.

I visited Ann Cluderay's family to discuss the funeral. They described her – with much love and laughter – as 'mad', 'an embarrassment'. A woman with 'no boundaries'. 'She would talk to anyone about anything,' her daughter Ruth said. I like the story they told of the hairdresser turning up to her house. 'Are you decent, Ann – can I come in?' 'Yes, I'm decent,' she replied. The hairdresser walks in to find Ann standing in a pair of knickers. That was her definition of decent. Ann wanted Bon Jovi playing during the service and demanded that I wear a Hawaiian shirt.

Wednesday 12 December

Neal has been quoted in *The Times* in a story about the latest Church of England census. It reported that only 60 per cent of the UK population now classed themselves as Christian. It went on: 'He (Neal) said his own church had been particularly poor, but in the short time he has been there, the congregation has doubled, from 60 to 120.' They've made Neal sound boastful. Arrogant, even. The opposite of what he's like. He's so embarrassed – so of course Irene and I teased him mercilessly.

I was interviewed by local Hull radio station KCFM about our Live Nativity plans. 'How will you top this next year?' the reporter asked. 'Elvis impersonators in Santa outfits parachuting into Trinity Square,' I replied.

Thursday 13 December

Student Danny's girlfriend Kirsty became a Christian at Holy Trinity today. I was dunking a fig roll into my brew when she breezed in wanting to go for it. We went in to the chapel and she said a prayer of commitment to Jesus with such feeling, as if she was accepting an invitation from the most special friend. Her lovely West Yorkshire accent rolled over the words. It was a beautiful moment.

Judi Murden, Radio Humberside's lovely faith and religion reporter, recorded us 'practising' for the Live Nativity tonight. It basically involved me trying to direct actor Daniel as he went through his Joseph bits. She recorded him banging on the door of the inn to ask if there was any room. Then I chipped in: 'Give it some more feeling, Daniel – your wife is about to give birth!' I love the fact I'm ordering around a former Royal Shakespeare Company actor. I'm winging this whole thing to a ridiculous extent. If I gave any deep thought and reflection to what we are embarking on, I'd be a complete wreck. I'm clinging on. A lovely member of the council events team is the one reason I think we can pull this off. She's calm, organized and makes helpful lists. She met us outside City Hall to walk the route. Our latest addition to the procession is an angel on stilts holding aloft a massive star.

I visited Gareth and Lyndsey at their home in East Hull tonight to talk about Sidney's (now Jesus's) baptism. They are looking forward to being the Holy Family at the Live Nativity. I feel a real love for them. I'd jokingly said I wouldn't come unless they had my favourite custard creams to eat. Lyndsey met me at the door with a huge bowl of them. How embarrassing. I had to scoff about five just to be polite. I showed them the cheesy Church of England baptism video. I wish I hadn't. It wasn't helpful. In the end, I turned it off and tried to articulate the meaning of baptism in different words, in a language that was more relatable. Lyndsey gave me a doggie bag for the remaining custard creams.

Friday 14 December

The *Church Times* ran a story about the Live Nativity today. "'I've created a monster, to be honest,'" one of the quotes said. "'It has got completely out of control, in a good way." Mr Woodcock – who has become known as the "camel man of Hull"' (no, I haven't – no one calls me that, literally no one) 'is a believer in doing things differently. "As soon as you take the story outside church, people engage with it like never before. Hull has really been struggling jobs-wise, and this has become something that people are really looking forward to."'

I watched the classic thriller *Heat* again tonight. It's well worth the three hours for that great scene in the cafe between De Niro and Pacino. Two of the greats going hard at it. 'I must take you down ... I won't hesitate.'

Saturday 15 December

I was a very reluctant Santa at the twins' club Christmas party. Heidi is a complete nightmare at the moment. She takes our fury levels into the red zone. The only words I remember saying this morning were, 'Heidi, no!' Over and over and over again. She wriggles and kicks and screams if she doesn't get her own way – usually among the people and in the places where it will cause the most embarrassment to us. Mum says she reminds her of someone. Ali the Brummie elf was a big hit at the grotto. Most of the dads who came looked so awkward. They hid behind their mobile phones while their wives 'ooed' and 'aahed'. Some dads were dug in the ribs. I heard other wives whispering swear words and death threats into their ear holes to get them to pay more attention. The girls didn't recognize me when they sat on my knee. That was until Heidi nearly pulled the Christmas tree on top of us after tugging on a bauble. 'Heidi, no!' I shouted.

I received a lovely email tonight. It sums up how so many people must feel about the possibility of coming to church:

Dear Reverend Matt

Recently, I've begun to feel compelled to 'go to church' which is odd as I have never been before (other than weddings and funerals!). Not only that, I feel drawn specifically to Holy Trinity. I would very much like to attend a service but have to admit to feeling a little anxious as the whole thing is totally unfamiliar to me. I've found myself wondering – what should I wear? Where should I sit? What do I need to do during a service? Please could you provide me with some guidance?'

The gist of my reply was: 'Fear not! We are on a mission at Holy Trinity to help people like you explore faith and church in a friendly, accessible way. We don't care what you wear, or where you want to sit etc. We are just thrilled that you want to come.' She said she'd come to our 9.30 a.m. service tomorrow. Excellent.

Sunday 16 December

The 9.30 a.m. service was buzzing. New people, lively worship, and kids everywhere! I was so happy to see my email writer had turned up. We talked afterwards and she said she'd enjoyed it. It felt like a significant morning.

Holy Apostles was more challenging. One of the grandmas, 'scary Kath', marched up to me and snarled: 'You bloody stink of garlic, Matt!' She then turned to our tiny congregation and said: 'Don't get too near Matt – he stinks!' Thanks, Kath. That made it a bit awkward during the Peace.

Monday 17 December

I'm poorly at the worst possible time. Why, Lord?! I somehow managed to drag myself down to church, but I was an achy, shivering mess of man flu. I couldn't swallow. I stuffed my face with Nurofen and went with our handyman David and cousin Ben to pick up our Live Nativity hay bales from a local farm. A choir mum goes horse riding there and sorted them out for us. I'm touched by how people are rallying round. The Live Nativity has caught their imaginations. I'm surrounded by willing philanthropists. But Ben wasn't happy when we unloaded the bales at Holy Trinity. The boot of his Citroën Picasso looked like a barn floor and stank of cow pats. He's slowly learning that there's usually an unpleasant catch to every favour I ask of him.

Waves of ill health washed over me once we'd sorted the bales. I was done. I sank into bed and had crazy dreams that seemed real. In one, I was married to three women. They each loved me the same and we all got on really well. My sheets became sodden as I went from shivering to boiling and back again.

On a happier note, I got a text to say all the nativity costumes are done. Our church cafe volunteer Maria is a magician with a needle and thread. Things are coming together.

Tuesday 18 December

I've been diagnosed with a throat infection. Thank heavens the doctor could see me at such short notice. He was sympathetic. I begged him to give me something just to get through the week. I left with armfuls of antibiotics and a special spray. Feel a bit less like I will die imminently now.

Wednesday 19 December

I was devastated to see the weather forecast for Saturday. I shouldn't have looked. Driving wind and torrential rain – *all day*. There's still time for God to do his thing.

I took Ann Cluderay's thanksgiving service at St Paul's Church in York today. I granted her wish and led the service wearing a garish Hawaiian shirt. Her daughter Ruth gave a lovely welcome speech. Pictures of Ann living out her adventures were beamed up on the big screen. Her smiling, full-of-life face was the only eulogy we needed, really.

Thursday 20 December

I received a lovely card of encouragement from two of our stalwart church welcomers. Proper Jesus people. It read: 'Thank you for bringing the wonderful story of the nativity to our city. Don't ever lose sight of the vision you first had. Saturday will be epic! And the wonder of Christ's coming will become so real and inspirational to the people of Hull. So let us say boldly: "The Lord is here. His Spirit is with us." What then is there to fear? Bless you, dear Matt.' I sobbed reading that.

It was the Live Nativity dress rehearsal tonight. Absolute mayhem. The sight of boxing coach Paul dressed as a shepherd, grim-faced and holding a toy sheep will make me smile for a long time. He gave me murderous looks. 'Why did I agree to this?!' I heard him mutter to someone. He wasn't alone.

There was terrible wind and rain all night. It was unrelenting. Dark pools gathered in our makeshift Bethlehem in the Holy Trinity car park. But the rehearsal was warm-spirited and full of light and joy. It radiated off people's faces. It felt like the Old Town had truly come together as a community. We tried on the costumes, got a group photo and I briefed everyone on what their role will be on the day. This isn't something we can really rehearse as such.

I went on Burnsy's Radio Humberside show to plug the event with Andy (Herod) and the Yardleys (the Holy Family). Gareth, playing one of our two Josephs, came out with the best line: 'If this rain continues, Burnsy, we'll be doing Noah's Ark.' A *Look North* reporter turned up for the rehearsal. His pay-off line was something like, 'I don't know about camels, but Matt's having kittens!' Yep.

Friday 21 December

I stayed in most of the day trying to keep calm. I'm convinced tomorrow will be a significant moment for Holy Trinity. I had a wonderful time with God this morning. I've missed him. I told him all my fears, and hopes. I prayed that somehow through the event, the people of Hull would catch a glimpse of the depth of God's love for them.

Gareth came round to drop his engagement ring off. He's nervous too. I'm not surprised. He's had the crazy idea that he will kneel down in front of hundreds of people dressed as Joseph and propose to his girlfriend (dressed as Mary) in their makeshift stable. 'I couldn't think of anywhere better to do it,' he said. 'That's fine, Gareth, but are you sure she'll say "yes"?' I asked.

'Well, we've been getting on just lately.'

Only in Hull.

Saturday 22 December

And so we arrive right back at where this book began. Standing in the pouring rain in a deserted Hull Trinity Square, just a couple of hours before the curtain went up on our Live Nativity, thinking 'B*gger. What have I done?' No one is going to come.

I looked to the heavens for inspiration. Surely God had some answers?

Back to the diary …

I remembered a little technique my spiritual director, Sister Cecilia, used to teach me for times of stress and panic.

'Breathe slowly in through the nose and out of the mouth,' she'd say. 'Breathe in Jesus, Matt. Breathe in his light. His hopeful spirit. Breathe out all that is not of him.'

I could hear my nun's soothing, manicured voice in my head. It helped. As I breathed and prayed, a strong feeling stirred. It sounds untrue when I write it down, but in that moment, in the middle of that deluged, stormy square, I knew God was with me. Knew that he'd called me to Hull for days like this. I felt charged with a new strength. I would carry on. I wouldn't grow despondent.

I would see this day through with a smile on my face and hope in my heart.

And I would walk those ****ing camels through Hull city centre if it ****ing killed me …

While I was wiping my eyes and blowing my nose, our massive North Star then turned up with Wayne's cherry picker. Leroy (Gabriel) soon followed to do his sound check. I arrived at City Hall aka Nazareth – just as a massive articulated lorry was turning in. I heard the camels before I saw them. Grunts and shuffling hooves. These animals have become a symbol for the beautiful madness of what we're trying to do at Holy Trinity. For me, they've come to represent what's possible if you don't let fear and safety and comfort rule. I've learnt that being careful gets you nowhere. It was like slow motion as they trotted out of the truck. They took my breath away. Three huge, glorious camels. The sheep and donkey followed. I threw my arms around their chief handler, Nathan. I stood back as he tethered them in the square. The most surreal, special sight. We were on.

I herded the Live Nativity cast into City Hall. A beautiful motley crew. We nervously got our costumes on. Our wise men were hung-over. The boxing shepherds bickering. I gave a final pep talk and we were ready. I peeked over the balcony. Queen Victoria Square was full. The people looked drenched but expectant. I was thrilled and heartened to see a few of the family had made it – Mum, Grandma, nephew Joel, niece Honor, Uncle Mike and Deb. Anna was there with the girls, waving furiously. Legends.

I said a final prayer to myself and before I knew it, we were off. Neal – resplendent in headdress, hessian robe and irritating fingerless gloves – stepped out onto the balcony to begin the narration. Gabriel – his gold costume flapping all over his face – sang the first song, 'Ave Maria'. It's all a bit of a blur after that. Mary and Joseph acted out all the Nazareth scenes and then we set off to Bethlehem. The boxing coaches led us out, their sheep on leads. I stayed at the back with the camels. It was a health and safety nightmare. Carving a path through the crowds was precarious. Everyone wanted selfies with the camels. For quite a small woman, our chief steward Justine was a giant presence. Seeing people's faces was the best bit. Pensioners walking out of Superdrug in Whitefriargate with the last of their Christmas shopping being greeted by a massive camel. Their look of shock and wonder. They'd frantically call friends on their mobiles: 'You'll never guess what I'm looking at!' The Christmas story was alive and incarnate on the streets. You couldn't ignore it. I didn't underestimate the glorious power of that.

The procession stopped outside a pub called The Bonny Boat. Joseph banged on the door. Mary, next to him in a pregnancy suit, going for Oscar glory, was hamming up the contractions. Colin the landlord came out at the top window looking like a grumpy Yasser Arafat. 'What do you want?!' he cried in a mash-up of Middle Eastern accents. 'We'd like a room for the night, please – my wife is about to have a baby!' Joseph shouted back.

'We are full. There is no room at the inn. Now be on your way!'

Colin shouted. Now people tell me he actually told us all to 'piss off' at that point but I never heard him. Then Hull's most famous chip shop owner, Bob Carver, spontaneously appeared in the path of the camels with a yellow tea towel on his head and wearing batter-splattered chef's whites. Well, spontaneous for us, not for Bob. The wily old fox knew press photographers were swarming everywhere. He soon had them eating out of his hands. The camels, too. He fed them chips, posing for every picture he could. I guarantee that's the iconic image of the day. Well done, Bob.

Then it was Lee's turn to appear at the top window of The Kingston. He looked white and sick with nerves. He informed Mary and Joseph that he had a stable round the back and we processed onto our car park. A massive crowd took their positions round it as the story unfolded. Our second Holy Family, Gareth and Lyndsey, were in place huddled in the stable. Baby Sidney was as quiet as a church mouse, swaddled and nestling on Mary's lap. The boxers really got into their parts. Their looks of amazement at the choir of angels and the shining star on top of the cherry picker were BAFTA-worthy. I could have cried with joy. Our choir led us in some traditional carols and some poignant moments passed between us all as we sang words of light and hope. Herod (Deputy Churchwarden Andy) and his hilariously scrawny henchmen (cousin Ben and student Danny) were booed in all the right places.

I got on the mic at the end to thank everyone and invite the crowd into church for a cake, a hot drink and a Christingle service led by Irene. 'That leaves just one more thing,' I said. 'Joseph has got something to ask Mary.' I passed the mic to Gareth. His hands were violently shaking like an alcoholic in search of his next dram. He got down on one knee next to the manger, pulled his ring out of his smock and said: 'This bit's not in the Bible but could be added in ... Lyndsey, I love yer. Will you marry me, please?' She said yes and burst into tears as he put the ring on her finger. Then this rough-faced, granite-hard welder from East Hull publicly cried his eyes out. The happiest of tears. The crowd went nuts. I love that he said 'please'.

It was all over. We'd done it. I waved the camels off, tidied up and collapsed. Nothing left. Thank you, Lord. An unforgettable day.

Sunday 23 December

The Sunday Times front page carried a story about the Live Nativity. I did an interview with BBC Radio Essex. I'm not sure the people of Romford or Billericay were ready to hear from such an excited, hoarse-throated northerner that early in the morning.

I'm still dazed. All that adrenaline has poured out of me and I feel like a wrung-out dish cloth. Holy Trinity was abuzz with the excitement of what we did and the response we got. I sense a renewed pride in the church. Gareth and Lyndsey said they were both violently sick in the middle of the night.

'Because of all the emotion and excitement?' I asked. 'No,' Gareth replied in the thickest Hull accent I've ever heard. 'Dodgy Chaaanese.'

I found homeless John fast asleep in our Bethlehem stable when I came out of church. The straw covered his cold legs. It was a timely reminder that Jesus was born into poverty and came to help and serve the poor. I could see John had been getting help. His shopping trolley was full of packets of mince pies that people had bought him. He woke up and we chatted while he smoked his roll-ups and drank tea from his pint glass.

Our candlelit Nine Lessons and Carols service was packed out tonight. The great and the good of Hull were all in. I gave the address and reflected on my former life as a news reporter. A section of the congregation booed me. It's not a popular profession round here. 'Don't boo – it's not a panto!' I shot back.

I got home and watched *It's a Wonderful Life* with Anna. We wept in each other's arms for the hundredth time. The power of human kindness and generosity never fails to move us.

Monday 24 December

Midnight mass is still my favourite service in the church year. A time when anybody and everybody – the sozzled pubgoers and the church stalwarts – come to Christ's table without shame or embarrassment. It's a picture of what it should be like all the time. We had record numbers. I've never seen the choir look so joyful or sound so relaxed and in tune. Earlier Anna made us a buffet tea and we grabbed a few precious hours together. I got my presents bought just as the last shop was being locked up. I've bought Anna a jumper she'll probably never wear and best friend Lee a curly wig and comedy nose from Hull's famous Dinsdales joke shop.

Tuesday 25 December

Anna presented me with a beautiful silver cross neck chain this morning. I'll treasure it. Lee says I look like P. Diddy. After preaching at Holy Trinity's Christmas Day Holy Communion, Anna and I sang Elton John songs all the way back to York. I legged it down to The Fox to meet friends and family. ''Ave another one, our Matt,' Grandma insisted long after I should have left. I made it back just in time to tuck into Anna's mum's sensational dinner. We told unfunny cracker jokes, ate too much meat, silently trumped, watched the Queen's Speech, played Wii Tennis and fell unconscious. Then we did it all again at tea time.

Wednesday 26 December

Another intense family day. I was barely conscious. I felt like I'd taken some heavy sedatives or something. The last few weeks have taken their toll. I'm in bed and it's only 9.30 p.m. That never happens. Uncle Ally's house was full for the family party. It was so good to see the girls running riot like we used to. We all backed a horse running at Wetherby Races called 'What's Up, Woody'. It came second. Back to Hull tomorrow.

Friday 28 December

Finally feel a bit more relaxed. Weight came off my shoulders today. No nails were nibbled. Not having the phone permanently attached to my ear is such a release. I got to enjoy just being present and pottering round the house. I went for a run for the first time in ages. I welcomed the fresh wind blowing my face to bits round Hull Marina. I took the girls to the café at the Deep aquarium for a scone. We moseyed round the Old Town. I bought a new diary, bike chain oil and a metal chest to store my writing treasures.

Later on, I learnt 'Don't Panic' by Coldplay on the guitar. I reflected on my huge new Picasso print 'The Old Guitarist'. Is the man lost in the misery of his grinding poverty or lost in the joy of his music despite his poverty? I can't decide. It's why I won't get bored of looking at it. I'm slowly becoming human again.

Saturday 29 December

Hull's Olympic boxing champ Luke Campbell is now a contestant on *Dancing on Ice*, alongside *Baywatch's* Pamela Anderson. He's come a very long way.

Churchwarden Tim sent us an encouraging email laying out what positive changes he'd witnessed this last year at Holy Trinity and the healthy numerical growth. He didn't mention the heartache, fall-outs, discouragements and general insanity that we went through to get us there. Probably for the best.

Sunday 30 December

Neal had a coughing fit at the altar during Holy Communion this morning. I had to jump in and take over.

Gareth and Lyndsey were at the service. They've asked me to marry them next Christmas. They want a nativity-themed wedding – with live animals. *Nooo!!*

Monday 31 December

Some year, then. I flicked back over these pages. I know I compromised too much family time. Gave my heart and soul to too many other things. Eighteen months in Hull and it already feels like ten years. I'll try to be less full-on next year. I'm increasingly convinced that if we say 'yes' to God, incredible things happen but it's not without consequences. There's always a cost to any kind of adventure.

I'll stop writing this in a bit. Brush my teeth, kiss the girls, cuddle Anna and finish my Jack Reacher. My hope is to stay as horizontal and in as much comfort as possible tomorrow. And no thinking about church. I've done quite enough of that.

Afterword

On 13 May 2017, the Archbishop of York, Dr John Sentamu, re-dedicated Holy Trinity Church as Hull Minster to reflect its importance and contribution to the local community it serves. The church has also undergone a spectacular £4.5 million development project to transform the building.

In 2018, a record 225,000 people visited Hull Minster. It's an amazing place to worship in and wander around.

For more information see: www.hullminster.org

I can also confirm that the pews have now been removed and it has proper heating.

Praise God.

Acknowledgements

To:

- Esther and Heidi
- Mum and Amy
- Dad
- Grandma
- The Sawyers, the Andertons and the Wrights
- The Reverend Canon Dr Neal Barnes and the Reverend Irene Wilson. For your laughter, friendship, patience and grace.
- The congregation, volunteers, staff and supporters of Holy Trinity/Hull Minster. An incredible place that taught me so much. Not least how cold a massive 700-year-old building can really be at 8 a.m. on a Sunday morning.
- The four Holy Trinity legends whose faithfulness, doggedness and sense of humour kept Holy Trinity alive for so long: Sam McGaw, Chris and Jean Fenwick and Tim Wilson.

I have tried hard to disguise the potentially embarrassed, change names and seek permissions where necessary.

I'm very grateful to the many people who gave me enthusiastic permission to tell their story so candidly, in particular to Sam and Jess (who now have two beautiful daughters).

- Find out more information about the work of Sands, the stillbirth and neonatal death charity, here: https://www.sands.org.uk/
- Donate to the incredible work of Martin House children's hospice here: https://www.martinhouse.org.uk/Donate

Thanks also to:

- Reverend Ben Brady, the greatest bass player in the Church of England
- Ollie Holliday

- Ruth Collins
- 'Dan the Tan' Adams
- Wayne, Louise and Harry Ede. The first ones in.
- Sarah Glenton and scary Kath (who insisted on the 'scary')
- Matthew Uney
- Jamie and John
- Luke Campbell, Paul, Mick Bromby and all at St Paul's Boxing Academy
- Lee and Charlotte at The Minerva
- Hull CAMRA comrades, particularly Angela, Bernie, Stewart, Mark and Paul
- Gareth and Lyndsey Yardley and Sidney
- Terry and Sharon Igoe. Fearless, ferocious and hilarious practitioners of the social gospel.
- Mark Keith. My favourite organist of all time.
- Danny and Kirsty Whittaker
- Daniel Morgan. Keep pushing that door.
- The fabulous journalists and presenters at BBC Radio Humberside, particularly Burnsy, James Hoggarth, Judi Murden and Amanda White
- Emma Wright for her *Hull Daily Mail* articles
- Meehan Media's finest, John and Janey
- Outrageous Alpha buddies Becky Shipman, Debs Stevo and fundraiser Phil
- Reverend Eve Ridgeway for teaching me to disagree gracefully
- Dan Broom
- David and Marie Howden
- Dave and Julia Allum
- Andy Basset-Scott
- Robin Alden
- The Holy Trinity development team for their drive, vision and wallet-loosening skills, particularly Dr Stephen Martin, John Robinson, Brian Gilliland, Jane Owen and Jonny Bottomley
- Dan Parker for filling that wall in

- Shaun Turner for those lively coffees and discussions about heresy
- John Lawson for my red Olmo bike
- Ace photographer and Hull's greatest purveyor of positive news, Jerome Whittingham
- Julian, Jo and Jack Wild. For your encouragement and hay bales.
- The former Bishop of Hull, the Right Reverend Richard Frith and his colleagues for having the faith and courage to let us loose on Holy Trinity
- The people of St Paul's, Holgate and St Barnabas, Leeman Road, York
- Peter Warry and the Diocese of York team
- The lovely *Radio 2 Breakfast Show* team
- My beautifully maddening and inspirational mentor and friend Reverend Robin Gamble. Such an influential, truth-speaking and hilarious voice in the Church of England over the last 30 years.
- LYCIG friends and colleagues.
- The Reverend Canon Anna Norman-Walker. Someone please make her a bishop.
- Retreat confidantes and companions, Ned Lunn, Andy Stinson, Russ Gant and Kuhan Satkunanayagam
- Jonny and Anne Wooldridge. Faithful friends, incredible godparents.
- The Corfu crew
- To those who read the original manuscript, commented honestly and encouraged me to keep going, namely: Pete Hale, Iain and Katie Ogilvie, John Lee, Al Chambers, Lisa Whitley, Alex Lloyd, Arun Arora and Liz Addy
- Editing wizard and *Pause For Thought* tormentor, Jonathan Mayo
- Thomas Allain-Chapman, Josie and all at CHP

But most of all thanks and as much love and respect as I can muster, to Anna. She's some woman.

In loving memory of the wisest and most well-spoken spiritual guide a wayward reverend ever had – Sister Cecilia Goodman.